Library of
Davidson College

IN THE SERIES
AMERICAN CIVILIZATION
EDITED BY ALLEN F. DAVIS

# Forever Wild

*Environmental Aesthetics
and the
Adirondack Forest Preserve*

In the Five Ponds Wilderness Area. Photograph by Richard Linke.

# Forever Wild

▲▲▲▲▲▲▲

*Environmental Aesthetics
and the
Adirondack Forest Preserve*

Philip G. Terrie

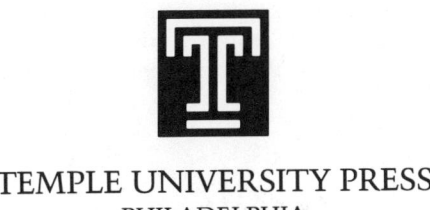

TEMPLE UNIVERSITY PRESS
PHILADELPHIA

**Library of Congress Cataloging in Publication Data**

Terrie, Philip G.
  Forever wild.

  Bibliography: p.
  Includes index.
  1. Adirondack Forest Preserve (N.Y.)—History.
2. Landscape protection—New York (State)—Adirondack Forest Preserve—History.  3. Nature conservation—New York (State)—Adirondack Forest Preserve—History.
4. Wilderness areas—New York (States)—History.
I. Title.
SD428.A2N79    1985        333.78′4        84-26803
ISBN 0-87722-380-7

Temple University Press, Philadelphia 19122
© 1985 by Temple University. All rights reserved
Published 1985
Printed in the United States of America

The lands of the state, now owned or hereafter acquired, constituting the forest preserve, as now fixed by law, shall be forever kept as wild forest lands. They shall not be leased, sold, or exchanged, nor shall the timber thereon be sold, removed or destroyed.

— Article XIV, Section 1, New York State Constitution

# Acknowledgments

Verplanck Colvin, nineteenth-century explorer and surveyor, probably knew the Adirondack wilderness as well as anyone. Yet one of his most telling comments on the character of that wilderness emphasized its elusiveness. "Few fully understand what the Adirondack wilderness really is," he wrote. "It is a mystery even to those who have crossed and recrossed it along its avenues, the lakes; and on foot through its vast and silent recesses." Colvin might well have added that the cultural historian who has read and reread the voluminous literature generated by and about the Adirondack wilderness has an equally difficult time in penetrating its mysteries. But to both the explorer and the historian, the joys of intimacy with the Adirondack wilderness are reward enough, even when its secrets remain just beyond his ken.

As any reader will quickly discover, this book is as much a polemic as it is an exercise in scholarship. I am a friend of the wilderness, and my biases are undoubtedly responsible for the faults that remain here—despite the efforts of many friends to eliminate them. I am grateful to Bernard M. Mergen, Roderick S. French, and William K. Verner, who read and criticized the first version of this study. Since then, my colleagues SueEllen Campbell and Janice Alberghene have read rewrites and new sections. Norman J. VanValkenburgh kindly lent me a huge collection of important documents. And William Verner, to whom special thanks are due, then reread the entire manuscript and saved me from numerous errors. Librarians at George Washington University, Bowling Green State University, the University of Michigan, the Library of Congress, the Adirondack Museum, and the New York Public Library were always helpful. This whole project really began more than ten years ago when I worked at the Adirondack Museum. Financial support for the book came from the Bowling Green State University Faculty Research Committee and the National Endowment for the Humanities. Parts of this book have been published as articles in the following journals: *American Studies, Environmental Review, Journal of the Early Republic, Journal of Sport History,* and *New York History.* To the editors I am grateful for permission to reprint here what originally appeared in their journals. I also thank the Adirondack Museum for permission to publish all of the illustrations in the gallery, pages 113–20. Several members of the Museum staff were especially helpful: Librarian Jerold Pepper, Curator William Crowley, and Registrar Tracy Meehan.

The person whose contribution has been the most important and to whom this book is dedicated is my wife Martha. She did not type the manuscript, did not help with research or editing, has not, in fact, even read this thing. But she was there, and that was indispensable.

# Contents

|   |   |   |
|---|---|---|
| | Introduction | 3 |
| I | First Impressions | 15 |
| II | Progress or Nature: Ebenezer Emmons and the Natural History Survey | 27 |
| III | Romantic Travelers and Sportsmen | 44 |
| IV | The Gilded Age: Murray, Colvin, and the Wilderness Breached | 68 |
| V | Wilderness Preserved: The Forest Preserve and the Irony of Forever Wild | 92 |
| VI | Wilderness and the Conservation Bureaucracy, 1895–1940 | 109 |
| VII | A Wilderness Aesthetic | 136 |
| VIII | The Institutionalization of a Wilderness Aesthetic | 150 |
| | Notes | 167 |
| | A Note on Sources | 197 |
| | Index | 203 |

# Forever Wild

*Environmental Aesthetics
and the
Adirondack Forest Preserve*

Adirondack Park. Map by Lee Floro.

# Introduction

On May 15, 1985, conservationists and historians will celebrate the one hundredth anniversary of the establishment of the Adirondack Forest Preserve. For conservationists, the Forest Preserve is a vast and scenic expanse of forests, lakes, and mountains, a home for wild animals endangered elsewhere, a retreat from the problems of the urban Northeast, and the largest publicly owned wilderness east of the Mississippi. For historians, the creation of the Forest Preserve a century ago represents a turning point in American environmental history, one of those pivotal moments when ideas about the land and the effects of human activity on it reached dramatic fruition. Throughout the hundred years of its existence, the Forest Preserve has been a special place to both scholars and hikers, and it has inspired both historical interpretation and spiritual reverie. The feature of the Adirondacks that has particularly appealed to men and women of all interests has been its wilderness—however vaguely they have defined that elusive term.

This book is not a history of the Adirondacks, not even an environmental history. It does touch on much of what has happened in the Adirondacks, and it pays particular attention to what has happened to the Adirondack environment. But it is mainly a study of how people have thought about one feature of the environment—a feature that in the Adirondacks has been and remains substantial. This is a study of how people have responded to the idea of wilderness in the Adirondacks. The basic argument is simple: attitudes toward wilderness have changed over the years. Throughout my discussion, there is an important but usually only implicit premise: what happened in the Adirondacks was typical of the rest of the nation.

At the opening of the nineteenth century, the Adirondack region of upstate New York was a blank spot on the map: its highest mountains were unclimbed and unknown; the headwaters of its rivers were unexplored; the community of its landscape, wildlife, and forests was unviolated by the incursions of Europeans. By the end of the century the Adirondack country had been crossed and recrossed by surveyors, travelers, and sportsmen; lumbermen had cut timber in some of its most remote valleys and had driven logs down its many fast-flowing streams; parts of it had been devastated by forest fires; stylish hotels had appeared on its lakes; politicians had haggled, worried, and postured about its future. In short, the region had come to occupy a prominent place in the consciousness of New Yorkers and other easterners.

Throughout the nineteenth century the aspect of the Adirondack landscape that especially struck the many writers, artists, scientists, and other visitors, the aspect that elicited the most comment—whether hostile, appreciative, or ambivalent—was its wilderness. And at the end of the century, New York voters approved—for reasons that remain ambiguous—a constitutional provision insuring that state-owned lands in the Adirondacks would be "forever kept as wild forest lands."

The twentieth century has seen refinement of nineteenth-century attitudes as well as new syntheses of old views. From romanticism, twentieth-century environmentalists have adopted the conviction that wilderness holds spiritual truths and the capacity to restore vigor to the mind and body. Drawing from late-nineteenth-century science, they have modified the emerging discovery of the interrelationships and interdependency of all living things, and have found scientific and naturalistic reasons for appreciating and preserving the wilderness.

In this century there have been two main groups whose opinions and attitudes have shaped policy and the condition of wilderness in the Adirondacks. These are the amateur environmentalists—mostly associated with clubs or lobbies like the Adirondack Mountain Club or the Association for the Protection of the Adirondacks—and the state bureaucracy mandated to oversee public lands in the region. The latter was created in the 1880s as the Forestry Commission, evolved through a number of similarly named agencies, and is now the Department of Environmental Conservation. The story of how these agencies have displayed changing attitudes toward the idea of wilderness is an important chapter in the history of the Adirondacks.

▲▲▲▲▲▲▲

When I refer to the Adirondack region, I mean that part of New York State now officially within the Adirondack Park. This is an area of some six million acres west of Lake Champlain and north of the Mohawk River. It runs from a few feet above sea level to several peaks whose summits are over 5,000 feet high and contains a complicated variety of ecosystems. The forests are mixed hardwoods and softwoods, varying according to elevation, soil, exposure, and history, among other factors. The predominant species—the trees one is most likely to encounter throughout the region—are American beech, sugar maple, eastern hemlock, balsam fir, and red spruce. Other common species include white pine, tamarack, northern white cedar, ashes, aspens, birches, and cherries. On the highest mountains—Marcy, Algonquin, and Whiteface, for example—hikers cross a timberline and find alpine species like Lapland rosebay, diapensia, mountain sandwort, and other plants common in Labrador and similar regions far to the north of New York State. All the alpine summits are in the area known as the high peaks, in the east central Adirondacks.[1]

Scattered through much of the region are hundreds of lakes and ponds. Some of these are substantial bodies of water; Long Lake, in the central Adirondacks, is fourteen miles long and nearly two miles across at its widest. Others are small ponds; Lake Tear of the Clouds, high on the slopes of Mount Marcy, is less than a quarter of a mile across. Many of the major lakes, connected by rivers or close enough for short carries (in the Adirondacks, one never says "portage"), stretch in a long belt running southwest-northeast. This central lake area was the focus of much of the recreational activity of the nineteenth century. Campers could start a trip in the Saranac Lake vicinity, in the north-central Adirondacks, and travel all the way to Old Forge—about seventy-five water miles away via the Raquette River and the Fulton Chain Lakes—with a few easy carries.

In addition to lakes and ponds, one also finds ubiquitous swamps, marshes, and bogs. Indeed, one of the distinguishing features of the Adirondacks is the variety of its terrain; during a day's walk, a hiker can travel from a hemlock-lined lakeshore, past a swamp noisy with insects and birds, up through hardwoods and then boreal conifers, and finally to an alpine summit high above the timberline. The Adirondacks has presented a complex host of images to the people who have journeyed through or lived in the region; these images have derived as much from the diversity of the terrain as from the uses to which the region has been put. Much of this terrain, for reasons to be discussed in this book, has been preserved in or has returned to a wild condition.

▲▲▲▲▲▲▲

The response to wilderness is a function of environmental attitude.[2] By environmental attitude, I mean the combined responses of the conscious intellect and the imagination to the landscape and its constituent parts. Arising from the confluence of culture and personal experience, but not always with full awareness of the cultural traditions behind it, environmental attitude involves both intellection and imagination. From their cultural heritage, people responding to the world around them impose on their perceptions a collection of conventions, prejudices, and preconceptions. Or, as Clyde Kluckhohn and Henry A. Murray have written, in a visual metaphor that particularly suits this study, "Culture directs and often distorts man's perceptions of the external world. . . . Culture acts as a set of blinders, or a series of lenses, through which men view their environments."[3] When people began to explore and respond to the Adirondack wilderness, they did so in ways that clearly showed their cultural background. Throughout the nineteenth and twentieth centuries, scientists, travelers, and sportsmen displayed attitudes shaped by cultural conventions concerning aesthetics and unproductive land.

In addition to responses to the physical arrangement or condition of the landscape, environmental attitude comprises beliefs about what the elements of the environment are good for, how they satisfy or fail to satisfy a wide variety of human needs, and how or whether they can or should be altered to meet those needs. The individual displays his environmental attitude in his personal response, which can be anything from writing a romantic poem, planting corn, or setting off on a primitive backpack trip to starting a forest fire or erecting a skyscraper. The aggregate of individual responses adds up to and creates society's response to the environment, which in America is often indicated through legislation, public policy, and the actions of various bureaucracies.

Obviously, given the infinitely great number of definitions of what constitutes anything so vague as "human needs" and given the complex cultural heritage brought by Americans to their contact with the Adirondacks, we should not be surprised to discover that the development of an environmental attitude in and toward the region has been marked—as it has nearly everywhere—by ambiguity and confusion. We find these ambiguities and confusions in the response of the individual, whose attitude toward the Adirondacks has sometimes seemed contradictory, and in those of society, which has always had a hard time making up its collective mind about what to *do* with the Adirondacks.

The word "Adirondack" was first applied to a geographic entity, the area of the region now known as the high peaks, some one hundred fifty years ago; geologist Ebenezer Emmons chose the name, which was an Iroquois word for the Algonquin tribes.[4] During the nineteenth century, the region of New York now known by this name brought to the minds of various observers an amazing diversity of images: a sterile, useless desert; a sublime and scenic temple where the regenerative powers of nature could restore both mental and physical health to members of modern, urban society; a land rich with dormant agricultural potential waiting to support a large population of industrious husbandmen; a source of apparently limitless mineral wealth; an arena for the unhampered pursuit of the manly sports of hunting and fishing; a place where the plutocrats of the Gilded Age could retreat to rustic yet lavish camps surrounded by thousands of acres of privately owned timberlands; a rich source of lumber and pulp to be either exploited quickly and ruthlessly or harvested scientifically; a watershed whose capacity to guard and gradually release the water essential to the state's canals and reservoirs was threatened by the irresponsible ravages of nineteenth-century lumbering; a forest preserve to be owned in perpetuity by the people of New York; and finally a state park where private and public lands abutted in a complicated patchwork whose very complexity derived from the diverse demands made on the region and symbolized the disparate nineteenth-century uses of the Adirondacks.

In the twentieth century many of these images persist and still exercise considerable influence on the public consciousness. But sometime in the 1920s, a substantially new way of responding to the wilderness began to appear. I call this development the emergence of a modern wilderness aesthetic. In brief, the modern love for wilderness combines respect for the integrity of the landscape; belief that human interference violates that integrity; appreciation of the total, dynamic, interdependent system of nature; faith in the capacity of the landscape and its natural constituents (including wildlife, plants, and landforms) to manage their own affairs, even when this involves the loss to human society of economically valuable resources; and respect for the smallest details of nature as well as appreciation of the grand prospect. All of these, which suggest the land ethic first promulgated by Aldo Leopold, add up to a wilderness aesthetic. While the Leopoldian ethic is limiting in that it restricts human behavior to that which respects the nonhuman members of the terrestrial community, a wilderness aesthetic liberates humanity's perceptions in that it extends our appreciative faculties to parts of nature, such as swamps and deserts, that conventional aesthetics have ignored.[5] It enables a person to consider the *condition of wilderness* as an appealing characteristic of a landscape. This is what I mean when I discuss the inclination to preserve wilderness *as such* or wilderness per se.

This collection of ideas differs significantly from the response to wilderness of the American romantics. For one thing it leads to the conviction that at least some of the landscape ought to be preserved in a state where only natural forces operate; this means no lumbering, wildlife habitat management, or any other human interference in the environment. American romantics, even those most struck by their era's supposed love of nature, seldom expressed such a hands-off attitude. For another, it emphasizes the details and dynamic processes of nature, not the residence of a pantheistic deity in a sublime landscape. The person who backpacks in the wilderness but goes only for the views from lofty summits, deprecating swamps and other places which do not satisfy a predilection for the scenic or picturesque, does not really love and respect wilderness. A genuine wilderness aesthetic acknowledges the perfection of any part of nature where humans have not interfered with nature's processes.

In the last few years several historians have written about the politics of wilderness preservation in the Adirondacks.[6] I do not intend to repeat, nor do I have anything new to add to, the story of the wars waged by preservationists against developers, bureaucrats, and others whose aim was in one way or another to dilute or eliminate wilderness in the Adirondacks. In the twentieth century the wilderness lobby has exercised considerable power in New York State, and the saga of its battles to protect wilderness in the Adirondacks is a stirring one. What interests me here is not its tactics, victories, or losses but how the twentieth-century appreciation of wilderness both builds on and differs from the attitudes of the previous century.

When I comment on the absence of a modern appreciation of wilderness among the many explorers, scientists, sportsmen, and travelers who visited and reacted to the Adirondacks throughout the nineteenth and twentieth centuries, I mean the degree to which they remained somehow short of the attitudes described above. I try to avoid condemning nineteenth-century persons for not having twentieth-century views. I do not mean to suggest that explorers like Ebenezer Emmons and Verplanck Colvin were at all shallow or unperceptive because they did not respond to wilderness the way I do. My point is that too many historians of the Adirondacks and of the American wilderness in general have failed to understand adequately the extent of the hostility or indifference toward wilderness felt by our ancestors.

This hostility has been recognized where we expect to find it: in Puritans, developers, farmers, purveyors of manifest destiny, and others who trumpeted the mission of American civilization to carry progress and domestic institutions across the continent. But a similar unwillingness to accept wilderness also informs the response of people who have been thought to feel otherwise. Particularly with respect to the Adirondacks, historians have been inclined to perceive far more appreciation of wilderness for its own sake than actually existed.

The one thread that runs through nearly all perceptions of the Adirondacks is the continuing association of the region with wilderness, however the word was defined. In the 1830s the scientists of the New York Natural History Survey, who were often exploring country never before seen by American settlers, spoke of the region as a wilderness. Sportsmen in the 1880s referred to the Adirondack wilderness, despite the presence of hotels, lumber dams, the unavoidable evidence of nonnatural forest fires, and other signs of human impact. And modern backpackers pursue their sport in large tracts of publicly owned land officially designated by the state as "Wilderness Areas." We must agree with Roderick Nash, who laments in the Prologue to his *Wilderness and the American Mind* that useful, intelligible definitions are hard to come by. As Nash points out, "One man's wilderness may be another's roadside picnic ground."[7]

The 1964 Wilderness Act, which culminated a legislative struggle of several decades, provides a good starting point for any search for a reasonable definition of wilderness:

> A wilderness, in contrast with those areas where man and his works dominate the landscape, is hereby recognized as an area where the earth and its community of life are untrammeled by man, where man himself is a visitor who does not remain. An area of wilderness . . . retaining its primitive character and influence, without permanent improvements or human habitation . . . generally appears to have been affected primarily by the forces of nature, with the imprint of man substantially unnoticeable.[8]

The language of this statute recognizes in its very first sentence that wilderness must be defined by what it is not as much as by what it is. Wilderness is not, clearly, the city, the suburb, or even the farm.[9] In short, the wilderness is not where people live or work permanently. By approaching a definition in this negative way, by contrasting wilderness with something that we can generally agree is *not* wilderness, we can find common ground with the writers and travelers who have described the Adirondacks throughout the last century and a half. For they nearly always employed the notion of wilderness to indicate something radically different from what they knew in their ordinary lives.

Although it could be argued that wilderness is any place inhospitable to humans and that there are thus many urban or rural areas that some people would *call* wilderness, the use of the word here depends on a perception of the landscape as fundamentally shaped by natural forces. To be sure, the idea that wilderness is inhospitable is an important element of attitudes toward the Adirondack area and explains much of the hostility that many nineteenth-century and later travelers expressed toward it. But equally important in most writers' use of the word "wilderness" in connection with the Adirondacks has been the sense of a landscape where the familiar forces of agriculture, internal improvements, and evidence of "man the builder" are more or less absent. The Wilderness Act, reflecting this attitude, thus emphasizes that wilderness possesses "primeval character," lacks "permanent improvements or human habitations," and "generally appears to have been affected primarily by the forces of nature."

The fascination with wilderness, therefore, involving both appreciation and hostility, arises from the perception of the wilderness as essentially different from civilization's usual environment. Civilized, Western peoples—with whom we are exclusively concerned here—inhabit a secondary environment, characterized by their additions to and improvements on nature. In the wilderness the very facts of physical discomfort and psychological disorientation emphasize the difference between "untrammeled" nature and the urban, suburban, or rural (i.e., agricultural) landscape. As long as this difference appears significant, the perception of a landscape as wilderness persists; it does not depend on virginity.

Land that has escaped the notice and therefore the imprint of humans is of course a wilderness, but land that people have touched is not ipso facto nonwilderness. This has two applications. First, it permits land that has been significantly affected by human forces but from which the operation of those forces has been removed to be legally classified as wilderness under the Wilderness Act. For example, land once lumbered and then left to reforest itself, where the marks of previous human activity are visible only to the expert botanist or ecologist, may be wilderness if it appears to the ordinary observer to have been affected primarily by the forces of nature.

More important for our purposes is the notion that wilderness is a relative concept. Wilderness is in the eye of the beholder. The landscape constitutes a wilderness to the extent that people perceive it to do so. Thus wilderness is both an objective, geographic entity, a physical place defined by the fact that the human is a visitor there, and also a subjective, psychological phenomenon, defined epistemologically by the mind of that visitor. Thoreau knew this well; writing of the Maine woods, he noted, "Generally speaking, a howling wilderness does not howl: it is the imagination of the traveller that does the howling."[10] The Adirondacks, pristine wilderness when first encountered, continued to be perceived as wilderness throughout most of the nineteenth century. During that time much of the region was lumbered, towns appeared, hotels and camps dotted parts of the landscape, and summer sportsmen thronged the woods. But people still spoke of going to the Adirondacks and going to the wilderness in the same breath. It is clear that significant changes took place between the days of the Natural History Survey in the 1830s and the era of early conservation in the 1880s and 1890s, but a substantial portion of the population of New York and the rest of the Northeast continued to perceive the Adirondacks, or at least large parts of the region, as wilderness. And this has continued to be the case throughout the twentieth century.

Despite enthusiastic appreciation of Adirondack scenery, the idea of wilderness as such met with a continuing and pervasive hostility throughout the nineteenth century. Surveyors, sportsmen, and travelers of all sorts responded positively to the scenic charms of Adirondack mountains and lakes and to the manly pleasures of outdoor recreation, but they often felt alien and psychologically disoriented in the wilderness, and they were overtly hostile to the idea of land that contributed nothing of commercial or agricultural value to American society. Yet in 1894 the people of New York adopted a new state constitution, one of whose provisions guaranteed forever the preservation of state-owned lands in the Adirondacks as "wild forest lands."

The language and intent of this constitution, however, did not reflect a decision to protect wilderness as such; it did not even include the word wilderness. To the framers of the 1894 constitution and to most of its earliest interpreters, the word "preservation" of a forest meant simply maintaining the forest to the extent of its established bounds. It did not mean, as it does to advocates of a modern wilderness aesthetic, that the primeval character of the forest was to be preserved. The 1894 constitutional provision represented an effort not to save wilderness for the sake of its inherent values but simply to prevent the destruction of the Adirondack watershed by lumbering and to preclude the consequent demise of New York's commercial waterways.

In the twentieth century, although attitudes toward wilderness changed, the forever-wild provision of 1894 has been incorporated in precisely the same language in every subsequent New York constitution. For most of the century, however, a wide divergence has persisted between the practical results of that provision and public feeling. The gap was most clearly manifested in the hostility toward wilderness long shown by the state conservation bureaucracy. But in recent years the preservation of wilderness for its own sake has been institutionalized in the state's plan for the future of the Adirondacks.

The constitutional protection of 1894 and the institutionalization of preservation sentiment in the 1970s provide the basic organizational pattern for this book. The first four chapters discuss attitudes to wilderness as they developed in the nineteenth century; they set up the discussion in the fifth chapter of the legislative and constitutional measures adopted in the 1880s and 1890s. Chapters VI and VII discuss twentieth-century attitudes, and the last chapter shows how the conservation bureaucracy (or at least part of it) finally accepted the idea of wilderness preservation and how that idea became part of the statutory mandate for the future of the Adirondacks.

# I
# First Impressions

▲▲▲▲▲▲▲

When people first started to think of the Adirondack region as a place, beginning late in the eighteenth century, they saw it through the lens of certain cultural preconceptions concerning wild, rugged country where human modification of the landscape was minimal or nonexistent. In the last few years, historians have been giving increased attention to the attitudes Americans have displayed toward all of what may be loosely classified as nature. Because of our contemporary concern with the quality of the environment and the deleterious effects of many activities of American society, it is important to understand how the Europeans who settled America have responded to, and what impact they have had on, the American landscape. Since a fundamental feature of our historical experience, moreover, was our confrontation with wild, uncultivated country, intellectual historians have recognized that an understanding of the dynamics of that confrontation is essential to any understanding of the American national character. Although historians have certainly not reached any agreement on a definition of the American character, they have produced a substantial secondary literature on the preconceptions Americans have brought with them to the wilderness.[1]

At the time of the first European encounter with the Adirondacks, the region *was* a wilderness. The timber, wildlife, and landforms showed virtually no sign of civilized activity. Before the first few land surveys were run in the latter half of the eighteenth century there is little evidence of any significant previous human penetration of the region. Common sense tells us that there must have been some contact—Indians and early settlers alike probably trapped beaver in the Adirondacks—but as far as written records reveal, the first Europeans to describe the Adirondacks depicted an area that was the product of natural forces.[2]

From the outset, Europeans responded to the Adirondacks with ambivalence. One of the most significant features of the American attitude toward wilderness is its mixture of hostility, indifference, appreciation, and wonder. Not only have some people responded positively while their contemporaries responded negatively, but even the response of a single individual has sometimes been a complex mixture of hostility and reverence. Roderick Nash traces the roots of this ambivalence to the beginnings of the Judaeo-Christian tradition. On the one hand, wilderness was the opposite of cultivated and therefore life-sustaining land; moreover, wilderness was a place where savagery flourished, a place of physical and spiritual peril. On the other hand, the wilderness was sometimes seen as a sanctuary from humanity's sinful ways. Hebrew and Christian fathers alike went into the wilderness to meditate and renew their dedication to the Lord, and whole tribes sometimes sought in the wilderness a refuge from those aspects of civilized life that distracted the faithful from their devotion to God.[3]

To this antagonistic combination of hostility and appreciation, which dominated European reactions to wild country until the time when settlement on this continent was well established, the American experience added the further element of a simple distaste for land that was unproductive. Because life for men and women in the New World had been for so long so precarious and so hard, and because whatever civilization Americans had achieved by the eighteenth century had literally been wrested from the wilderness, Americans came to think of wilderness as the special enemy of civilized society on this continent. And not only did the wilderness resist the efforts of settlers to turn the New World into a land of farms, but its native inhabitants, the Indians, seemed to the settlers to represent the barbarous savagery to which they themselves might revert if they dwelt too long in the wilderness.[4]

Thus Americans, because they had too recently been actually involved in a life-or-death struggle with the wilderness, were not likely to change their attitudes toward it as easily as Europeans were to do in the eighteenth century. As the romantic temperament emerged from the Enlightenment, some Europeans began to evince a taste for wild scenery, to derive aesthetic pleasure from the contemplation of unimproved nature. In English poetry and painting, country that retained its wild character came to be viewed positively.[5] James Thomson's *The Seasons*, for example, written early in the eighteenth century, described the spiritual joys of intimacy with a nature with which one communed but which one did not try to subdue. Americans lagged behind Europeans in adopting this attitude. As Tocqueville noted more than a hundred years after Thomson's *Seasons* had shown the nascent European appreciation of nature,

> in Europe people talk a great deal of the wilds of America, but the Americans themselves never think about them; they are insensible to the wonders of inanimate nature and they may be said not to perceive the mighty forests that surround them till they fall beneath the hatchet. Their eyes are fixed upon another sight: the American people views its own march across these wilds, draining swamps, turning the course of rivers, and subduing nature.

Of course, like any generalization, this one is not without exceptions; Jefferson's famous encomium on the beauties of the confluence of the Shenandoah and Potomac rivers represents the adoption by culturally alert Americans of certain European views.[6] But most Americans remained indifferent or hostile to wild country until well into the nineteenth century.

Those Americans like Jefferson who displayed an admiration for wild country were strongly influenced by a formal school of English aesthetics whose canons were most clearly expressed by Edmund Burke in his *Philosophical Enquiry into the Origins of Our Ideas of the Sublime and the Beautiful*. With the rationality characteristic of the Enlightenment, the book is an analysis of, among other things, how man perceives and reacts to the natural world. Natural scenery, according to Burke, could be divided into two categories—the beautiful and the sublime. The beautiful included most of what had traditionally been associated with cultivated, delicate, pleasant nature; its features were typically small, smooth, gently curving, light in color, fragile, and "founded on pleasure." The sublime landscape, on the other hand, was characteristically vast, rugged, straight or angular, dark and gloomy, solid and massive, and "founded on pain."[7] Thus a formal English garden or a pleasant bucolic landscape would have been called beautiful; a wild mountain scene, sublime.

Despite the ostensibly negative features of the sublime, the eighteenth-century temperament found it a fascinating subject. Although writers usually described sublime scenery with adjectives like "awful," "gloomy," "painful," and "terrifying," they associated the sublime with the infinite powers of God. The ability of the wild mountain panorama to envelop the soul of the viewer, to put everything else out of his mind, reminded Burke of God's power to enthrall the worshiper. The chief attribute of sublime scenery was its incomprehensible greatness:

> The passion caused by the great and sublime in *nature*, when those causes operate most powerfully, is Astonishment; and astonishment is that state of the soul in which all its motions are suspended, with some degree of horror. In this case the mind is so completely filled with its object, that it cannot entertain any other, nor by consequence reason on the object which employs it.[8]

Burke's classification of the properties of the sublime proved extensively influential among viewers of mountain scenery in North America in general and in the Adirondacks in particular; they routinely invoked the Burkean vocabulary in their descriptions.

Among the features of this aesthetic was the inclination to reduce the consideration of mountain scenery to an analysis of its constituents, described in the most precise terms. William Gilpin, an English clergyman who wrote a number of books on aesthetics, explained that his aim was to "teach the eye to admire justly": that is, to teach his readers exactly what proportions of variety, ruggedness, grandeur, angularity, etc., constituted the ideal sublime scene.[9] This line of thinking led viewers to judge the rugged landscape as though they were rewarding excellence at an art exhibition. Paradoxically, writers could describe the terror educed by a particular sublime view and then in the same paragraph coldly and rationally analyze the scene according to the canons of Burke and Gilpin. Many Adirondack writers, in fact, discussed scenery exactly as they would have described landscape painting, praising the placement of a gnarled tree in just the right corner and criticizing the lack of color in another. Their response showed an intimacy with the standard works of the cult of the sublime, and they described the sublime Adirondack view with a stock, derivative vocabulary.

Their fascination with wild scenery, however, did not mean that they (or Burke, for that matter) were replacing the traditional hostility to wilderness with a positive response founded on the Enlightenment association of God and nature. Burke and Gilpin were chiefly interested in the process by which human perceptions translate the disparate elements of the natural world into a unified picture of nature. This interest often assumed an almost mechanical detachment. And in its single-minded concern with the senses—mainly sight—it never intended to suggest that wilderness per se might offer a positive spiritual experience. Adirondack observers who participated in the cult of the sublime could write glowingly of the mountains, yet maintain the traditional American hostility to unproductive, uncultivated, and uncultivatable land.

Persistent hostility notwithstanding, the influence of the cult of the sublime was an important early ingredient in the eventual accommodation between some Americans and the wilderness; the suggestion that there was anything positive there exercised a growing influence on how people perceived the Adirondacks and all American wilderness. It was not a very long step from the Enlightenment position that in the grandeur of the sublime view one could sense the vastness of the power of God to the romantic belief that God is omnipresent in nature. The mechanistic rationalism of the eighteenth century, in fact, by which Burke and others dissected the constituents of sublimity and beauty, helped to usher in the mystical pantheism of the nineteenth.

Adirondack tradition holds that the first European to see the region was Jacques Cartier, peering to the south from Mont Royal on an October day in 1535; and that Samuel de Champlain, the first to set foot in what is now the Adirondack Park, did so in 1609. Nevertheless, Adirondack history remained a virtual void until the eighteenth century. In the meantime the Dutch belief that that part of New Netherlands near the St. Lawrence was inhabited by unicorns indicates, as does the blank spot on early English maps of New York, that the Adirondack region was a mysterious terra incognita. Even when Englishmen began to pay some notice to the area in the middle of the eighteenth century, it was chiefly to say what they did not know about it.[10]

Lewis Evans, whose 1755 a *General Map of the Middle British Colonies in America* was the most accurate, detailed map of the pre-Revolutionary period, was able to provide more information about the Ohio frontier than he could about the Adirondacks; he was forced to leave a conspicuous void in that part of New York north of the Mohawk and write lamely across the area, "This Country by Reason of Mountain Swamps and drowned Land is impassable and uninhabited." And in his *Analysis* of the map, published the same year, he wrote, "The Country between the *Mohocks* and St. *Laurence* Rivers is entirely impassable by Reason of Ridges of Hills, not being yet broken, to drain the vast drowned Land and Swamps."[11]

Evans' comments are interesting for two reasons: first, the description of the Adirondacks as a marshy, mountainous wasteland would remain common in certain observers' reports for the next eighty or ninety years; second, he implied that the reason for the region's "impassable" condition was the fact that improvements had not yet been worked on the rough landscape to "drain the vast drowned Land and Swamps." Evans was the first of many to suggest that the barren Adirondack terrain wanted only the imposition of human genius to change a useless wilderness into something that human industry might make productive. The suggestion would appear with greater and greater frequency in the years to follow.

Most observers, however, saw little or no potential. Sir William Johnson, who from his seat near the modern city of Johnstown ranged over much of the land on either side of the Mohawk, wrote in 1770 that the terrain in the southern Adirondack foothills was "so verry [sic] mountainous & barren that it is worth nothing. The Snow was 5 feet deep on these Mountains the 30th of March." A similar response appears in the field notes of Archibald Campbell, who ran the north line of an early Adirondack land purchase in 1772 and provided the earliest written record of a reaction to the central Adirondacks. As Campbell made his way through the wilderness, marking trees with blazes, he noted in a journal the character of the terrain. For the most part he found it inhospitable and without agricultural potential, writing, for example, "Land stoney & Rocky," "high poor Land," "poor Land with Spruce Timber," and "the Land is Poor and Rocky here." Occasionally, however, Campbell came upon areas that he felt could be converted to farming, writing at one point, "This is a fine Land for to make meadow."

Campbell and Johnson represent an attitude that has remained influential throughout Adirondack history. In this view, lands appear interesting or valuable only to the extent that they are potentially productive; wilderness, therefore, is a condition to be eliminated as quickly as possible because it impedes the progressive thrust of civilization.[12]

Despite Campbell's survey, the Adirondacks remained mostly unknown. In 1784, Thomas Pownall's *Topographical Description*, written to be published with a reissue of Evans' 1755 map, noted in passing,

> (rather to mark my Ignorance than presuming to give Information) . . . that the Country, lying to the West of these Lakes [George and Champlain], bounded on the North West by Canada River [the St. Lawrence], and on the South by the Mohawks River, called by the Indians Couxsachrage, which signifies the Dismal Wilderness or Habitation of Winter, is a triangular, high mountainous tract, very little known to the Europeans; and although a hunting Ground of the Indians, yet either not much known to them, or, if known, very wisely by them kept from the Knowledge of the Europeans. It is said to be a broken unpracticable Tract; I own I could never learn anything about it.

Borrowing from Evans' *Analysis* the position that the region was probably useless, as well as the Indian name "Couxsachrage," Pownall added further credibility to the notion that the Adirondacks was not worth exploring. At the same time, he demonstrated with admirable honesty the extent of European ignorance about the Adirondacks.[13]

Although this ignorance persisted until well into the nineteenth century, it did not prevent gazetteers and other sources of geographical information from printing bold inaccuracies: it was commonly asserted, for example, that the Catskills were the highest mountains in New York. And Whiteface Mountain, known because of its proximity to the settlements at North Elba and Wilmington, was usually said to be no higher than 2,700 feet above sea level, whereas its true height is 4,867 feet.[14]

The principal rivers of the region often received similarly inaccurate mention. Since by the early decades of the nineteenth century, settlements had appeared all around the margins of the Adirondacks, the mouths of the Raquette, the Saranac, the Hudson, the Ausable, the St. Regis, the Oswegatchie, and other streams were recognized to be the outlets of rivers that rose somewhere in the heart of the wilderness. Little else was known, although what details the gazetteers did provide indicated that some explorers had begun to penetrate the central Adirondacks. Macauley, for example, in tracing the course of the Raquette, wrote that it passed through a long lake running northwest-southeast. This body of water must have been Long Lake, which actually runs southwest-northeast. Macauley also wrote that the Raquette flowed "out of a lake eight or nine miles long, and from two to three broad, situated in the northwestern part of the county of Hamilton"—a nearly accurate description of Raquette Lake. However, he continued, "we are but little acquainted with the dreary and desolate region through which this river flows, before it reaches the low country neighboring the St. Lawrence," apparently subscribing to and encouraging the persistent perception of the Adirondack region as barren, useless land.[15]

In a more favorable tone, Macauley noted that "the scenery around Lake George is exceedingly magnificent and picturesque." He was not the first to say so. Thomas Jefferson, for example, who visited the lake in 1791, wrote to his daughter:

> Lake George is, without comparison, the most beautiful water I ever saw; formed by a contour of mountains into a basin thirty five miles long, and from two or four miles broad, finely interspersed with islands, its water limpid as crystal, and the mountains sides covered with rich groves of thuja, silver fir, aspen, and paper birch down to the water edge; here and there precipices of rock to checker the scene and save it from monotony.

Jefferson's judgment of the scene is typically eighteenth century; he lists the elements of the view and then judges their arrangement according to contemporary aesthetics.[16]

What made the Lake George area interesting to both Jefferson and Macauley, and what distinguished it in Macauley's mind from the "dreary and desolate" course of the Raquette River, were the precipices that in Jefferson's opinion saved the scene from monotony. Although the wilderness surrounding the Raquette was repugnant to most people in the late eighteenth and early nineteenth centuries, they could react positively to a scene that satisfied certain preconceptions about natural scenery, and the terrain around Lake George happened to do so. The fact that it remained relatively unsettled and in its original character was incidental, or even a shortcoming.

A number of early nineteenth-century visitors were lured by the lake's reputation for remarkable scenery. One of the better known and more articulate of these was Timothy Dwight, president of Yale College, who every summer traveled to some interesting part of New England or New York and in 1802 paid his first visit to Lake George. Although Dwight considered the landscape sublime rather than beautiful, his response is nonetheless characteristically Burkean. He described the water and soil, speculated on how the lake might have been formed, and then analyzed the scenery mechanically, telling his reader how to find the "three best points of view." He commented on the lake's light, variety, grandeur, and all the stock attributes; in a passage typical of the cult of the sublime he emphasized "the sudden promontory, the naked cliff, the stupendous precipice, the awful chasm, the sublime and barren eminence, and the vast heaps of rude and rocky grandeur which [are] thrown together in confusion and piled upon each other by the magnificent hand of nature."[17] The vocabulary is standard, with words like "naked cliff," "stupendous," and "awful" all leading to a confirmation of the powerful deity behind the forms of nature.

But like other writers who responded to the scenery at Lake George, Dwight saw nothing positive in the *idea* of untouched nature. The sheer cliff may have been an essential element in the sublime scene, but Dwight felt that the natural setting alone lacked an important ingredient:

> To complete the scenery of this lake, the efforts of cultivation are obviously wanting. The hand of the husbandman has already begun to clear these grounds, and will, at no great distance of time, adorn them with all the smiling scenes of agriculture. It does not demand the gift of prophecy to foresee that the villas of opulence and refinement will, within half a century, add here all the elegances of art to the beauty and majesty of nature.

The emphasis on the scenic attributes shows a response not to nature but to how that nature appears and how its appearance could be improved. Dwight was merely the first of many who foresaw a thriving agricultural future for the Adirondack region and whose vision of this development dwelt on the scenic changes it would necessitate; his vision of the future also provided for the establishment of luxurious summer homes, in which respect he showed himself more prescient than most observers of his time.[18]

Dwight's prediction, hinted at by Evans and Campbell, that the Adirondacks could support a population of farmers was to be echoed frequently over the next fifty years. It was a common American response to insist that in the interests of civilization the wilderness must be broken by the plow. The American vision of turning a continental wilderness into a garden peopled by thrifty husbandmen has been well elaborated and analyzed by scholars, and Dwight's participation in this tradition comes as no surprise.[19] What is pertinent here is that the agricultural vision follows so closely a rapturous description of a wilderness. To Dwight, the sublime scene was more a passing oddity than an item of intrinsic value. It was a sight worth traveling to see, but its very existence suggested that the region was tardy in entering the mainstream of American life. Wherever it was found, wilderness implicitly condemned the slack spirit of the few settlers in the neighborhood. Any American landscape unadorned by the cottages, neatly tilled fields, and well-tended livestock of an agricultural population was simply incomplete.

Henry Nash Smith calls the faith in the almost sacred mission of the American farmer the "myth of the garden," while Leo Marx includes it within the rubric of the "pastoral ideal" and associates it with the Jeffersonian concept of the "middle landscape" or the bucolic dimension between the grim exigencies of industrialism and the savage threat of the wilderness.[20] I propose to call the point of view, of which Dwight's hopes for agriculture at Lake George were an early example, the *middle-landscape ideal*. In the context of this study, it involves the conviction that agricultural productivity is the best possible use to which any land can be put. Thus, in a sense, I have slightly redirected the emphasis of the Jeffersonian concept from the farmer to the farm. The conventional American faith in the virtues and wisdom of the hearty husbandman put the emphasis on the farmers and their families, and on the ability of these tillers of the American soil to maintain a wholesome and stable democracy. In this study of environmental attitudes, however, I want further to emphasize the land itself, the earth, the water, and the hoped-for fruits of productivity. The

American ideology of agrarianism, in addition to its social and cultural impact, had aesthetic and environmental implications; it helped to determine how Dwight and his contemporaries reacted to the appearance of the American landscape.[21]

In the early years of the nineteenth century, a few pioneers in the Adirondacks were trying to realize Dwight's vision of agricultural prosperity. Along with iron miners, trappers, and a few early loggers (substantial logging in the region did not begin until 1850 and did not peak until the end of the century), they constituted the only incursions on the wilderness when the state undertook its first systematic examination of the Adirondacks—with the New York Natural History Survey of 1836–40. By the 1830s the Adirondack region had been carved into several huge blocks by speculative land purchases; a few families had settled in the interior; and county and some town lines had been drawn. Political subdivision, however, had meaning only on official state maps: the land itself remained, for the most part, unexplored and uninhabited. The story of land purchase and subdivision was largely one of speculation on the part of businessmen who never set foot in the Adirondacks. Their tracts were often surveyed, and some knowledge of the region resulted, but in most of the Adirondacks the wilderness remained.[22]

Throughout the nineteenth century a pattern evolved: lands were purchased from the state, either used for a while or never used at all, and then allowed (intentionally or through oversight) to revert to the state for unpaid taxes. Some parcels went through this process repeatedly. Although much of the prime hunting and camping land was thus from time to time privately owned, most people who came to the area for recreation perceived it as public domain. Before the day of the no-trespassing sign, sportsmen did not care that they might be camping on nominally private property; until late in the century, the owners did not care either.

Some of the early purchases were developed, however, and settlements did appear. Keene Valley had its first settler by 1797; Newcomb by 1810; Saranac Lake by 1819; and Long Lake by 1830. These scattered hamlets consisted of marginally productive farms; the Adirondack soils and climate made successful farming nearly impossible. As a state commission examining the condition of the forests in the 1880s noted, "All attempts at settlement of the Adirondack plateau by an agricultural population . . . have resulted in disastrous failure. Abandoned homes and fields are scattered everywhere along the borders of the forest, while the scanty population which still struggles to compel the inhospitable soil to yield it a miserable existence too plainly shows the hopelessness of the task." The farmers themselves would probably have given up the fight had not their woodcraft and knowledge of the local geography permitted them to remain and make money as guides for the sportsmen who began appearing in the Adirondacks in the 1840s. Adirondack iron was also luring settlers and developers. These were important not because they succeeded financially (they did not) but because the hopes for success for these ventures weighed so heavily on the minds of early explorers, and because one enterprise—the McIntyre development near Newcomb—was the starting point for the expedition that in 1837 made the first ascent of New York's highest mountain.[23] Still, except for widely separated pockets of civilization, the primordial forest covered all. A surveyor wrote in 1840 that the Adirondacks was "as little known and as inadequately appreciated as the secluded valleys of the Rocky Mountains, or the burning plains of Central Africa."[24]

# II

# Progress or Nature:

## Ebenezer Emmons and the Natural History Survey

Early in 1836, New York Secretary of State John Adams Dix submitted to his legislature a report on the need for a survey of the state's natural resources. Such a survey, argued Dix, would benefit New York in two ways: first, it would encourage the exploitation of mineral and other resources; second, it would add to the body of scientific knowledge. The legislature responded enthusiastically, and the New York Natural History Survey began field explorations that summer. Both the annual reports filed with the New York Assembly and the elaborate final reports published after the completion of fieldwork emphasized the dual mandate: the Survey was to assist in the utilitarian development of the state, and it was at the same time to be an exercise in intellectual advancement.[1]

The fieldwork occupied five years, 1836–40, and the final reports began appearing in 1842. The scientists engaged in the Survey were among the country's most prominent scholars. Ebenezer Emmons has been called the most important American geologist of the nineteenth century. John Torrey was one of the two foremost American botanists of the day, the other being his collaborator, Asa Gray. James Hall, who began working for the Survey as Emmons' assistant and was subsequently appointed its paleontologist, eventually achieved world renown. The Survey itself was one of the most ambitious efforts of nineteenth-century American science; it "engaged the services of a number of prominent naturalists and earned the plaudits and approval equally of politicians and scientists." In short, it became "the classic model of the state survey."[2]

In their response to the wilderness of the Adirondacks, these men, particularly Emmons, revealed a self-contradictory extension of their dual mandate. In the recesses of the Adirondack forests, on the summits of mountains they were the first to ascend, on the uninhabited shores of Adirondack lakes, they perceived the joys of intimacy with untouched wilderness and asserted the value to a busy civilization of the spiritual forces immanent in wild nature. But they also recommended a variety of exploitative schemes that would have entirely compromised the wilderness experience they elsewhere extolled. To them, the wilderness was simultaneously the temple of a pantheistic deity, a natural curiosity deserving the notice of both scientists and tourists, an impediment to efficient fieldwork, and finally an obstacle to progress itself: a primitive remnant of a former world to be replaced as soon as possible by farms, canals, roads, mines, and other features of American commerce and industry. The utilitarian mentality dominated the reports, but in the attitude of geologist Emmons, at least, it also led to a plea for conservation of natural resources and thus initiated the kind of reasoning that effected the establishment and protection of the Adirondack Forest Preserve later in the century.

The reports of the Natural History Survey are worth studying both because they display the complexities and paradoxes of the Jacksonian response to nature and because they anticipate the multifaceted, ambivalent, often contradictory perceptions of the Adirondacks that have influenced popular attitudes and policy ever since. Although the scientists of the Survey were products of the elite, educated class and thus do not necessarily represent the attitudes of the majority of Americans, their response to the wilderness is nonetheless important because this class has largely determined public policy relative to the Adirondacks and all of the diminishing American wilderness throughout the nineteenth and twentieth centuries.

The New York Natural History Survey was but one part of a national phenomenon. Beginning in the 1820s various states in the East and South had commissioned prominent scientists, mostly geologists, to supervise statewide surveys of natural resources. The most comprehensive of these earlier efforts was the Massachusetts Survey, which began fieldwork in 1830 and produced its final reports in 1833. Under the leadership of Edward Hitchcock, the scope of its research included botany and zoology as well as geology. The New York Natural History Survey followed the Massachusetts example and borrowed one of Hitchcock's most efficient workers: Ebenezer Emmons, who had been the chief zoologist in Hitchcock's corps, was named geologist of the second geological district of New York—an area embracing most of the Adirondacks. Emmons acknowledged that his work in New York was the local manifestation of a popular enthusiasm for science and of national pride in the foresight and intelligence of the American people: "The Survey of New York was indebted for its projection and execution to a movement in science—a movement which pervaded the entire thinking community. It was one of those natural results which mark the progress of truth, and in itself was an evidence of the progressive intelligence of the human mind."[3]

Emmons is the key figure in the story of the Natural History Survey. In addition to leading the first recorded ascent of New York's highest mountain and bestowing the name "Adirondack" on the region, he composed thoughtful and revealing reports, which commented far more fully on the character and potential of the wilderness than did those of any of his colleagues. Born in Middlefield, Massachusetts, in 1799, Emmons received his primary education in the local schools and then studied at Williams College, where he subsequently became a professor of natural history. In the 1820s he was also teaching at the newly established Rensselaer School (now Rensselaer Polytechnic Institute) and the Albany Medical College, and was practicing medicine. His entire life was devoted to the natural sciences; he taught and studied chemistry and geology, and in 1855 he published a widely used geology textbook.[4]

Emmons' writings on the Adirondacks show him to have been an industrious, perceptive man, sensitive to the wonders of the wilderness he was exploring as well as to the practical needs of a growing state. Though Emmons devoted most of his attention to the need to replace the wilderness with progressive enterprises like mining and agriculture, he also showed a romantic faith in the beneficence of nature. He knew well that his country depended on the efforts of farmers, miners, and entrepreneurs of all sorts for its continuing prosperity, but at the same time he discovered in the Adirondack wilderness a source of spiritual power and a hint that all the frenzy of the Jacksonian economy might in the long run be threatening to both society and nature.

In writing of the Adirondack scenery, Emmons subscribed to the aesthetic distinctions of Edmund Burke and his popularizers and divided most of the terrain into Burke's two categories—the sublime and the beautiful; his descriptions of any place satisfying Burke's definition of the sublime emphasized the gloomy, frightening, overpowering features. "The Ausable river... flows through deep and frightful chasms," Emmons wrote. And his colleague William C. Redfield thus described the trap dyke—a towering, natural chimney—on Mount Colden at Avalanche Lake: "The scene on entering the chasm is one of sublime grandeur and its nearly vertical walls of rock, at some points actually overhang the intruder, and seem to threaten him with instant destruction." Though such descriptions reflect the Burkean fascination with landscapes whose chief attribute was a capacity for inspiring terror, Emmons nonetheless recommended that tourists seek out such scenery, noting with approval that newly constructed steps made the gorge at Ausable Chasm more accessible. And Redfield's immediate response to the Colden trap dyke was to climb it.[5]

In the lake country of the central Adirondacks, Emmons found scenery corresponding to Burke's other category—the beautiful. Of Indian Lake, Emmons wrote, "The scenery is fine, and such as characterizes a northern region, [with] forests of deep green pines and spruce, intermixed with the lighter hues of the white birch and poplar; these when contrasted with the purple skies and reflected from the bosom of some lake, create a scene of unrivalled beauty." All of the lakes of Hamilton County, he suggested, "form a beautiful addition to the scenery of our country," and he compared the central Adirondacks to the lakes and mountains of Scotland.[6]

Emmons was not locked into the rather mechanical distinctions of the Burkean aesthetic, however, and did not, as did some of his contemporaries, dwell on the merely scenic at the expense of spiritual values. Calling the Adirondack region a land "unrivalled for its magic and enchantment," he went on to say:

> It is not, however, by description that the scenery of this region can be made to pass before the eye of the imagination: it must be witnessed; the solitary summits in the distance, the cedars and firs which clothe the rock and shore, must be seen; the solitude must be felt; or, if it is broken by the scream of the panther, the shrill cry of the northern diver, or the shout of the hunter, the echo from the thousand hills must be heard before all the truth in the scene can be realized. These are elements in the landscape, all of which are felt when there, but are lost in the words of a description, and untransferable by the pencil of the artist.[7]

By emphasizing the solitude, the sensation of being surrounded by an apparently endless wilderness, and the ultimate appreciation of "the truth in the scene," Emmons has suggested that the wilderness itself, of which the scenery is an important but not the only constituent, offers spiritual sustenance to the soul. He was too careful a writer to use "feel" for "believe" or "perceive"; his use of that verb twice in this passage signifies that he was describing more than intellection or perception. His response to the wilderness, at least as he accounted for it here, involved a mixture of emotion and even religion. To speak of "elements in the landscape," immanent but ineffable, is to suggest the existence of a pantheistic presence.

But Emmons, as both a Wordsworthian pantheist and a progressive utilitarian, seemed at times to recognize the twofold nature of his response. In August of 1837, shortly after leading the first known ascent of Mount Marcy, he climbed Nippletop, a peak several miles to the east of Marcy and in those days equally difficult of access. After an arduous hike of three days through a pathless forest, the expedition reached the summit just as a morning mist was breaking up, gradually revealing the surrounding peaks. In his report to the Assembly for that year, Emmons wrote:

> Wishing to obtain the bearing of the more important mountains in the vicinity, we watched, with an interest in which it is difficult to say, whether our love of science or admiration of the intrinsic beauty and sublimity of the scene more participated; the lifting up of the cloudy envelope from the neighboring summits, one after another, in the order of its elevation, presented its outline, dim or well defined, according to the distance, until the profile, in every direction but that of a single mountain, was complete.[8]

In asserting the importance of *"intrinsic* beauty and sublimity," Emmons recognized something inherent in the landscape, something beyond the ken of the measuring, weighing, judging faculties of the scientist. But he admitted the competition between his "love of science" and his spiritual response to natural magnificence. The scientific inclination is akin to the practical and utilitarian, and in Emmons' double vision we find precisely the ambivalence that has characterized attitudes to the Adirondacks in particular and to the American wilderness in general ever since. Emmons the romantic admired the beauty, but Emmons the scientist welcomed the dissipation of the mist so that he could proceed to use his telescope, barometer, and the other instruments that reduced nature to cold data.

Emmons displayed a similar double vision at Indian Pass, which appealed to his aesthetic sense as the essence of sublimity: "We look upon the falls of Niagara with awe, and a feeling of our insignificance; but much more are we impressed with the great and sublime, in the view of the simple rock of the [Indian] Pass." Thus it was truly "worthy of a visit by lovers of magnificent scenery." But Indian Pass, with its sheer cliffs, its virtually impassable gorge, its chaos of huge boulders and thick forest, was also "merely a natural curiosity." While Emmons appreciated the sublime view, he also perceived Indian Pass as a remnant of something primitive. It was a visual lesson in geology: of the gigantic boulders on the floor of the pass, Emmons wrote, "It is from facts like these, that we learn what mighty forces operated in former times." In addition to showing that Emmons remained a catastrophist in the face of mounting evidence proving the principles of uniformitarianism, this statement suggests that the area of Indian Pass is both ancient and at the same time atavistic, having escaped the mellowing forces that shaped the less imposing terrain more familiar to most New Yorkers.[9] If the high peaks and Indian Pass reveal how ancient forces worked to shape the earth's surface and if their effects were not visible elsewhere, then the natural sequence of geological events must have stopped in the Adirondacks. Indian Pass, then, was both an object of aesthetic appreciation and a curiosity exciting scientific wonder.

Other members of the Survey found the Adirondacks to be full of similar oddities pointing to the primitive nature of the region.

Zoologist James DeKay noted the persistence of several animal species in the Adirondacks that had been extirpated in the rest of the state. The fisher, which once was common in New York, was then "confined to the thinly settled northern districts. . . . In Hamilton county it is still numerous and troublesome." The wolverine was "still found in the districts north of Raquet lake." Likewise, wolves were "still numerous in the mountains and wooded portions of the state, and, we believe, are most numerous in St. Lawrence and the adjacent counties."[10] To DeKay, the absence of the wolf in most of the state was an obvious sign of civilization and progress, while its survival in the Adirondacks indicated how backward the region was.

To John Torrey, chief botanist for the Survey, the discovery of rare northern plants like diapensia or Lapland roseboy reflected the topographical and climatological strangeness of the region. Of one alpine species that he found on the summit of Mount Marcy, he wrote, "This plant has not been found elsewhere in the United States, except on the highest peaks of the White Mountains of New-Hampshire. It occurs in Labrador, in Arctic America, and in the northern regions of Europe." The discovery and subsequent publication of the existence of such flora helped to establish a picture in the popular consciousness of the Adirondack wilderness as an unusual place, unlike the familiar remainder of New York. The notion was encouraged by Torrey's comments on the black spruce: "The largest trees of Black Spruce that I ever saw, were in the valleys of the Essex mountains . . . where there were several that measured nearly three feet in diameter."[11] Torrey's remarks promoted a view of the region as a natural curiosity, where certain plants unknown to ordinary New Yorkers thrived and where familiar species reached unheard-of size.

Participants in the ascent of Mount Marcy commented on another indication of the climatological strangeness. On the morning of August 5, 1837, when the party scrambled over the last rocky ledge to reach the highest point in New York, Torrey, James Hall, and Redfield were all amazed to find patches of ice.[12] Like the continued habitation of the area by wolves and the existence of alpine flora, ice on the summit of Marcy in August further emphasized the difference between the Adirondacks and the civilized parts of the state.

For the most part, however, the men of the survey viewed the wilderness less as an oddity or a scenic wonder than as an obstruction to the proper course of both the Survey itself and American civilization. Despite the admitted pleasures of working amid the "picturesque scenery," they often complained of "the toil and fatigue, the peril and privation" that accompanied their research. Of his seven northern counties, Emmons wrote, "A very large proportion of this surface is uncultivated, and covered with forests of a dense growth. The conditions under which the survey has been executed were therefore unfavorable in more respects than one." "The progress of the survey is necessarily slow in wooded and uncultivated districts, especially where there is so much territory inaccessible except on foot." And Hamilton County, Emmons said, "is yet a wilderness, and consequently we labor under great disadvantages in attempting to explore its mineral riches."[13] The wild condition of the Adirondack landscape, of course, was a genuine physical impediment to fieldwork, but the emphasis of the surveyors on this fact suggests their belief that whatever inhibited efficient exploration also delayed progress itself: whatever made the discovery of mineral deposits difficult also made their exploitation that much more problematic.

▲▲▲▲▲▲▲

The idea of mineral wealth in the Adirondacks was one of the major stimuli to the creation and public support of the Survey; it had intrigued New Yorkers from the time of their first knowledge of the region. "Looking upon their barren district," reported Emmons, "they infer, that inasmuch as Nature had stinted, or has been sparing in the bounties which accompany a fertile soil, [the mountains] must of necessity abound in something else that is valuable." In particular, people hoped that the Survey would turn up evidence of "coal, iron, silver and other precious metals." And John A. Dix had written, "This district, still almost entirely unexplored as to its mineralogical character, probably contains a larger amount of valuable metals than all the other counties of the state combined."[14] Thus even before the Survey began its fieldwork, great hopes were placed on mineral extraction to help eliminate the wilderness.

Emmons proceeded to bolster these hopes. Most of his plans for mineral exploitation involved iron deposits, but he suggested that certain other minerals also held economic potential, including limes, clay, and firestones. The glittering green hypersthene, common in the Opalescent and other brooks of the high peaks, appealed to Emmons; he suggested that it could be sawed into slabs, like marble, and used in "tables, mantel pieces, and other ornamental useful purposes." "If cut into thin tables, and polished, it would form one of the most ornamental articles for parlors which can be imagined. Especially those which are opalescent. Nothing of the kind has yet been in market." This utilitarian proposal, which Emmons may have borrowed from iron developer David Henderson, who had made a similar suggestion several years earlier, illustrates his eagerness to see practical benefits emerge from his work.[15]

The major focus of interest in Adirondack iron was the McIntyre development near Newcomb. After rigorous exploration, Emmons became convinced that the Sanford Lake area represented a significant source of iron: "The most extensive beds of this kind of ore in the district, and perhaps in the world, are found at Newcomb, in the vicinity of Lake Sandford [sic], but a few miles from the source of the Hudson river." Emmons waxed ecstatic about the economic potential of the deposits, declaring that the Sanford vein alone was worth over $300 million and that it was perfectly located, being surrounded by virgin forests whose trees could furnish all the charcoal needed for smelting: "Never was a vein so favorably situated . . . where so little capital will be required to obtain the ore." It was a find of national importance: "Now the Adirondack [Sanford] ores, it is believed, if any exist in this country, are the great source from which our most valuable iron is to be drawn. It is here, if any where, it can be made in this country; and the whole Union, if true to herself, will encourage its manufacture." This iron was so essential to the welfare of the nation, thought Emmons, that he suggested bringing in convict labor to build roads, mine the ore, run sawmills, and perform the other heavy jobs in producing the iron.[16]

Emmons' vision encouraged a popular perception of the Adirondack region as endowed with valuable physical attributes that could enrich investors and contribute to the state economy, if only the proper means for exploitation could be developed. As it turned out, the McIntyre deposits would be deserted within twenty years; the expense of transporting the iron across the rugged Adirondack terrain proved too great.[17] But for the time being the Emmons reports promoted the notion that the Adirondacks possessed limitless wealth waiting to be exploited. At first, hopes were pinned on the iron; by the end of the century, many people saw the region only in terms of the timber it could supply to the state's lumber and pulp mills. Emmons' predictions for the profits to be realized in iron were merely the first of many concerning the capacity of the Adirondack landscape to enrich the wise investor.

Emmons also did much to foster hopes for the emergence in the Adirondacks of a Jeffersonian middle landscape with a hearty agricultural population working busy farms. In the reports of the Natural History Survey and other surveys conducted in the Adirondacks at about the same time—mainly to investigate possible routes for canals and railroads—the middle-landscape ideal occupies a prominent position. From initial optimism concerning the rich agricultural future of the region, the ideal eventually evolved, in the minds of many Adirondack landowners, to a criticism of the state for failing to open up the region with state-subsidized roads and canals.[18]

The middle-landscape concept embraces much of the ambiguity of the man-nature relationship. It is positive toward nature in that it emphasizes the virtues of living close to the soil, yet it is anti-wilderness in its utilitarianism. According to this ideology, life on the farm avoids the evils inherent in both the city and the wilderness; the city harbors vice and all sorts of human suffering, while the wilderness is simultaneously useless and malignant. Despite Emmons' occasional appreciation of the wilderness, he remained uncomfortable with the thought that any land might remain unused. His more practical side explicitly condemned the continuing existence of wilderness and insisted that some productive use must be found for the Adirondacks. Thus, once the trees were removed, Emmons wrote of Hamilton County, there "will be found an excellent country for grazing, raising stock, and for producing butter and cheese." Emmons' ideal scene for the Adirondacks involved a New England-like landscape where livestock grazed beside neat clapboard farmhouses and barns at the feet of treeless hills.[19]

In order for the middle-landscape ideal to succeed imaginatively, it had to displace the image of the Adirondacks fostered by early geographers and gazetteers, who had described the same Hamilton County for which Emmons entertained such high hopes as "broken and sterile, abounding with swamps and clothed with dreary forests." Emmons responded specifically to such descriptions, insisting that Hamilton County's rivers and lakes were "not the pestilent miasma of dead marshes, but pure water, the emblem of life." Other writers also tried to demolish the old conception of the region as cold and useless. An 1840 surveyor for the state Canal Board wrote, "As far as I penetrated it, I could find no wild and barren tract, covered with impenetrable bogs and marshes, as represented on the old maps of the State." And as late as 1855, an Adirondack geographer felt constrained to say, "Hitherto, very erroneous opinions have been entertained in regard to this portion of the State; by many it having been considered a *cold, wet, swampy, barren country.* "[20] This insistence on the relative absence of any type of wetlands parallels the repugnance that contemporary tourists felt when they actually encountered such terrain. For the surveyors, wetlands suggested that the landscape might be useless; for romantic travelers, as we shall see (Chapter III), swamps and marshes differed too much from conventionally appreciated scenery. In either case, the distaste for wetlands illustrates the depth of the hostility toward wilderness as such.

The purveyors of the middle-landscape ideal acknowledged that the Adirondack climate was indeed cold, but they believed that there was a way to improve it: "A great and good result will take place, when the forests of all that region are removed, and the soil opened to the sun. The mean temperature will then be increased, and the frost will be less common in the season of vegetation." This idea enjoyed wide currency and also appealed to Emmons: "When the country is settled extensively, and the timber and wood removed, there will be an amelioration of climate; it will become drier and less frosty, and the summer warmer and better suited to the raising of corn." The primordial Adirondack forest, which both symbolized and was the major physical feature of the wilderness itself, was thus seen as a tangible obstacle to progress and productivity. "At present the forest, which might be made a source of wealth to the country, is a barrier to its settlement." The hills of the Adirondacks, wrote Emmons, "will afford good pasturage, and herds of cattle and flocks of sheep may one day give life and animation where the silence of the day is broken only by the rustling of the wind through an unbroken forest."[21] Silence and the absence of human institutions, therefore, are to be condemned, while the prospect of bustling husbandry is anticipated enthusiastically.

Nor was Emmons the only person demanding the destruction of the Adirondack forest or seeing that forest as an obstacle to civilization and progress. The Canal Board surveyor of 1840 wrote, "*Until* that *forest crop* be disposed of, the great and perpetually progressive value of the territory, as being eminently well fitted by nature for a *grazing* country, can never be realized." The same writer went on to foresee a "hearty, vigorous and wholesome population." In one of his most extravagant pronouncements on this development, Emmons wrote:

> The axe has been laid at the foot of the tree, and ere long where naught now greets the eye, but a dense, and to appearance impassable forest, will be seen the golden grain waving with the gentle breeze, the sleek cattle browsing on the rich pastures, and the farmer with well stored granaries enjoying the domestic hearth.[22]

This statement, in telling contrast to Emmons' discovery of "truth" in the wilderness, reveals more than an idle longing for the arrival of agriculture in the Adirondacks. Although secular in intent, it carries a quasi-religious connotation of faith in the American mission to subdue nature and make it productive. And it is profoundly antiwilderness. The axe symbolizes our technological capacity to conquer the darkness of the wilderness, while the dense and impassable forest represents everything that is primitive, uncivilized, and hostile to the legitimate needs of humanity. The georgic scene envisioned by Emmons is of the harvest, the time when nature's subjection to human will is most apparent: the cattle are sleek, the grain golden, the granaries full. Such a vision involves the promise of fecundity and security against the privations imposed by an uncultivated land, while the continued existence of the wilderness connotes the fear of starvation. The virtues and wholesomeness of the "domestic hearth" are explicitly contrasted with the dense and impassable forest, whose impassability, we infer, obstructs not only the passage of the explorer but also, metaphorically, the prosperity and happiness of society itself.

But all this prosperity depended on the establishment of a suitable transportation system by which, observed Emmons, the "almost inexhaustible stores of wealth might be transported to market." An extensive system of canals was part of his grand vision of dairy farming and rural commerce for the Adirondacks. A cogent statement of how badly the region needed efficient transportation was an 1846 report to the New York legislature by Farrand Benedict, a professor of mathematics at the University of Vermont, on the feasibility of a combined railroad-steamboat route from Lake Champlain to Oneida County. Benedict had been exploring the central Adirondacks since the beginning of the Natural History Survey, to which he was not officially attached but to which he contributed some work. In 1846 he was commissioned to survey a route through the Adirondacks and reported that the absence of a useful transportation system alone accounted for the persistence of the wilderness. The soil, timber, and minerals, wrote Benedict, were valuable and ripe for exploitation, provided that the state would see to the construction of roads, railroads, and canals. It was the state's shortsightedness, implied Benedict, that was responsible for the failure of businessmen to tap the resources of the Adirondacks. Another observer wrote, "From repeated examinations, this country wants only communication with the markets to give it rank among the best of agricultural districts." And, ironically, just as the McIntyre mine was being abandoned, a correspondent to the *New York Times* insisted that the completion of a railroad to the mine would make it "the largest and most profitable works of the kind in the United States."[23]

Once new routes were established, suggested Emmons and Benedict, the Adirondacks would no longer be excluded from the mission of progress being pursued by New York. Emmons noted that building canals from the Mohawk Valley to the summit of the Adirondack plateau would be difficult, involving a gain of some 1,500 feet of elevation. But if such a project could be undertaken, "a large and important territory is as it were acquired and annexed to the State." In Emmons' view the Adirondacks was to New York what the great plains were to the nation. The construction of canals was one more necessary step in eliminating those characteristics—isolation and primitiveness—that distinguished the Adirondacks from downstate terrain. As the 1840 Canal Board surveyor noted, when canals joined the Adirondacks to more progressive areas, they "would awaken a spirit of agricultural enterprise which would soon put a new face on the whole region."[24]

The potential for canals appealed to a number of entrepreneurs, and Farrand Benedict actually began work on one that would have joined the Hudson and Raquette (and thus the St. Lawrence) watersheds by linking Long Lake, which is part of the Raquette system, to Round Pond, which discharges to the Hudson. This project was quickly abandoned; the realities of Adirondack topography generally precluded the construction of useful canals. Roads did gradually penetrate the region, however; by midcentury, tourists could reach Saranac Lake or Old Forge by wagon. Another popular route to the interior was from Lake Champlain (navigated by steamboats) to the McIntyre mine. Railroads did not arrive until after the Civil War. In 1871, the Adirondack Railroad (bought by the Delaware and Hudson in 1889) stretched from Saratoga to North Creek on the upper Hudson. By 1875 a line hugged the west shore of Lake Champlain. Other lines followed; their period of greatest use was the late nineteenth and early twentieth centuries.[25]

Behind these schemes for agricultural, mineralogical, or commercial exploitation lay an understanding—usually implicit, sometimes overt—that certain resources of the Adirondacks were finite, that although great wealth would reward the bold investor, some care ought to be exercised in the realization of exploitative schemes. Even in the era of the Natural History Survey, when most thoughts about the future of the Adirondacks involved development and the elimination of the wilderness, we can see the emergence of a conservationist impulse. The impulse was utilitarian, to be sure, stemming from a desire to see that the resources of the region were properly exploited and not wasted; but the kind of thinking it revealed was to play an essential role in the substantive conservation measures effected later in the century. It is important to note that the conservation impulse in the Adirondacks appeared early in the nineteenth century and that it first arose from practical concerns.

For example, when Emmons noted that one useful attribute of the McIntyre site was the proximity of hardwoods that could be reduced to charcoal for smelting the iron ore, he also pointed out that the developers should exercise caution lest they abuse the apparent limitlessness of the forest:

> It is a measure of policy as well as wisdom, to proceed in cutting the timber with a rigorous system. To secure a sufficiency of wood for the future, only a given area should be devoted to the axe yearly, and on this enough of the small trees should be left standing to support the soil and prevent its washing.

Three years later he remarked on the same subject, "There can be no lack of fuel for a long period, if these resources are properly husbanded." These early warnings from Emmons, the first serious effort to forestall the unenlightened use of Adirondack natural resources, were consistent with contemporary exhortations about the finitude of resources throughout the country. As Lee Clark Mitchell has noted, many observant Americans in the Jacksonian period were aware that just as eastern farms had become exhausted through profligate agricultural methods, so all the natural resources of the young nation were finite. Despite the boosterism of Jacksonian rhetoric and despite an American West that truly seemed limitless, some Americans, of whom Emmons was clearly typical, recognized that some resources could run out.[26]

Emmons implied a further criticism of the frenetic character of Jacksonian commerce and life when he discovered his last utilitarian possibility for the Adirondacks—as a wilderness retreat where the physically tired and spiritually jaded businessmen from eastern cities could restore vigor to body and soul. In his final report he commented:

> I would remember that in a community constituted like ours, many individuals require recreation during certain seasons; and while I am occupying time and space [with geology], I am also making known a new field for relaxation from business—one which has peculiar advantages and many resources for restoring health and spirits, such as are unknown at the more fashionable watering places. . . . The breezes of Hamilton are invigorating; the lake scenery is magnificent, and the exercise it calls forth is healthful; and the invalid who, after reaching these romantic wilds, makes a rational use of the forests and lakes and the skies which invest them, and returns dissatisfied with what he has received, I should pronounce not only difficult to please, but mistaken in the objects of his search and the character of his wants.

Thus Emmons changed the distinction between the primitive Adirondacks and the more progressive countryside into a positive feature; the same attribute that made the Adirondacks a curiosity also offered something useful to a society entering the traumas of urban, industrial capitalism. While maintaining his utilitarianism, Emmons assumed the characteristically romantic position that civilization, in the "more fashionable watering places," ignored the regenerative powers of nature. Earlier, in a description of the beauties of Raquette Lake, he also favorably contrasted the solitude and peace of the Adirondacks with the anxiety-producing stresses of city life: "It is finely fitted for the temporary residence of those who are troubled with *ennui,* or who wish to escape for a time during the months of July and August from the cares of business or the heat and bustle of the city."[27]

In these passages and others like them, Emmons maintained that the romantic distinction between the city and the country was real, and that the course taken by American society toward industrialism, commerce, and urbanism would place great emotional and spiritual stress on the businessmen who controlled it. Such a society would need a place where people could escape the pressures of their ordinary lives. And his explorations in the Adirondacks showed him that the region could play an important role in American life by providing just such an escape. Whereas the absence of the bucolic landscape of neat farmhouses and waving stalks of grain usually inspired in Emmons and others a hostile reaction and a wish to see the wilderness eliminated as soon as possible, here Emmons perceived the wilderness condition as a virtue. This kind of thinking would become increasingly significant as the century grew older.

Emmons saw no contradiction between his hopes for exploitation and development and his faith in the powers of the Adirondacks to work their positive medicine on the weary soul of the nineteenth-century business class. The Adirondack wilderness appeared extensive enough both to satisfy the contemplative needs of the urbanite and to provide tillage for the farmer. But to Emmons' fellow geologist, Lardner Vanuxem, the recreational attributes of the Adirondacks merely supplied a temporary use while the more important task of clearing away the trees and diverting the entire tract to farming was being accomplished. In Vanuxem's view, tourists might as well enjoy the scenery in the meantime, but only until the elimination of the forest opened up the area for more serious economic exploitation.[28]

Vanuxem represents the extreme utilitarian view, a position never entirely absent in the emerging attitude toward the Adirondacks, while Emmons' hopes for a mixture of the practical and the contemplative are marked by ambivalence toward the best possible use of the region. Vanuxem hoped to see the Adirondack forest leveled, the wilderness eliminated, and the entire region devoted to the worthy pursuit of agriculture. Emmons' position was more complex, more interesting, and more illuminating in its anticipation of the various attitudes that have shaped the region's destiny. Emmons saw tourism as a permanent industry in the Adirondacks; he predicted the establishment of hotels and resorts to cater to the needs of tourists and travelers.[29] Yet all his hopes for recreation were surrounded by a utilitarianism nearly as pervasive as Vanuxem's. Emmons' various plans for the future of the Adirondacks appear mutually exclusive. The same hills and forests of Hamilton County whose beauties he foresaw uplifting the tired spirit of the businessman, he elsewhere condemned to the indiscriminate axe. The wild scenery he proposed as the cure for the *angst* of a commerical society, he elsewhere suggested should be eliminated in favor of grazing stock and grainfields.

All of this is not to suggest that Emmons was a fool or a hypocrite. On the contrary, he was an intelligent, progressive man of his time. His responses to the wilderness of the Adirondacks reflected the ambiguities and confusions that inevitably occurred in a mind sensitive to the beauties of nature and at the same time aware of the needs of a growing country. To Emmons, the Adirondacks held enormous potential in many different domains of human activity. The region was full of mineral wealth, it offered rich rewards to the hard-working farmer, and its natural beauties could provide succor to the jaded spirit. Subsequent events have shown that it has often been difficult to reconcile these apparently conflicting expectations.

# III
# Romantic Travelers and Sportsmen

Sometime in the 1840s, Joel T. Headley—Protestant minister, popular historian, journalist, author of biographies of Napoleon and George Washington and a guide to Italy—took the first of his several camping trips in the Adirondack wilderness. He later wrote that an "attack on the brain . . . drove me from the haunts of men to seek mental repose and physical strength in the woods," thus affirming the romantic faith in the redemptive powers of nature. In 1849 he published *The Adirondack; Or, Life in the Woods*, a book that was reissued, reprinted, expanded, and plagiarized in numerous editions over the next thirty years. It was a prime example of one of the nineteenth century's most popular genres, the illustrated volume of romantic travel literature. More exactly, it typified a distinct vein of romantic writing: books and articles devoted exclusively to the American wilderness. Headley's book included all the standard apparatus of the Adirondack sporting and touring narrative: instructions on how to reach the woods and how to prepare for a camping trip, exciting descriptions of hunting and fishing, meditations on the meaning of life in the wilderness, stock responses to scenery, discoveries of the deity in nature, and detailed accounts of day-to-day life in the woods with guides.[1]

Expeditions like Headley's and the many narratives they inspired were part of a cultural phenomenon. During the three or four decades before the Civil War, comfortably affluent, educated easterners were fascinated with the wilderness and eagerly repaired to what was left of it in the East: the White Mountains in New Hampshire, the Green Mountains in Vermont, the Rangeley Lakes in Maine, wild parts of Appalachia in Pennsylvania and the Virginias, and both the Catskills and the Adirondacks in New York. The intellectual climate of the day promoted nature as the place where modern people could invigorate body and soul, where they could restore their physical, mental, and moral fortitude. And when educated men sat in their drawing rooms on Washington Square and Beacon Hill and pondered nature, they apparently saw little distinction between nature and wilderness, assuming that wilderness was but the most natural of nature's possibilities. When the same people, however, sought the answer to their physical and spiritual needs in the wilderness—as many of them did— they found that wilderness as an actual place was far less appealing than the wild landscapes so glowingly depicted in romantic literature and art.[2]

In this chapter I focus on the romantic response to the Adirondacks, one of the most popular camping grounds of the antebellum era; I am interested in seeing how a particular group of people—literate eastern men who actually camped in and achieved intimacy with a wild landscape of mountains, forests, lakes, and rivers—responded to the wilderness they encountered. My emphasis is thus on the actual experience of traveling in the wilderness for reasons other than exploration or emigration. I want to find out how the wilderness affected those men (before the Civil War very few women went camping for recreation) who left their comfortable homes in New York or Philadelphia and spent a few weeks roughing it in the Adirondacks.

For the most part, therefore, I am dealing with popular romanticism and how it reflected in written expression its response to a specific wilderness. By popular romanticism I mean the loose collection of assumptions, ideas, and values of culturally aware but not extraordinary men and women. Popular romanticism contains much that reminds us of the more complex thinking of men like Emerson and Thoreau, but it is not the same thing. In studying the romantic response to the Adirondack wilderness, however, we can compare the popular romanticism of Headley and the high or complex romanticism of no less a figure than Emerson himself, who camped there for a few weeks in 1858. In both cases we find a profound ambivalence about the existence and the future value of wilderness.

The typical Adirondack camping trip of this period usually involved several weeks spent in the woods. Generally, a party consisted of a group of some three or four city sportsmen and the same number of guides, who were hired at the small settlements on the edge of the wilderness. The intricate system of connecting rivers and lakes provided easy access to the heart of the wilderness; romantic travelers seldom hiked. Arriving by boat at a pleasant spot on a lake or river, the party would establish a base camp; then they could spend their time hunting, fishing, meditating, and admiring the scenery.

The sportsman brought with him all his personal gear, including clothing, blankets, gun (either rifle or shotgun), fishing rod and flies. Nearly every author of a book on the Adirondacks felt obligated to provide a detailed list of necessary gear, as well as the usually ignored warning against packing too much. Since everything had to be stowed in each man's guideboat, and it all had to be transported over the carries that connected the hundreds of miles of interlocking lakes and rivers, one was wise not to include too much gear.[3] But most sportsmen, expecting the guides to do the carrying, seldom denied themselves any extra comfort or convenience.

Among hundreds of accounts of such trips, none is so eloquent as Emerson's; his poem, "The Adirondacs: A Journal Dedicated to My Fellow Travellers in August, 1858," commemorates his sojourn in the Adirondack wilderness with a group of Concord-Cambridge notables including the scientist Louis Agassiz, the poet and editor James Russell Lowell, and the artist and journalist William James Stillman. Having arrived by wagon at Martin's Hotel on Lower Saranac Lake, the party hired guides and guideboats and set out for the wilderness.[4]

From Lower Saranac the party of ten, with their guides, rowed their way to the point where the outlet of Follensby Pond enters the Raquette River. Then, according to Emerson's poem,

> Northward the length of Follansbee [sic] we rowed,
> Under the low mountains, whose unbroken ridge
> Ponderous with beechen forest sloped the shore.
> A pause and council: then where near the head
> Due east a bay makes inward to the land

Between two rocky arms, we climb the bank,
And in the twilight of the forest noon
Wield the first axe these echoes ever heard.
We cut young trees to make our poles and thwarts,
Barked the white spruce to weatherfend the roof,
Then struck a light and kindled the camp-fire.

Emerson's facility with iambic pentameter was more reliable than his sense of direction: a glance at the United States Geological Survey's Long Lake quadrangle shows that the only direction one can row from the outlet is south.[5]

Otherwise his description of the establishment of an Adirondack camp is accurate, though brief. Arriving at a likely spot, the sports sat around while their guides constructed a shanty or leanto facing the site selected for the campfire. They built a frame out of whatever saplings were handy and thatched the sides, back, and roof with fir, spruce, or hemlock boughs or—better still—with sheets of spruce or hemlock bark. To obtain the bark, the guides cut a circle around the base of a tree, another as high as they could reach, and a vertical cut joining these two horizontal incisions. Next they forced a knife or axe blade into the long vertical cut and peeled the bark away from the tree. Needless to say, stripping the bark like this killed the tree; by 1895, people understood the wastefulness of this and it was illegal to bark any tree on state land.[6] Inside the leanto (or tent, if the party carried one) beds were made of piles of balsam or hemlock boughs, on which were stretched blankets or shawls. Fishing rods, creels, rifles, kitchen gear, and other pieces of equipment were scattered about inside the shelter or hung from the branches of the surrounding trees.

The hunters were after white-tailed deer, the animal that came to symbolize in the minds of most sportsmen the wildlife of the Adirondacks. There were two main methods of bagging the deer—hounding and jacklighting. The former involved sending out hounds trained to pick up the scent of deer and drive them to water, where the guides and their clients would be waiting in boats. After the deer had swum well into a lake, the guides would row to within shooting distance and keep close until the hunters had made their kill. Once in the water, the deer had little chance of survival: a well-rowed boat can always catch a swimming deer. If the hunter turned out to be a wretched shot, as many apparently were, the guide could even grab the deer's tail and hold on while his client blasted away. If the shooter proved unable to achieve even this degree of marksmanship, the guide sometimes beat the deer over the head with an oar and then cut its throat with a knife. For obvious reasons, hunting deer with hounds was not everyone's idea of fair play. As Charles Dudley Warner, who camped often in the Adirondacks after the Civil War, put it, "The dogs do the hunting, the men the killing."[7]

In jacklighting, the sport and his guide set off in their boat after dark and coursed along the shore of a lake or pond, looking for deer drinking or feeding on the aquatic vegetation of the littoral. The key to this brand of hunting was the jacklight, or torch, placed on a stick standing in the bow of the boat. A piece of bark or a reflector behind the light prevented it from disclosing the occupants of the boat. Since a deer, spotting a bright light after dark, will become mesmerized by it and unless startled will stand perfectly still. The only trick was for the guide and sport to remain as quiet as possible while rowing up close, and for the hunter to fell the beast with his first shot: in jacklighting there was no second chance.[8]

The assistance of jacklight or dogs that most Adirondack hunters required to bag a deer testifies to their incompetence in the woods and their willingness to employ whatever technological or other leverage they could dream up in order to exercise their "gentleman's right" to exploit the wilderness. Yet in the attitudes of the Adirondack hunter toward his victim, we can see all the ambiguities and confusions of the romantic urbanite's attitudes toward nature—anthropomorphic, sentimental, and exploitative—and their place in it. The Adirondack deer symbolized the goodness of nature as well as its bounty. It appeared to be a gentle, intelligent, harmless creature, whose life in the wilderness—so far as the hunters knew—was easy and untroubled. Its bovine brown eyes, delicate form, and vegetable diet contributed to its image as one of God's perfect creatures living in the natural paradise of an untouched wilderness. Unlike the carnivorous animals such as wolves and panthers, which appeared to be vicious and out of place in such a paradise, the herbivorous deer, apparently at peace with its fellow creatures, appealed to the romantic mind as typical of the goodness inherent in the natural world.[9] The hunters continually spoke of noble bucks, attributing to them all sorts of human characteristics and describing them as monarchs of a wilderness domain—yet the same sportsmen spilled the blood of noble bucks and does with appalling energy. While the occasional hunter may have been aware of the paradox in his sentimental attitude toward the deer and his simultaneous impulse to eat it for dinner, this perception seldom kept him from hunting. Headley, for example, experienced some regret over having killed a buck driven to a lake by dogs but appeared to justify his sport by invoking the doctrine of the survival of the fittest. After the deer was dead, Headley

> raised him by the horns, and towed him slowly along toward the shore. The excitement of the chase was over, and as I gazed on the wild, yet mild and gentle eye of the noble creature, now glazing in death, a feeling of remorse arose in my heart. I could have moralized an hour over the beautiful form as it floated on the water. The velvet antlers . . . gave a more harmless aspect to the head than the stubborn horn, and I almost wished to recall him to life. It seemed impossible that, a few minutes before, that delicate limbed creature was treading in all the joy of freedom his forest home. How wild had been his terror, as the fierce cry of the hound first opened on his track—how free and daring his plunge from the rock into the wave! How noble his struggles for life. But the bold swimmer had been environed by foes too strong for him, and he fell at last, where he could not even turn at bay. The delicate nostril was relaxed in death, and the slender limbs stiff and cold.[10]

Some hunters did fear that the Adirondack deer herd might suffer from hunting pressure too great for its numbers, but most believed in the infinite capacity of nature to supply *their* needs and considered the use of dogs and jacklights to secure a wilderness supper sporting and humane. What worried them was the imminent danger of the herd's extinction if *other* hunters were allowed to go on wasting deer.

Indeed, it soon became evident that nature could not always keep up with the sportsmen's demands. The seven men who formed the Piseco Trout Club in 1842, for example, fishing for an average of less than nine days each year, for only nine summers, took from Lake Piseco, in southern Hamilton County, more than 6,000 pounds of trout. In one twenty-four hour period in 1844, one man caught over forty-four pounds of brook trout at a single hole. Even allowing for a measure of fish-story exaggeration in these figures, they tell a tale of horrible waste. Little wonder that when the club disbanded in 1852, one of the reasons given was an incipient scarcity of trout.[11] Throughout the nineteenth century, deer were slaughtered by summer jacklighters and left to rot on the shores of

Adirondack lakes, and the bark was stripped from spruce and hemlock for temporary shelters while the trees were left to die. Nearly every account of hunting and fishing expeditions to the Adirondacks during this period demonstrates an implicit yet pervasive assumption of the inexhaustibility of nature.

▲▲▲▲▲▲▲

But the sportsman never really felt at home in the wilderness; he depended on an insulating barrier of technology, civilized comforts, and psychological buffers to keep himself from being overwhelmed by the vastness of nature, by an environment in which he perceived himself to be somehow out of place. Although the romantic temperament encouraged him to seek spiritual satisfaction in the wilderness, his experience as a city dweller made it difficult for him to feel psychologically comfortable in the setting to which the cultural atmosphere of the age sent him.

To try to reconcile the conflict between the search for spiritual regeneration and the sense of alienation, the romantic sportsman and traveler brought with him mementos of the civilized world he pretended to leave behind. These were important both to keep him physically comfortable and to prevent his feeling that his connections to home life had been severed. He carried civilized artifacts like neckties and champagne to keep up appearances and to avoid the sense of living in an uncouth or barbarous way. He applied a civilized vocabulary to his wilderness campsite and activities to make them seem less hostile. One chronicler noted that his party referred to its bark shanty as the "hotel" and to their eating area as the "dining saloon." Ordinary pursuits, like eating a meal, were described in elevated language; one wilderness meal was described as

> a royal dinner—venison broiled, roasted and fried, pork and beans, a course of finer game consisting of frogs' hind legs, capped off with a dessert of pancake and rice pudding, coffee, cigars, whiskey, brandy, and a delicious glass of West India Shrub, the recollection of which still makes the teeth water. We finish up the day with a game of whist.[12]

The sportsman's efforts to accommodate himself to the wilderness are strikingly portrayed by Arthur Fitzwilliam Tait, an English artist who camped and worked in the Adirondacks during the Civil War and for many years thereafter.[13] In his painting, "A Good Time Coming" (1862), the campsite represents an isolated pocket of civilization surrounded by an untouched wilderness. We see the sportsman wearing a necktie and well-cut clothes easily distinguishable from the rough shirts and trousers of the guides. Behind him is the typical bark shelter, jagged pieces of bark drooping over its front; at his feet lie all sorts of civilized paraphernalia: pots and pans, jugs, baskets, and eating utensils. While the sport peacefully watches a guide frying a mess of trout, he pours himself a cup of champagne. That the champagne is to be drunk from a tin cup rather than from crystal measures the extent to which he is willing to sacrifice the comforts of civilization during his stay in the wilderness.

Another device by which romantic travelers reduced the wilderness to a tolerable phenomenon was their lavish and enthusiastic appreciation of one of the wild landscape's more obvious features—its visual magnificence. Their raptures fill page after page of Adirondack travel narratives and suggest a genuine love of wild scenery. And in a sense that love is there, but the descriptions of scenery also contain the most significant strategy whereby romantic travelers could accept the wilderness itself: the conversion of the landscape from topographical, biological, and geological reality into an object of aesthetic appreciation. Invoking the aesthetic vocabulary of the cult of the subline and the beautiful, romantic travelers imposed Edmond Burke's response to nature on their own response to the Adirondacks.[14] Testimonials to the grandeur of Adirondack scenery appear in virtually every account of visits to the region, typically reflecting stock Burkean attitudes but nonetheless revealing an honest effort to address a magnificent landscape. Even from the otherwise skeptical pen of Thomas Bangs Thorpe, the southwestern humorist, the Adirondacks elicited praise: after a camping trip that took him up the Fulton Chain in John Brown's Tract, Thorpe wrote, "I question if there is in the wide world a place where the natural scenery so strongly combines every possible variety of expression to gratify the eye and call forth admiration." And John Todd, a minister from Massachusetts who paid several visits to Long Lake and the central Adirondacks in the 1840s, commented, "The scenery on these lakes is grand and beautiful beyond any thing of which I ever conceived."[15]

Travelers who made their way to the high peaks and Indian Pass responded to the scenery there in terms emphasizing the influence of the cult of the sublime. The great cliffs on Wallface at Indian Pass, which Headley called "the most remarkable gorge in the country, if not in the world," particularly excited a consciousness of sublimity in the souls of visitors. The journalist Charles Fenno Hoffman wrote that Indian Pass "was one of the most savage and stupendous among the many wild and imposing scenes at the sources of the Hudson. . . . It is a tremendous ravine, cloven through the summit of a mountain." Headley's reaction was similar: "Majestic, solemn and silent, with the daylight from above pouring all over its dread form, it stood the impersonation of strength and grandeur." Standing at the height of the pass, Headley felt that "there was something fearful in that mysterious, profound silence." Likewise, Jervis McEntee, an artist who visited Indian Pass in 1851, explicitly underscored Burke's observation that one of the features of the sublime was its capacity to remind the viewer of the omnipotence of God: "It is one of those wild scenes so full of majesty and sublimity which the Creator has formed for us to look upon that we may the better comprehend his boundless power." In a description of the view from Mount Marcy, Headley emphasized another of Burke's points, that the response to a sublime scene is "founded on pain"; standing on the summit, Headley found himself

> in the centre of a chaos of mountains, the like of which I never saw before. It was wholly different from the Alps. There were no snow peaks and shining glaciers; but all was grey, or green, or black, as far as the vision could extend. . . . grand and gloomy . . . a background of mountains, and with nothing but the most savage scenery between—how mysterious—how awful it seemed!
>
> Mount Colden, with its terrific precipices—Mount McIntyre with its bold, black, barren, monster-like head.[16]

In the less imposing, more gentle scenery around the lakes of the central Adirondacks, in country accessible by boat, romantic travelers discovered Burke's second landscape category—the beautiful. Headley's description of the scene at Forked Lake provides a revealing contrast to his account of the view from Marcy:

> All was wild but beautiful. The sun was stooping to the western mountains, whose sea of summits were calmly sleeping against the golden heavens: the cool breeze stirred a world of foliage on our right—green islands, beautiful as Elysian fields, rose out of the water as we advanced; the sparkling waves rolled as merrily under as bright a sky as ever bent over the earth, and for a moment I seemed to have been transported into a new world. I never was more struck by a scene in my life: its utter wildness, spread out there where the axe of civilization had never struck a blow—the evening—the sunset—the deep purple of the mountains—the silence and solitude of the shores, and the cry of birds in the distance, combined to render it one of enchantment to me.

In this passage Headley emphasized the serenity of the scene in an explicit counter to the menacing violence dormant in the high peaks. Amid the wilderness of Forked Lake, Headley felt safe and peaceful. As he was rowed across the lake, he enjoyed the openness of the scene, not threatened as he had been by the closeness of the cliffs of Indian Pass or the peaks surrounding Marcy. Indeed, one of the features of the lake country that appealed to Headley and others was the absence of the sense of claustrophobia they experienced in the high peaks. When the wilderness was too close, it seemed oppressive; when, on the other hand, Headley was able to view the high peaks from a distance, he could integrate their hard lines into a more pleasant perception. For example, from Owl's Head, a low mountain on the shore of Long Lake, he observed that, "to the left, shoot up into the heavens the massive peaks of the Adirondack chain, mellowed here, by the distance, into beauty."[17]

Although both sublime and beautiful landscapes evoked rapturous responses from romantic travelers, the beautiful was clearly preferred. Comparing their relative attributes, Headley wrote:

> The gloomy gorge and savage precipice, or the sudden storm, seem to excite the surface only of one's feelings, while the sweet vale, with its cottages and herds and evening bells, blends itself in with our very thoughts and emotions, forming a part of our after existence. Such a scene sinks away into the heart like a gentle rain into the earth, while a rougher, nay, sublimer one, comes and goes like a sudden shower.[18]

This response suggests an important source of the preference for the beautiful. Although Headley elsewhere responded positively to the absence of marks of civilization and the opportunity to settle into a reverie of introspective solitude, here he indicates his faith in the likelihood or at least the possibility that the beautiful landscape—gentle, rolling, peaceful—could be turned into a cultivated middle landscape, thus eliminating the implicitly useless wilderness.

Romantic writers repeatedly suggested that a huge improvement in the Adirondacks would be effected by the emergence of a scene of farms and fields—a change seen as inevitable and positive. Todd explicitly stated that it was a sin against God's grand design not to subject the wilderness to the plow: "It is God's plan and will that the earth should be tilled and thus yield food for man and beast. Any people who fall in with this plan, and till the earth shall prosper. Any people who will not, shall perish." Although Todd admired certain of the characteristics of the woodsmen he encountered in the Adirondacks, he eagerly predicted their disappearance as the region became more settled. Another observer, echoing Crèvecoeur, was less kind to the backwoodsmen who did not live by agriculture; finding a few homesteads at Raquette Lake, this man was appalled to learn that the inhabitants did not till their land but lived by "hunting and fishing rather than . . . farming.[19]

These predictions of an agricultural future for the Adirondacks confirm the mythic quality of the middle landscape ideal in the American consciousness. The elimination of the wilderness was clearly part of the American mission to establish—even in "these glorious mountains"—"a virtuous, industrious and Christian population." Then, according to S. H. Hammond (whose views on this development underwent a later revision), the Adirondacks would be a land of "beautiful and productive farms. Where meadows and green fields would stretch away from the river towards the hills, and where fine farm-houses and barns would be seen, and flocks and herds would be grazing in rich pastures." In addition to reflecting the mythic significance of the middle landscpe, Hammond's prediction also suggests that a chief virtue of the evolution from wild to georgic was the visual change. When writers like Hammond imagined this alteration in the land, they commonly dwelt on its scenic elements. To the romantic traveler the notion of actual or imagined scenic vistas was more important than the reality of the wilderness itself, and the exercise of the visual imagination emerged as one of the critical strategies for taming the wilderness.[20]

This is more than simply deeming the landscape picturesque. It involves the imposition of cultural, aesthetically defined standards on nature and reflects the need of the romantic travelers to reconcile a fear of the wilderness with a predisposition to love all of nature. It allowed them to isolate or at least distance themselves from the physical reality of the wilderness. When romantic travelers expressed a genuine appreciation of the wild scenery of the Adirondacks, they were responding to *scenes*, to certain arrangements of natural elements—trees, rocks, mountains, water—that were familiar in paintings. As Burke's popularizer, William Gilpin wrote, "*Picturesque beauty* is a phrase but little understood. We precisely mean by it that kind of beauty which *would look well in a picture.*"[21]

To some travelers, then, nature was more or less perfect according to the extent that it satisfied the criteria of landscape painting. Thomas Cole, the most important artist to visit the Adirondacks before the Civil War, wrote of the terrain in the Schroon Lake vicinity, "I do not remember to have seen in Italy a composition of mountains so beautiful or pictorial as this glorious range of the Adirondack." Cole, despite his glowing tone, was judging the landscape according to how well the "composition" of the peaks would fit on a canvas. Another traveler wrote of the Saranac River: "One view particularly pleased us, soon after our departure from the Lake House: A graceful curve of the stream, lost at either end in woods with one dry jagged tree slanting athwart, the only sign of decay amid the overflowing life." The curving river and the blasted tree are common elements in the paintings of romantic American landscape artists. This visitor unconsciously transferred the motifs of familiar paintings to the reality of the Adirondack wilderness and found that reality most pleasing when it conformed to the conventions of those paintings.[22]

Writers often suggested, moreover, that the wilderness was in fact an impediment to the observer of fine vistas. Thomas Cole, wandering through the woods near Schroon Lake and looking for a good spot from which to paint Schroon Mountain, wished that the forest had been lumbered to make his view clearer. Likewise, Headley, on Owl's Head, "wanted to set fire to the trees on the summit of the mountain, so as to present an unobstructed view, but the foliage was too green to burn." Jervis McEntee observed that reaching Indian Pass required an arduous hike: "They who look upon it must endure no little toil for the privilege for its gateway is of the rugged rock and the tangled forest and the feet that pass through it are few as the hardly discernible path will attest." "He who sketches Indian Pass," further remarked McEntee, "will have to work for it[,] for it is a toilsome work to it." The solution to this difficulty, as proposed by T. A. Richards, author of an 1859 account of an Adirondack camping trip, was to build a road through the pass, from which "the traveler may be able to see the wonders which now, in the denseness of the forest, he can only infer." Louis Noble, Cole's first biographer, who accompanied the artist on an 1846 trip to the Adirondacks, suggested that scenery, not wilderness, was the attraction:

> It is not, perhaps, generally known that, to this day, a jaunt through that region of the State of New York will ordinarily subject the tourist to more privation and fatigue than almost any other he can take in the United States, this side of the Mississippi. The wilderness, haunted by the great moose, the wolf, the bear, the panther, seems almost interminable, and nearly houseless: the mountains, some of them reaching into the sky, ragged, rocky pinnacles, and robed with savage grandeur, are pathless and inaccessible without a guide: the lakes, which are every where, and often strikingly beautiful, repel by the oppressive loneliness in which they slumber.

Noble undoubtedly exaggerated the hardships of Adirondack camping in order to show what perils his friend Cole was willing to endure in the name of art, but at the same time he clearly showed that he thought of wilderness itself as irrelevant or dangerous.[23]

The growing taste for wild scenery evinced by Cole and others was, to be sure, a critical element in what eventually developed as the modern appreciation for wilderness, but it was most certainly not the same thing. The modern wilderness aesthetic promotes the appreciation of any area where the signs of human activity are substantially absent. While scenic beauty is almost invariably associated with such an area, it is not the sine qua non. To the modern wilderness purist, natural beauty often derives simply from the fact that the processes of the natural environment appear unaffected by any human interference.

When romantic travelers found themselves in parts of the Adirondacks that conformed to their definitions of neither the sublime nor the beautiful, they were unable to employ any mediating strategy and responded with nearly unqualified hostility. In the swamps and thick forests away from the lakes and high peaks, they discovered landscapes for which the Burkean aesthetic did not provide a ready-made vocabulary and for which landscape paintings had not prepared them, and their descriptions of this part of the region are thus not couched in derivative terms. The reactions of several visitors to the area around the head of the Bog River, where they went searching for the even then rapidly disappearing moose, show particularly well how raw, untouched nature, when it failed the aesthetic test, horrified the romantic traveler. Because this region was accessible by boat from Tupper Lake, travelers were willing to visit it; but once there they discovered a dark and forbidding terrain of thick timber and many marshes. The presence of dead and decaying trees particularly offended the senses of these men. S. H. Hammond noted both the absence of appealing scenery and the (to him) oppressive presence of process:

> Of all the lakes I have visited in these northern wilds, this [Mud Lake] is the most gloomy . . . no tall mountain peaks, reaching their heads toward the clouds, overlooking the water, no ranges stretching away. . . . It is in truth, a gloomy place . . . [with] so sepulchral an air of desolation all around, that it brings over the mind a strong feeling of sadness and gloom.

A. B. Street responded to the region in much the same way; it had, he said, a

> lonely and funereal aspect. In every direction, also, dead pines and hemlocks thrust up their pallid, rough raggedness, dripping with grey moss. . . . Over the whole brooded an air of utter loneliness, which, aided by the dull, heavy sky, rested with a depressing weight upon my spirits.

Street reacted similarly to a cluster of small, isolated lakes west of Upper Saranac: "The scene . . . was as utterly lonely and desolate and wild as could be imagined. The shores, unlike those of the other lakes and ponds in this alpine region, were low, belted with swamp and disfigured with dead, ghastly trees." Finally, wrote Street, "as this profoundly desolate scene smote my sight, I felt a weight deeper than I had ever experienced in the forest."[24] Not only was the absence of conventionally approved scenery repugnant, but the ubiquity of natural processes, wherein new life depended on death and decay, reminded the mid-nineteenth-century traveler too much of his own mortality. In an age when the "manifest destiny" of American civilization, moreover, demanded the conquest of the continent's wilderness, the combination of loneliness, gloom, and death suggested that America's mission would be difficult, perilous, and perhaps impossible.

Thoughts of the deep woods, away from the comforting shores of the larger central lakes, also evoked a terror of getting lost. The fears expressed by travelers of this period approach hysteria and show, beyond a reasonable apprehension about losing one's way, the horror of the wilderness itself and of the actively malicious powers attributed to it. Meditating on the more isolated parts of the Adirondacks, Street wrote, "I was more and more impressed with the utter savageness of the scene, and my entire helplessness should I be left alone. The few paths, if not of deer, could only be of bear, wolf, or panther, and tended doubtless toward their fearful haunts." John Todd displayed a similarly high-pitched fear: "The sensation of being lost in this vast forest is horrific beyond description. No imagination can paint the bewilderment and terrific sensations which you feel when you are alone and fairly lost. . . . It is probably as near derangement as can be, if there is any difference."[25]

In one sense, the notion that the Adirondack wilderness was a place where one could actually get lost and disappear was part of the attractiveness of the region. It was a function of the wilderness similar to the sublimity of mountain scenery, fascinating in its very terribleness. But the source of this fascination and of the fears expressed by writers like Street and Todd lay in the conviction that in the wilderness a man would be particularly likely to lose his mind, that the wilderness was a hostile environment where his rationality might desert him in the face of irrational forces. Such suspicions reflect vestiges of the old Puritan fear that life in the wilderness can lead to mental or moral degeneration. With enthusiastic trust in its veracity, Todd recounted a story told him at Long Lake about a man "of liberal education, and fine promise" who became lost in the woods and went insane. Todd offered this tale as proof of the pernicious effects of being alone in the woods without the protection of comrades against the wilderness's inherent malignity. Nor did one have to be lost to suffer the loss of rationality. The artist William James Stillman, whose feelings toward the wilderness were generally far more positive than those of most of his contemporaries, observed that he could easily imagine a solitary life in the forest "leading to insanity."[26]

But romantic travelers did not venture into the wilderness alone, nor did they stay long enough to lose their sanity. Although travelers commonly rehearsed the familiar arguments about how an urban society demands the redemptive powers of nature, the brevity of their visits also implied that they did not feel altogether comfortable with having abandoned, even temporarily, the progressive reality of American life. Behind the pleasures of being away from ordinary responsibilities lies a reluctance to be too long away from the exciting world of politics, technology, and all civilized activity. Headley described the unmasked enthusiasm with which he devoured a recent newspaper after a long trek through the wilderness: it put "into my hands again the links of the great chain of human events I had lost—rebinding me to my race and replacing me in the mighty movement that bears all things onward."[27]

The paradox inherent in repairing to the wilderness for spiritual regeneration but simultaneously admiring the material and scientific achievements of nineteenth-century technology apparently escaped Headley. But Emerson did not fail to note the ambivalence suggested by such a contradictory set of responses. In his long poem describing his reactions to the Adirondack wilderness, Emerson also recorded a startling event that took place while he was in the woods: the laying of the first transatlantic cable, one of the premier achievements, in Emerson's view, of nineteenth-century American technology.[28] Receiving this news, Emerson found himself in a situation analogous—but not identical—to that of other romantic travelers; although aware of the irony implicit in his reaction, he too needed some sort of imaginative mediation to reconcile antagonistic yet attractive impulses.

Emerson's response to the Adirondack wilderness is particularly important because he was, on the one hand, one of the purveyors of the romantic sensibility that so clearly influenced less creative men like Headley. On the other hand, Emerson's trip constituted the only extended experience of his life with genuine wilderness, and his reaction to what he saw and felt made him a romantic traveler in the wilderness for the first and only time.[29]

Assessing Emerson's reaction to the Adirondack wilderness, we see that nature as concept and nature as place are not necessarily the same thing. To confuse them is to misinterpret Emerson, who uses the terms "nature" and "wilderness" interchangeably as philosophical concepts in *Nature*, probably the most-quoted, best-known, and most comprehensive of American transcendentalist manifestoes. Immediately after the now-famous "transparent eyeball" passage, Emerson writes, "In the wilderness, I find something more dear and connate than in streets and villages." He thus advances the familiar romantic distinction between the country and the city, affirming the romantic inclination to find virtue and meaning in the natural while deprecating the ostensible degradation of the urban. Emerson seems further to be insisting that a particular kind of natural setting, the wilderness, that landscape where man's impact is either nonexistent or unnoticeable, is most likely to possess the truths inherent in all of nature. But when he composed these words, he had never seen a wilderness; the word was to Emerson a philosophical abstraction, not a term denoting geographical reality. His experience with nature was limited to the tame woods around Concord—until he camped in the Adirondacks.[30]

In 1858, Follensby Pond was as isolated and untouched as nearly any spot east of the Mississippi River. Accessible only by boat or a tortuous hike across many miles of unmapped territory, it was surrounded by a vast tract of virgin timber and showed absolutely no trace of human activity. Describing his party's campsite, Emerson ran through the characteristic romantic litany of the virtues of nature and a life close to it. He and his friends adopted the rigorous regimen of farmers, rising with the dawn and dining on hearty, simple fare. Beyond the reach of letters, visitors, advertisements, and all the commercial intrusions of urban life, they "were made freemen of the forest laws." Observing the woodcraft of the Saranac Lake guides, Emerson concluded (perhaps ironically) that his own intellectual prowess was inferior to the practical knowledge of people who lived in the bosom of nature:

> Look to yourselves, ye polished gentlemen!
> No city airs or arts pass current here.
> Your rank is all reversed; let men of cloth
> Bow to the stalwart churls in overalls:
> *They* are the doctors of the wilderness,
> And we the low-prized laymen.

As his stay in the wilderness lengthened, Emerson reacted more and more positively to it, finding there a peace and freedom that his life back home denied him:

> Lords of this realm,
> Bounded by dawn and sunset, and the day
> Rounded by hours where each outdid the last
> In miracles of pomp, we must be proud,
> As if associates of the sylvan gods.
> We seemed the dwellers of the zodiac,
> So pure the Alpine element we breathed,
> So light, so lofty pictures came and went.
> We trode on air, contemned the distant town,
> Its timorous ways, big trifles.

Sinking into a reverie of introspection prompted by nature's "visitings of graver thought," Emerson found spiritual truths in the wilderness:

> Nature spoke
> To each apart, lifting her lovely shows
> To spiritual lessons pointed home,
> And as through dreams in watches of the night,
> So through all creatures in their form and ways
> Some mystic hint accosts the vigilant,
> Not clearly voiced, but waking a new sense
> Inviting to new knowledge, one with old.

But one day some of his party rowed to Tupper Lake to examine the scenery and encountered another group of men, who relayed the news of the transatlantic cable; from the entire party a great shout arose to celebrate this most recent evidence of man's continuing triumph over nature. The announcement of this accomplishment had a profound impact on Emerson: "We have few moments in the longest life / Of such delight and wonder." The news of such a triumph of civilization suggested that his earlier musings on the spirituality of the wilderness were insignificant in the grand scheme of American progress. The mission of American civilization was to subdue nature:

> The lightning has run masterless too long;
> He must to school and learn his verb and noun
> And teach his nimbleness to earn his wage,
> Spelling with guided tongue man's messages
> Shot through the weltering pit of the salt sea.

Emerson began to rethink his earlier response to the wilderness; the guides do well enough in their element, but the men truly important are scientists like Agassiz:

> We flee away from cities, but we bring
> The best of cities with us, these learned classifiers,
> Men knowing what they seek, armed eyes of experts.
> We praise the guide, we praise the forest life:
> But will we sacrifice our dear-bought lore
> Of books and art and trained experiment,
> Or count the Sioux a match for Agassiz?
> O no, not we!

Emerson thus found himself faced with the same dilemma that confronted other romantic travelers. Preconceptions emphasized the positive features of the wilderness experience, and Emerson himself initially adhered to a conventional response. Then, though for reasons different from those of ordinary romantic travelers, he subsequently discovered some reason for deprecating the wilderness. In order to deal with these conflicting demands, Emerson too employed a mediating strategy. The nature of his strategy, though, shows that he was not repelled by wilderness to the extent that other romantic travelers often were. Indeed, when he saw the flat, visually unexciting marshes surrounding the route into Follensby Pond, he described the scene in relatively neutral terms:

> a small tortuous pass
> Winding through grassy shallows in and out,
> Two creeping miles of rushes, pads, and sponge.

Nonetheless, Emerson needed to reconcile ostensibly contradictory attitudes toward the wilderness. His solution was the conceit that the wilderness understood the joyous shout which greeted the news of man's technological achievement, that such exultation was not "unsuited to that solitude." The wilderness itself, according to this strategy, acknowledged human accomplishment and conceived its own

> burst of joy, as if we told the fact
> To ears intelligent; as if gray rock
> And cedar grove and cliff and lake should know
> This feat of wit, this triumph of mankind;
> As if we men were talking in a vein
> Of sympathy so large, that ours was theirs,

> And a prime end of the most subtle element
> Were fairly reached at last. Wake, echoing caves!
> Bend nearer, faint day-moon! Yon thundertops,
> Let them hear well! 'tis theirs as much as ours.

The news of the transatlantic cable was not the only reminder of the relative virtues of civilization compared with the wilderness; on another day, rowing with his guide on the Raquette River, Emerson was startled to hear the wilderness silence broken by the strains of Beethoven. Near the river was a log cabin inhabited by a man of evident education and other genteel attributes; he had managed to drag a piano to his wilderness retreat. The sound of the music was similar to the news of the cable: both confirmed the need to employ art, science, or whatever mediation was effective in eliminating those features of nature that seemed menacing or irrelevant to a progressive age. On hearing the Beethoven, the listener cries,

> Well done! . . . the bear is kept at bay,
> The lynx, the rattlesnake, the flood, the fire;
> All our fierce enemies, ague, hunger, cold.

Science and art—these are humanity's truly significant discoveries, not spirituality in the wilderness.

After suggesting that the wilderness approves of human accomplishments that continuously diminish both its power and extent, Emerson retreated further from his earlier sense of transcendence. He too invoked the notion that camping in the wilderness is somehow failing to participate in the momentous achievements of modern life. His description of his departure implies a need to get back home before something else important happens:

> The holidays were fruitful, but must end;
> One August evening had a cooler breath;
> Into each mind intruding duties crept;
> Under the cinders burned the fires of home;
> Nay, letters found us in our paradise.

Stillman, too, noted the transient nature of the idyll on Follensby Pond and observed that Emerson particularly perceived the need to return to the pressing demands of Concord:

Our paradise was no Eden. The world that played bo-peep with us across the mountains came for us when the play-spell was over; this summer dream, unique in the record of poesy, melted like a cloud-castle, and Emerson was one of the first to turn back to the sterner use of time.[31]

We must not forget that when the romantic traveler displayed a negative reaction to wilderness, this was but one side of a dual response, an ambivalence. Both Emerson and Headley were representatives of a busy, progressive age; to discover their participation in the enthusiastic anticipation of a technologically oriented future should come as no surprise. Likewise, to discover that an American romantic shared his ancestors' fears of the malignant or depriving aspects of wilderness is no shock. In the long run, what is remarkable is that men like Headley kept returning to the Adirondacks—and he did, throughout the 1840s and 1850s. Compromised as his attitude was, it nonetheless contains a perception of the power of the wilderness. The response to scenery may have been a meticulously constructed strategy for making the wilderness tolerable, but the very necessity for effecting the strategy in the first place shows that the romantic traveler did infer God's presence in the landscape. Hammond and Street may have been repulsed by the swampy terrain around Bog River, but the failure of one particular part of the landscape to satisfy their overall expectations did not eliminate the inherent capacity of the wilderness to work its mystical medicine. Although neither Headley nor Emerson, despite the romantic predisposition to see virtue in all of nature, could fully accept the imposing reality of wilderness as such, both did perceive positive values there. The chief characteristic of the romantic response to wilderness is its ambivalence, an endlessly interesting mixture of sympathy and fear, of love and hostility, of the impulse to embrace and the equally powerful urge to flee.

Romantics in the Adirondacks did not forget their conviction that nature was the dwelling place of God, offering cures for both physical and spiritual woes. In language reminiscent of the natural pantheism of Wordsworth or Emerson, Street speaks of finding God in nature: "The wilderness is one great tongue, speaking constantly to our hearts; inciting to knowledge of our selves and to love of the Supreme Maker, Benefactor, Father. . . . Here, with the grand forest for our worshipping temple, our hearts expanding, our thoughts rising unfettered, we behold Him, face to face."[32]

The romantics also saw the wilderness as a place where they could relax. Although they may have felt uncomfortable, they nonetheless recognized that they were away from the strictures and restraints of civilized society—a society they often described as sinister and repressive—from which the Adirondack camping trip provided a therapeutic escape. Camping on the shores of Upper Saranac Lake, Street observed, "Far away was the world with all its darkening sorrows and corroding cares. Here, I thought, would I abide and forget that world, that torturing, maddening world—here close to the heart of nature."[33]

In the wilderness the sportsman had the opportunity to be like a child again; the joys of shedding the responsibilities and burdens of adulthood are frequently recorded in Adirondack sporting narratives. At Emerson's Follensby Pond campsite, his companions "fancied the light air / That circled freshly in their forest dress / Made them to boys again."

Camping in the Adirondacks was an escape from the commercial, urban life even then coming to typify American society. For many people from the eastern cities, the Adirondacks represented their only hope for a few weeks of relaxation away from the demands of their quotidian lives. Although they were unable to leave behind them their dependence on the civilized amenities and forms to which they had grown accustomed, and although they abused the wilderness and wasted its resources, they found in the Adirondacks a temporary escape from a society they increasingly perceived as spiritually empty. But their enjoyment of the wilderness was often measured by the extent to which they could control it, to which they could apply a limited technology without being aware of the pressures of a truly technological society. Thus their importation of civilized ways and tools, as part of their efforts to reject briefly the society that produced them, contains a certain irony. Even while these sportsmen extolled the virtues of primitive life in the wilderness, they were unmistakably products of an urban, sophisticated society.

It was inevitable that sportsmen and travelers who discovered solutions to their modern woes in the wilderness would anticipate with some misgiving the elimination of that wilderness; when they observed real threats to the integrity of the wilderness, they feared the loss of something important. By the middle of the nineteenth century, loggers were working in the central Adirondacks; as early as 1855 their shanties could be seen along the remote Bog River. Though many romantics found them merely a picturesque addition to the primitive scene, others considered them an unfortunate incursion of civilization. William James Stillman, on one of his earlier trips, encountered evidence of logging and condemned it for destroying the aesthetic appeal of the landscape. Along the Raquette, "where the traces of the lumberman began to appear . . . the river lost much of its solemnity." Another writer gloomily predicted the triumph of utility over the wilderness: "Enterprise had already penetrated with its winter hordes and axes into the hitherto unprofaned sanctuary of the sacred woods; and we afterwards saw . . . the shanties and desolate clearings of the lumbermen."[34]

The culmination of the romantic perception of virtues in the wilderness occurred in the writings of S. H. Hammond, the only man of his day who both recognized the fragility of the wilderness and proposed that legal steps be taken to preserve the Adirondacks in a wild state. Although initially as ambivalent as other romantics, Hammond later offered the first solid plan for extensive conservation in the Adirondacks. In *Wild Northern Scenes*, published in 1857, he elaborated a traditional romantic catalog of the virtues of the wilderness, decrying "worldliness, greed for progress, thirst for gain," and the mentality that believed "everything in the heavens, or on the earth, or in the waters, were [sic] to be measured by the dollar and cent standard, and unless reducible to a representative of moneyed value, to be thrown, as utterly worthless, away." Hammond feared the civilizing impulse and the elimination of the last wilderness; in a crucial, and for its time radical, passage he went on to say:

> When that time shall have arrived, where shall we go to find the woods, the wild things, the old forests, and hear the sounds which belong to nature in its primeval state? Whither shall we flee from civilization, to take off the harness and ties of society, and rest for a season, from the restraints, the conventionalities of society, and rest from the cares and toils, the strifes and competitions of life? Had I my way, I would mark out a circle of a hundred miles in diameter, and throw around it the protecting

aegis of the constitution. I would make it a forest forever. It should be a misdemeanor to chop down a tree, and a felony to clear an acre within its boundaries. The old woods should stand here always as God made them, growing until the earthworm ate away their roots, and the strong winds hurled them to the ground, and new woods should be permitted to supply the place of the old so long as the earth remained.[35]

Not the least interesting feature of this passage is its acceptance of process. Whereas the romantic mind routinely appreciated wild scenery, Hammond did not even mention the attributes of sublime landscapes, choosing instead to emphasize the endless cycle of death, decay, and rebirth. He was ahead of his time, but the elements of a wilderness aesthetic implicit in Hammond's radical proposal reappeared during the nineteenth century and would achieve cultural and political legitimacy in the twentieth.

# IV
# The Gilded Age:
## *Murray, Colvin, and the Wilderness Breached*

Between the Civil War and the 1890s, the Adirondacks underwent enormous changes. In 1865, the region was still largely unexplored forest, dotted with marginal settlements and known but to a relative handful of sportsmen, surveyors, and local guides and trappers. By the last decade of the century, thousands of hunters and fishermen had rowed and tramped throughout its length and breadth; luxurious hotels had appeared on lakes uninhabited in 1865; huge chunks of the region had been locked up in private preserves owned by Gilded Age robber barons; other large parcels had been devastated by irresponsible lumbermen and by the fires that often succeeded their operations; and, finally, important steps had been taken toward conserving what was left of the forest.

During this period two men particularly contributed to the ways in which the region was perceived. The first, W. H. H. Murray, a Congregationalist minister, popularized wilderness camping and began what has been an ever-increasing boom in outdoor recreation in the Adirondacks. The second, Verplanck Colvin, surveyor and conservationist, scrutinized the growing threats to the wilderness and, more important, made significant strides toward a wilderness aesthetic.

When Murray published *Adventures in the Wilderness* in 1869, he was minister of the Park Street Congregational Church in Boston. Born at Guilford, Connecticut, in 1840, Murray developed an early love for the outdoors. After graduating from Yale in 1862, he attended the East Windsor Theological Seminary and assumed his first pastorate in 1864. During the next four years, he served in several Connecticut towns before receiving a call from the Park Street Congregational Church, at that time one of the most important in New England. Its invitation to Murray indicated that he had, in just a few years, shown himself to be a rising star in the New England ministry.

Meanwhile, Murray was pursuing his sporting and outdoor interests. The date of his first visit to the Adirondacks is not known, but it is certain that he stopped at the Raquette Lake House in September of 1866.[1] And in 1867 his first sketches of Adirondack camping, hunting, and fishing adventures appeared in a local newspaper. These became the nucleus of *Adventures in the Wilderness*, which the distinguished Boston house of Fields, Osgood, and Co. published in the spring of 1869. Murray's life after the publication of this, the first of many books, was a series of ups and downs. His nontheological interests eventually led to his leaving the ministry, and in addition to various forms of writing, he tried his hand at breeding horses and selling buckboard wagons. In 1879 he suffered serious financial reverses and was forced to leave Boston. His spirit was apparently unbroken, however; the next few years saw him traveling, ranching in Texas, running an oyster restaurant in Montreal, and lecturing to lyceum audiences all over the United States. In 1886 he returned to his family homestead in Connecticut, where he spent the remaining years until his death in 1904.

*Adventures in the Wilderness; Or, Camp-Life in the Adirondacks* is one of the most important books in the Adirondack canon. Although it is hard to measure exact sales, it was apparently one of the best-selling books of the spring of 1869. Compared with most of the Adirondack volumes that preceded it, Murray's *Adventures* was quite short. It opened with a brief description of why he chose to visit the wilderness, repeating the familiar praise of the "magnificent scenery" and the beneficence of intimacy with nature. An important difference between Murray and most of his predecessors was that while they had tended to emphasize the hardships of travel in the wilderness, Murray wrote, "there is no . . . exertion known here. It is the laziest of all imaginable places, if you incline to indolence. Tramping is unknown in this region. Wherever you wish to go your guide paddles you. Your hunting, fishing, sightseeing, are all done from the boat." Among the many healthful attributes that Murray claimed for the wilderness was a curative effect on consumption. He told a suspect tale about a young man, apparently about to die from this scourge of the nineteenth century, whose life was miraculously saved by a stay of some weeks amid the "healing properties of the balsam and pine." Within a few years of the publication of Murray's *Adventures*, the Adirondack region had become a well known resort for consumptives, and sanitaria appeared in the Saranac Lake area.[2]

Murray followed his general description of the wilderness with some very practical advice on expenses, camping gear, fishing tackle, guides, hotels, Adirondack weather, insects, and provisions. These descriptive, informative sections occupied about one fourth of the volume. The rest was devoted to ten separate chapters, which could be read in any order and at one sitting. Except for the last (which really had nothing to do with the Adirondacks at all but told a rousing story of a man trapped in a freight car with a mad horse), they were vignettes of the sporting life in the Adirondacks, one telling of the incredible fishing at "The Nameless Creek," another relating the dangers of "Running the Rapids" at some unidentified waterfall, and yet another describing the excitement of "Jack-Shooting in a Foggy Night." These sketches were full of color and vivid detail, but to their credit they lacked much of the bombast and melodrama that had marked earlier accounts of camping trips in the Adirondacks. Murray wrote a simple, forthright, vigorous prose and avoided the excessive ornateness that the modern reader often finds so cloying in romantics like A. B. Street. And also unlike his predecessors (except for Thomas Bangs Thorpe), Murray told his Adirondack stories with a touch of warm, self-mocking humor.[3]

The effect of this book was recognized almost immediately. Throngs of tourists appeared in the Adirondacks in the summer of 1869, and Murray was generally credited with having enticed them there—to the extent that these hordes of often ill-prepared visitors were dubbed "Murray's Fools," and Murray himself for the rest of his life bore the sobriquet "Adirondack" Murray. Years later, the sporting journal *Forest and Stream*, in an editorial introducing an issue devoted to the Adirondacks, observed, "It was reserved for 'Adirondack' Murray to draw such attention to the forest as Headley and Street had failed in doing. His facile pen and wonderfully vivid imagination gave him superior advantages. His writings opened the various gateways to floods of people." The crowds in the Adirondacks that summer were the subject of articles in the Boston and New York papers, the authors of which reported back in considerable detail how Murray's Fools were faring in the wilderness. The correspondent to the *Boston Daily Advertiser*, "Wachusett," wrote:

> Mr. Murray's pen has brought a host of visitors into the Wilderness, such as it has never seen before—consumptives craving pure air, dyspeptics wandering after appetites, sportsmen hitherto content with small game and few fish, veteran tourists in search of novelty, weary workers hungering for perfect rest, ladies who have thought climbing the White Mountains the utmost possible achievement of feminine strength, journalists and lecturers of both sexes looking for fresh material for the dainty palate of the public, come in parties of twos and dozens, and make up in the aggregate a multitude which crowds the hotels and clamors for guides, and threatens to turn the Wilderness into a Saratoga of fashionable costliness.

Other observers also remarked on the sudden appearance of crowds; one sportsman, writing from Long Lake in July, commented, "Those who entertain strangers say there has never been such a rush of visitors."[4]

Although many of Murray's Fools found the woods to be full of black flies and mosquitoes rather than deer and trout, and although many of the neophytes who entered the wilderness that summer were sorely disappointed by their experience, Murray and his *Adventures in the Wilderness* had begun a recreational revolution that was to have profound effects on the Adirondacks. After the summer of 1869, the wilderness was never the same again. After (and perhaps because of) Murray, one of the most important elements in the public perception of the wilderness was the possibility of sudden, unalterable change, the threat of loss. The rapid growth of the popularity of camping and fishing brought invitable shifts in the region's image. The most obvious of these came from the throng of hunters and anglers themselves. Others emerged from the proliferation of hotels and the construction of railroads, which in turn drew even more people to the Adirondacks for various forms of recreation. Many people objected bitterly to the changes that Murray and his followers caused. They hated the crowds, the hotels, and the railroads, and they longed nostalgically for the good old days when the wilderness was known only to a few.

One reaction to Murray and the crowds his book produced was

a feeling of proprietary elitism on the part of sportsmen who asserted that the wilderness should be enjoyed only by the few, that Murray's Fools violated the wilderness by their very numbers. Thomas Bangs Thorpe articulated this position during the first year of the Murray era, making a distinction between the "genuine sportsman and true lover of nature" and the "people listening to the fashionable twaddle" put forth by Murray. Thorpe called Murray's book "nonsense" and maintained that its readers had "profaned" the woods, having "neither skill as sportsmen, nor sentiment of piety enough in their composition, to understand Nature's solitudes." The opinion expressed by Thorpe appeared with increasing frequency in Adirondack literature as the century progressed (and has continued to manifest itself up to the present). Deriving from a fundamentally correct observation that the wilderness was fragile and could withstand only limited use, it quickly fell into the exclusive view that only the "right" people should be allowed to use it.[5]

Charles Dudley Warner expressed the elitist attitude with particular effectiveness: according to him, only "those who are most refined and most trained in intellectual fastidiousness," only the "most highly civilized" find "the real enjoyment of camping and tramping in the woods." These people, insisted Warner, were able to enjoy the spiritual features of the wilderness without abusing them, but the hoi polloi, whom Warner wished to keep out of the woods, were "they who have strewn the Adirondacks with paper collars and tin cans." The editors of *Forest and Stream*, who throughout the journal's existence took a special interest in Adirondack problems, lamented that "for one real hunter or angler who comes into the woods there are hosts who care little for either pursuit." An 1888 editorial entitled "Adirondack Abominations" declared: "Between the fish-hog, the railroad, the Italian railroad hand, the night-hunter, the pseudo-sportsman and the like, this grand region is becoming yearly less and less like its old self and a few more years will witness its entire destruction from a sportsman's and nature-lover's point of view." Here we see only too clearly how certain people perceived the threat to the Adirondacks to be not so much overuse as use by the wrong people.[6]

Undoubtedly, there were sportsmen who protected the resource and those who abused it. But behind the grim visions of destruction purveyed by Thorpe, Warner, and *Forest and Stream* was the implication that the wilderness and field sports were the exclusive province of white, Anglo-Saxon, well-to-do men. The traditions of hearty masculinity—of roughing it in the woods and escaping the trappings of civilized society—which had always appealed to Adirondack campers were threatened by crowds and by all the facilities that served them. The understandable response of some Adirondack enthusiasts was to insist that the changes in what they had come to consider as their own private preserve were the result of the intrusion of the wrong kind of people—people who simply did not grasp the traditions of outdoor life in the Adirondacks.[7]

It is interesting to note that sportsmen who knew the Adirondacks in the 1860s claimed in the 1870s that the old days were gone, that the wilderness had been destroyed by Murray's Fools. And sportsmen of the 1890s were crying just as shrilly that the changes of the 1880s had at last wiped out the wilderness. Behind all this fear of losing the old Adirondacks, of course, lay a perception of the Adirondacks—if preserved somehow—as embodying some special quality of a lost past. Just as Hammond and Headley in the years before the Civil War had found the Adirondacks holding reminders of a carefree youth, so the sportsmen of the Murray era saw the wilderness as part of the image of the golden age of the Adirondacks. For each generation, the current state of wilderness seemed only a fraction of the wilderness earlier campers had enjoyed. This notion became and remained a fundamental article of faith with many Adirondack writers.[8]

The intolerance of these changes, moreover, did not stem simply from a wish to preserve nature in a wild state. The reluctance to accept the steamboat, the hotel, and the neophyte hunter arose not so much from an appreciation of the wilderness as such as from the mythologization of the whole pre-Murray scene of the genteel hunting party accompanied by local guides spending several weeks hunting and fishing in the wilderness. This pervasive subscription to the image of a golden era and the concomitant belief in its apparent decline explain why so many writers feared and belabored the growing popularity of the region and often ignored the real threat posed by logging operations, which were becoming more and more widespread and destructive. While *Forest and Stream*, for example, showed in editorials that it was aware of the wasteful, destructive practices of Adirondack loggers, it spent far more energy in lobbying for changes in the Adirondack deer laws, maintaining with grave urgency that if the New York Assembly did not outlaw hounding or adjust the open season, then what was really important to the region—the gentlemanly art of killing the white-tailed deer—would diminish and eventually disappear.⁹

The only feature of logging that especially alarmed sportsmen was the construction of dams at the outlets of various Adirondack lakes; these controlled the flow of water in the spring when logs cut over the winter were run down the rivers to mill towns like Glens Falls. The typical sportsman seldom traveled far from the waterways and might have been more or less unaware of logging operations taking place in the deep woods, but when lumber companies constructed dams at the outlets of popular lakes and thus killed many of the trees lining the shores, the sportsman considered such action an unpardonable offense to his aesthetic sensibilities. The popular outdoor writer George Washington Sears, known by his pen name, "Nessmuk," described the scene on First Lake in 1880: "Stretching away to the dense green timber of what is now the mainland, there is a desolate waste of dead, decaying trees, lifting their bare, broken arms toward heaven in ghastly protest against the arborean murderers who tortured them to death by slow drowning." Elsewhere, he suggested that the local guides ought to acquire some dynamite and blow up these dams.¹⁰

One might expect sportsmen who complained about the effects of logging on the landscape to demand state ownership or at least controls on how the logger managed his lands. But most sportsmen, although they condemned the dams as a blight on the landscape, avoided the connection between logging and a shrinking wilderness; they still feared the inexperienced hunter more than they did the lumberjack. One correspondent to *Forest and Stream* argued that hunting and fishing in the Adirondacks suffered little from logging operations; rather, the tourists coming to the region on the railroads built by the lumber companies were more likely to diminish the capacity of the wilderness to supply game and fish for the gentleman sportsman. A correspondent echoed this sentiment, writing that the threat to the "Adirondacks as a sportsman's resort" came from "the so-called city sportsmen and the railroads."¹¹

On the other hand, some observers argued that the wilderness was equally the province of all people and that no group had any special rights to it. Kate Field, a popular lecturer and author of the day, visited the Adirondacks to investigate the phenomenon of Murray's Fools and wrote to the *New-York Daily Tribune*:

> Many sportsmen are rampant because their favorite hunting grounds have been made known to the public. The greatest good to the greatest number is, I believe, the true democratic platform, and if several hundred men think that the life-giving principles of the North Woods was [sic] instituted for the benefit of a few guns and rods, they are sadly mistaken.

Others agreed with Field and maintained that it was an overall gain for society if more people came to the Adirondacks, even though the wilderness solitude of a few people might be diminished. Murray himself accused elite sportsmen of intentionally keeping secret the region's beauties and benefits; many of the letters in the eastern press condemning him and his book, he said, were part of the plot of "certain interested parties, chiefly sportsmen, who selfishly wish to appropriate the Wilderness to their own uses."[12]

Murray insisted that the Adirondack wilderness belonged to everyone; he was glad, he wrote, "if the woods are filled with people, and I trust that thousands will visit them yearly. . . . Indeed I do not look at the Wilderness as belonging to sportsmen or any other class; it belongs to the country at large." There was plenty of wilderness in the Adirondacks to go around, and the deer and trout would last for many years, he maintained. It was thus his duty to the oppressed souls of modern man to popularize a region where their urban woes could be alleviated, especially since this posed, he thought, no real threat to the wilderness itself.[13]

Without knowing it, Murray was fostering an inevitable dilemma. The attribute of the Adirondacks that he most appreciated and believed would be most beneficial to visitors was wilderness. Yet by encouraging ever increasing numbers of people to come to the Adirondacks, he was helping to diminish the wilderness he loved so much. The actual effects of too many people in the woods became apparent even to him soon enough. He abandoned his camping grounds on Raquette Lake and began exploring the then little known territory around Cranberry Lake; undoubtedly, part of the reason for this move was the crowd on Raquette Lake, which his own book had attracted.[14]

Murray's democratic, anti-elitist position and that of the many writers who agreed with him was based on a utilitarian attitude toward wilderness—unspiritual and, in its effect, anti-wilderness. It was a shift from the practical, exploitative mentality of the Natural History Survey, with its perception of the commercial and agricultural needs of an expansive society, to a conviction about society's recreational needs. In either case there is an implicit indifference to the notion of wilderness as such. Both positions argue for the practical *use* of the wilderness, and while the deleterious effects of the former are more obvious, the latter equally fails to consider the fragility of the wilderness or appreciate that its spiritual benefits are compromised just as much by the presence of crowds as by the mine shaft or the cornfield. To be sure, one can easily understand why Murray and Kate Field would be offended by the smug condescension with which some writers attacked the misadventures of neophytes in the woods. Because of their patronizing tone, those horrified by Murray's Fools were seen to be espousing an essentially un-American position. When Thomas Bangs Thorpe or Charles Dudley Warner argued that some people by going to the Adirondacks helped to destroy what made the region attractive in the first place, their warnings seemed to many to originate in an exclusive, status-conscious attitude. With Murray and Field, as with many Americans, the notion of exclusivity did not sit well.

In their hostile reaction to this exclusivity, Murray and others showed that preservation of wilderness was of less concern to them than was the popular enjoyment of the land. While the rapidly growing interest in field sports that Murray both represented and stimulated has been cited as a crucial factor in the eventual appreciation and protection of the American wilderness, the attitude of these hunters and fishermen emphasized the utilitarian at the expense of the aesthetic.[15] Getting large numbers of visitors previously unfamiliar with the wilderness into the Adirondacks, where they could observe the region's natural wonders, undoubtedly worked to the benefit of the region when the conservation battle began. It was an important contribution to the eventual accommodation between some Americans and what remained of their wilderness. But Murray's wilderness-for-the-people approach involved a decision—conscious or otherwise—to emphasize the practical and popular functions of recreation at the expense of the spiritual and aesthetic importance of solitude and undeveloped open space.

Into the conflicts over crowds in the wilderness and the inchoate perception of the potential threat of logging came Verplanck Colvin. Surveyor, amateur scientist, conservationist, and indefatigable promoter of the Adirondacks, Colvin became the single most knowledgeable and articulate spokesman for the region. For roughly three decades, between the late 1860s and the end of the century, he explored parts of the Adirondacks never before described and likely never even seen—except, perhaps, by Indians. Colvin publicized the many threats facing the Adirondacks and actively advocated conservation. After he was commissioned by the state to conduct a comprehensive survey of the Adirondacks, his annual reports glorified the wilderness experience and suggested a response to wilderness which built on but was different from that of the romantics who had preceded him.

The narratives of romantic writers created an image of an idealized landscape where the very mountains and lakes radiated the immanence of God, while they often ignored or deprecated features of nature, such as swamps, thick forests, and rainy weather, which interfered with their appreciation of scenery and their discovery of the Deity in nature. Colvin undoubtedly read many of the romantic travel narratives, and his own writings show certain romantic characteristics, but he extended the romantic aesthetic to a unique combination of spiritualism and naturalism, of epic adventures and grinding hardships in the wilderness. His explorations in the Adirondacks became quests for the meaning of the wilderness, a meaning inherent in both the grandeur of mountain scenery and the tiniest of insects.

But Colvin's wilderness aesthetic remained incompletely formed and was inconsistently applied. His genuine love for the wilderness was eventually less cogent in his thinking than his commitment to progress and the needs of a progressive civilization; thus the same narratives that glorified intimacy with the wilderness often contained suggestions for development that would have compromised forever the capacity of the Adirondacks to supply a wilderness experience. Colvin recognized the threats to the wilderness posed by the increasing demands of lumbermen and sportsmen, yet he welcomed both. He believed that a progressive civlization depended on continuing exploitation of natural resources, and he, like Murray, maintained the democratic position that all citizens should have access to the wilderness. When it came to policy, Colvin was a conservationist, but he was never a preservationist, even though his own narratives of exploration were implicit arguments for preserving the wilderness.[16]

▲▲▲▲▲▲▲

Of Dutch and Scottish heritage, Colvin was born in Albany, New York, in 1847. After he attended private schools and the Albany Academy he began the study of law in his father's office. But the young Colvin was more interested in science and in working outdoors than he was in pursuing a legal career. By 1872, after several years of self-supported exploring in the Adirondacks, Colorado, and the South, he was appointed Superintendent of an Adirondack Survey; his mandate was to produce the first official and accurate map of the Adirondacks. This map was never completed, but for twenty-five years Colvin explored the Adirondack wilderness and submitted annual reports—often book length—to the legislature. A reporter for the *New York Daily Tribune* described Colvin in 1883 as "an athletic-looking young man of dark complexion, whose features tell of resolution, pluck and ability." In the field Colvin drove himself and his assistants through crushingly long days of surveying and arduous hikes across rugged, trailless terrain. His reports are punctuated by accounts of perilous nighttime descents from steep Adirondack peaks and of bivouacs deep in the woods away from base camp or supplies. His obsessive urge to gather topographical data led him and his men to winter camps and dangerous adventures on frozen lakes.[17]

The rigors of Colvin's fieldwork and the dictatorial nature of his relations with his assistants derived from his sense that it was his mission in life to plumb and interpret the secrets of the Adirondacks. Although Colvin prided himself on his scientific proclivities and described much of his work with the detached prose of a man simply reducing natural phenomena to cold data, the single most telling feature of his narratives is his discovery that wilderness is mysterious. As he wrote in 1874,

> Few fully understand what the Adirondack wilderness really is. It is a mystery even to those who have crossed and recrossed it by boats along its avenues, the lakes; and on foot through its vast and silent recesses.... Yet, though the woodsman may

pass his lifetime in some section of the wilderness it is still a mystery to him. Following the line of the axe-marks upon the trees; venturing along the cliff walls of the streams which rush leap on leap downward to form haughty rivers; climbing on the steep wooded slopes of lakes which never knew form or name on maps, he clings to his trapping line and shrouded and shut in by the deep, wonderful forest, emerges at length from its darkness to the daylight of the clearings, like a man who has passed under a great river or arm of the sea through a tunnel, knowing little of the wonders that had surrounded him.[18]

Exploring previously unseen parts of the Adirondacks became for Colvin a mystical experience. To contemplate the wilderness was to fall into a reverie—not the romantic reverie of introspection but a reverie produced by the appreciation of the vastness and ultimate elusiveness of the totality of nature: a "strange thrill of interest and of wonder at what may be hidden in that vast area of forest, covering all things with its deep repose."[19] His fascination with the Adirondack wilderness was not with an immanent spirit dwelling in scenic nature but in the innumerable facts of natural process. In the vast and varied workings of nature itself lay the region's greatest mystery.

Colvin's obsession with knowing every detail about the Adirondacks led him to climb the high peaks again and again, from every conceivable direction, in every kind of weather. Having made his first ascent of the Gothics, he was enraptured by the different perspective it afforded him of the surrounding peaks, dwelling on how the new view in effect created new features of the landscape: "all the black, frost-crested mountain billows—revealed from this new station in strangely different contour—with new passes, new gorges, and new chasms." Colvin's intimacy with the mountains especially struck the popular outdoor writer Fred Mather, who spent a season in the field with Colvin in 1882:

> I have been much interested in talking with Mr. Colvin, the superintendent of the survey, and had no conception that so much was to be learned about mountains and the water systems which drain them. He has made a study of their characters, and delights in getting hold of a new "nest" of them. Facts concerning their elevation, shape, and their position in regard to other mountains, are all noted down, so that each mountain has an individuality of its own to him, and he knows them as a herdsman knows the members of his flock.

Shrewdly, Mather recognized the depth of Colvin's knowledge as well as the proprietary, animating features of his attitude. Not only was Colvin intimate with physical details of geology and topography; he also saw the unique arrangment of these details in each peak. The individuality of a mountain arose not from the presence of a romantic *genius loci* or pantheistic spirit, however, but from the complex variety of natural phenomena.[20]

As Colvin strove to become more and more knowledgeable about the Adirondacks, gathering more data, exploring farther into the recesses of the wilderness, his labors assumed the tenor of an epic quest. Once, working in the northwestern Adirondacks—country hitherto overlooked by sportsmen and lumbermen and thus virtually unknown even into the 1870s—he learned from an old wolf trapper of a group of uncharted lakes. Immediately, although winter had begun and travel was difficult and dangerous, he set out to find these lakes. In that area, he later wrote,

> eventually new fields were entered upon . . . the most important discoveries were made in the region of the western lakes, where, in the course of an extended exploring expedition, with my guides—through a wilderness, trackless, save by wild beasts—numerous bodies of water new to the maps were found, and the courses of the rivers and forms of the lakes ascertained.[21]

The discovery of a previously uncharted pond in the remote wilderness of the western Adirondacks was far more to Colvin than a simple addition to geographical knowledge; it was an event of preeminent importance. Colvin felt that his surveying was in effect locating the mountains and waters of the Adirondacks for the first time. The translation of field data to maps and tables was a labor of creation, an enterprise whereby unknown—and by implication hitherto useless—features of the world achieved a new and more real existence. The physical processes of orogeny, glaciation, and erosion made the Adirondacks, but until Colvin announced exactly where the mountains and lakes were, they did not fully exist: "unerring maps shall be prepared which will show the region reproduced in true miniature, that all who see may read."[22] An example of Colvin's compulsion for absolute accuracy was his method for fixing the precise altitude of Mount Marcy, the highest point in New York. Since barometric measurements gave only an approximation, Colvin decided that a line of chains and levels would have to be run from Lake Champlain to the summit of Marcy, the precise height of each station being calculated to the thousandth of a foot. By the time the job was finished, Colvin's crew had established a line of levels over forty miles long with more than eight hundred stations. As the men approached the summit, an October blizzard began. Against the advice of guides and assistants, and despite extreme cold, freezing rain, and the possibility of being trapped in Panther Gorge by deep drifts, Colvin pushed the work forward; the simple exigencies of safety had become irrelevant in the face of his obsession. The night after the final reading was taken on the summit, back in Panther Gorge, "joy reigned in the camp to-night, for we had accomplished the work in the face of the greatest difficulties; when the most experienced guide had ventured to say that it was for this season impossible."[23] While the source of Colvin's joy may have been the achievement of his goal, that of the guides was doubtless the knowledge that the next day they would be leaving that wintry wilderness alive.

Behind Colvin's monomaniacal urge to assimilate the data that partially explained the physical reality of the Adirondack landscape was a complex attitude toward the wilderness. Moving beyond the romantic love of wild scenery and pantheistic perceptions of the deity, his wilderness aesthetic involved an acceptance of the dynamics of wilderness and an appreciation of the processes of undisturbed nature. A major influence was undoubtedly George Perkins Marsh and his seminal *Man and Nature*. Although Colvin did not cite Marsh directly during the period of his greatest influence in Adirondack affairs, it is clear that Marsh had a powerful impact on his thinking. As early as 1872, Colvin had warned that the destruction of Adirondack forests would lead to diminished flow in New York's rivers; one of Marsh's primary concerns was the deleterious effects of indiscriminate lumbering on the role of mountain forests in regulating watershed. *Man and Nature*, first published in 1864, within ten years became, as Marsh's twentieth-century biographer and editor has written, "an American classic of international reputation." While Marsh intended his work to point out the dangers to humankind, in strictly utilitarian terms of agriculture and climate, of physical abuse of the natural environment, there are also important aesthetic implications in his view of nature.[24]

The connection between Marsh's science and aesthetics was noticed by James Russell Lowell in an early review: in Lowell's opinion, one of the book's chief virtues was that it would "lure the young to observe and take delight in nature." And Marsh himself hoped that this "delight" would be the result of a new way of looking at nature:

> To the natural philosopher, the descriptive poet, the painter, and the sculptor, as well as to the common observer, the power most important to cultivate, and, at the same time, hardest to acquire, is that of seeing what is before him. Sight is a faculty; seeing an art. . . . This exercise of the eye I desire to promote, and, next to moral and religious doctrine, I know no more important practical lessons in this earthly life of ours . . . than those relating to the employment of the sense of vision in the study of nature.

To see nature with new eyes depended on accepting Marsh's thesis that interference with nature can lead to catastrophe. The logical implication of this concept was that nature when left completely alone presents a marvelous nexus of perfectly meshing processes. The fundamental point of *Man and Nature* was that untouched nature exists in harmony, and that man commonly disturbs this harmony. In addition to warning of the ruinous effects of human activity on the watershed that was essential to crop production, therefore, this point could lead, as it did for Colvin, to an implicit disposition to prefer that portion of nature showing no signs of having been tampered with. The observer of nature who finds beauty in its details and admires the perfect sum to which these details add does not look for Wordsworthian moral lessons, recognizing that doing so is imposing an anthropocentric construct on nature. An extension of Marsh's objection to physical interference in the natural world was an objection to metaphysical impositions as well. And for the most part, Colvin approached nature—and loved it—mindful of the perfection of its material existence, not for any spiritual presence behind it.[25]

Being concerned with reality, then, rather than romanticized ideality, Colvin could deal in his narratives with subjects that had seldom appeared in pre-Civil War accounts. His reports of weather, for example, reflected the realities of the Adirondack climate of rain, haze, and occasional clear days, not the virtually endless succession of sunny, idyllic days apparently bestowed on romantic writers. Likewise, the dead trees, sedge, open swamp, and mud that surround many Adirondack lakes—from which romantic travelers had recoiled—struck Colvin as integral parts of a natural scene governed by natural processes. On a rainy day in 1872, for example, high on the slopes of Mount Marcy, he discovered the highest lake source of the Hudson, a small marshy pond surrounded by gnarled and dead trees. Colvin's account of this event is a characteristic mixture of discoverer's exhilaration and sympathy for the utter wilderness of the scene:

> But how wild and desolate this spot! . . . There is no mark of ax, no barked tree, nor blackened remnants of fire; not a severed twig, nor a human footprint. . . . Skirting the shores, we seek the inlet, and find that the numerous subterranean streams from different directions feed its waters. The meadow at the eastern, upper end is full of wide-winding openings, in which deep streams are gliding, and it is remarkable that, while the water of the lake is warm, the water of the subterranean streams is delicious, icy cold. The spring rills which feed these streams come from far up on the sides of the surrounding mountains, the water dripping from the crest of Marcy. First seen as we then saw it, dark and dripping with the moisture of the heavens, it seemed, in its minuteness and its prettiness, a veritable Tear-of-the-Clouds, the summit water as I named it.[26]

Colvin thus emphasizes the wilderness, finding "desolation" to be no demerit, and admires the ever-surprising ways in which natural processes work. Compare Colvin's response to Lake Tear with the reactions (quoted in Chapter III) of romantic travelers to similar, though less elevated, terrain at the head of the Bog River. There the romantic dwelt on the fearfulness and the suggestions of mortality; Colvin, though also emotionally impressed, was equally aware of the significance of natural process in the perpetuation of life and creation of the totality of the landscape.

Colvin's appreciation of natural process partly stemmed from his understanding that nature is as interesting, as complex, and as wonderful in its tiniest detail as in the sum of these details. Colvin was fascinated equally by insects and sublime views. This shift from the romantic preference for conventional scenery and the broad view derived from Marsh's argument that nature makes no distinction between large and small, that in the natural world all phenomena, all creatures, all organisms contribute to the harmonious balance on which all life depends. As Marsh wrote, "It is a legal maxim that 'the law concerneth not itself with trifles,' *de minimis non curat lex*; but in the vocabulary of nature, little and great are terms of comparison only; she knows no trifles."[27]

To the mind attuned to the significance of details, then, as Colvin's was, the wilderness—the place where the details of nature most perfectly work together to maintain nature's harmony—was full of secrets. But only a mind both sensitive to details and trained in the ways of the wilderness could penetrate these secrets. One day when Colvin was exploring south of the Oswegatchie River, he spied a natural deer lick,

> the first and only natural deer lick which I have observed in the Adirondacks. It was not remarkable in its appearance, and other than a hunter's eye would have noticed merely the shapely footprints in the clay and not the inconspicuous smooth spots licked by the tongues of the deer.

Colvin responded with similar delight when, near Beaver River in October, he discovered on a south-facing snowbank "a small black insect, the *podura*, or 'snow flea.' These singular winter insects, the guides assert, are sure indications of a thaw. Is this not a wonderful region, indeed, where insects sport upon the snow!"[28] The only insects ever mentioned by romantics were the annoying ones—mosquitoes, black flies, and punkies.

A significant feature of George Perkins Marsh's recognition of the harmony of undisturbed nature was his observation of the continuous, self-sustaining cycle of death and regeneration. To Marsh—and to those, like Colvin, who grasped the aesthetic implications of this discovery—this dynamic attribute of nature was one of its chief glories. That undisturbed nature was both balanced and dynamic was a source of great comfort to Marsh as well as a warning against human capacity to upset this balance. In a description of the New England landscape before British settlement, Marsh emphasized the harmonious combination of succession and balance:

> The unbroken forests had attained to their maximum density and strength of growth, and, as older trees decayed and fell, they were succeeded by new shoots or seedlings, so that from century to century no perceptible change seems to have occurred in the wood, except the slow spontaneous succession. . . . Trees fall singly, not by square roods [*sic*], and the tall pine is hardly prostrate, before the light and heat, admitted to the

ground by the removal of the dense crown of foliage which had shut them out, stimulate the germination of the seeds of broad-leaved trees that had lain, waiting this kindly influence, perhaps for centuries.[29]

This acceptance of process and the concomitant rejection of conventional scenic criteria led Colvin to reject the old fears about how the wilderness could destroy moral character or evoke barbarism; on the contrary, he suggested, intimacy with the wilderness and acceptance of the natural processes of death, decay, and regeneration could calm humanity's inherently savage nature. In language strikingly similar to Marsh's, he described a moment of insight in the western Adirondacks:

> Alone in the heart of the western forest—far from trails—among nameless and unmapped mountain ranges; all shut in by the tangled forest where living trees grow savagely, in the very sepulchre of their ancestors; where the black spruce towering above beeches and maples winds its sinewy roots around the gigantic rocks and throws out tendrils to feed upon the prostrate trunks that died and fell to earth a century ago ... where from ragged cliffs the curious explorer looks down into wild gorges and pathless valleys of which his guides can tell him nothing—there on those wild crests as we rest on the luxuriant ferns and gaze out over the sea of forest-covered mountains, men feel what words cannot convey—the wildest men are quieted and hushed—a grand and beautiful solemnity and peace makes its way into the soul, for human strife and discord seem here to have passed away forever.[30]

Although Colvin's use of the word "savagely" in connection with a tree reflects the romantic tradition, the passage as a whole offers a contrast to the reaction of the romantic traveler—to the point that Colvin can experience positive sensations even where he feels "all shut in by the tangled forest." The romantic might have been thrilled by the fearful sublimity of such a wilderness but would have couched his reaction in a different vocabulary, one dwelling on the loneliness, the oppressiveness of process, and the claustrophobia-inducing closeness of the forest.

This passage is of further interest because of Colvin's suggestion of the spiritual influence that the wilderness exercised on the consciousness of the observer. His treatment of this traditional function of the contemplation of nature contains important differences from similar treatments in romantic narratives. Since Colvin did not subscribe to the existence of immanent spirits in nature, the spiritual experience which he describes results not from the recognition of the pantheistic quality of nature itself but from an analytical and calm acceptance of the natural facts of biological and geological process. The source of the spiritual experience, then, is not nature itself but the sensitive mind's comprehension of nature's reality.

Colvin's appreciation of the wilderness thus depended on his acceptance of the traditional distinction between man and nature. Like Marsh, he insisted that man was not *of* nature but above it. The ability of the sensitive mind to comprehend the harmonious glories of the wilderness was the same characteristic that separated man from nature and which enabled him to subdue it. Like Marsh, then, Colvin believed that humanity's relationship to nature must ultimately be one of manipulation and control. Like Marsh, he never explicitly advocated preservation of wilderness.[31] He violated the integrity of the wilderness with casual indifference, and his reports were full of utilitarian schemes which, if implemented, would have forever compromised what remained of the Adirondack wilderness. Colvin seemed unwilling to accept fully the implications of his own wilderness aesthetic; to move from appreciation to preservation was a step beyond his psychological and cultural capacity.

One sign of his inconsistency was the cavalier abandon with which he approved the felling of trees. On Blue Mountain, a peak in the central Adirondacks that he had chosen as a major station in the system of triangles with which he was fixing precise locations, he ordered the entire summit shorn of its timber cover. Blue Mountain has a rather flat summit, and the amount of cutting necessary to open up the views Colvin needed for sighting his angles was considerable. The practice of clearing mountain summits continued throughout the existence of the Adirondack Survey: in 1878, wrote Colvin, "the summits of seven lofty mountain peaks were chopped clear of forest." He also advocated continuous timber yield to the state's lumber and pulp mills, along with mining where feasible, railroads, the growth of the tourist industry, and even the tapping of Adirondack lakes to supply water for New

York City. In discussing potential timber productivity, Colvin adopted a familiar utilitarian, anti-wilderness stance, writing that the region's forests could "yield a noble income to the State from lands hitherto deemed wild, valueless and worthless." During most of his career, Colvin's only criticism of Adirondack logging was that it was unscientific in its methods; he hoped that through the intervention of the state, the logging industry could be encouraged to see the virtues of exploiting the region's forests on a continuous-yield basis.[32]

Most of Colvin's exploitative schemes, however, involved water. In 1873 he proposed the construction of a huge aqueduct to reach all the way from the Adirondacks to the lower Hudson Valley, and he referred to this scheme periodically thereafter. Another project that fascinated Colvin, as it had others before him, was a proposed system of canals that would join the lake and river systems of the Adirondack tableland. Noting the interrupted work on a canal between Long Lake and Round Pond that would have united the Raquette and Hudson watersheds, he suggested that nearly all the lakes of the western Adirondacks could be made to flow into the Hudson via such a channel. Linking the region's lakes in this way, Colvin insisted, could turn an "agriculturally worthless" wilderness into "the arbiter of empire." Raising his expectations for such canals to mythic dimensions, he suggested that with their completion the nation would finally have realized the elusive dream of the northwest passage.[33]

The inconsistency of these schemes with wilderness, if Colvin failed to notice it, did not escape at least one other writer. Nessmuk, who condemned the lumber companies' construction of dams on Adirondack lakes, found Colvin's canal project equally offensive. Nessmuk considered Colvin no better than the "illogical hoodlums" who built those dams, and accused him of rank hypocrisy for singing the "praises of the Adirondacks, as a finer more romantic land than the Swiss Alps" while explaining "how the waters that, by nature, seek the St. Lawrence, may be dammed, backed up and turned, to flow into the Hudson." The catastrophic results of Colvin's plans, wrote Nessmuk, were perfectly apparent to "any man, with as much brains as a hen-turkey." He was no more enamored of the aqueduct proposal: "If Verplanck Colvin's proposition of a grand aqueduct from the headwaters of the Hudson to New York City (supplying the Hudson Valley) should ever become an accomplished fact, it will change the entire character and status of the wilderness."[34]

One reason for this hostility to Colvin's utilitarian suggestions was that Nessmuk spent nearly all of his time on the Fulton Chain to Raquette River route, where tourism was booming and where the changes in the landscape ushered in by the combination of hotels, private camps, and lumber dams were most apparent. Thus, while to Nessmuk the final destruction of the wilderness seemed imminent, to Colvin the Adirondack wilderness seemed a much larger entity, one that could suffer diminution in certain spots yet still not lose its essential wildness. The changes that were becoming more and more apparent merely emphasized the "wildness of the remainder," while "the unvisited wilderness centres or cores are still left in all their sylvan purity."[35]

Early in his career Colvin expressed some regret that wilderness must inevitably disappear before the demands of progress and civilization: "To the explorer . . . it is pleasanter to imagine the wild mountain crest, or mirrored lake which he was the first to reach, remaining as unvisited, in all its aspects as unchanged as when he first beheld it." But the more progressive side of his nature could not accept the notion of preserving wilderness as such. If change occurred, he assumed it had to be for the better. Thinking about the crowds who followed Murray to the Adirondacks, he concluded:

> The woods are thronged; bark and log huts prove insufficient; hotels spring up as though by magic, and the air resounds with laughter, song and jollity. The wild trails, once jammed with logs, are cut clear by the axes of the guides, and ladies clamber to the summits of those once untrodden peaks. The genius of change has possession of the land; we cannot control it. When we study the necessities of our people, we would not control it if we could.[36]

Behind Colvin's willingness to see change in the wilderness was his commitment to the American dream of progress and the sanctity of private property. In 1890, when publicity about the wasteful abuse of Adirondack landscape and timber by loggers was causing considerable criticism, he delivered a speech in New York City, insisting that logging was beneficial to the region, which was "too vast and too magnificent to be destroyed so easily." The felling of Adirondack trees was a necessary feature of a progressive age, and one could not regret that "charming spots, that were day dreams of picturesque delight, are now laid waste." With the conservative's reverence for the rights of property owners, he maintained that "we must not begrudge the toiling owner his reward."[37]

Colvin's rather jingoistic faith in the virtues of American progress and private property prevented him from ever fully realizing the inconsistency of his attitudes. Even when—five years after this speech—he encountered shocking evidence of the threat to nature posed by private enterprise, he refused to acknowledge the import of what he saw. Surveying boundaries near Ampersand Lake, he was dismayed to find the shores marred by the existence of a logging dam: "Great forests of arbor vitae (white cedar) along the southerly shores of the lake were drowned and killed by water. . . . It was painful to see great masses of these typical forest trees now dead, lifeless and going to decay." These trees were dead not because of natural processes but because of human interference in the environment.

But this was just the beginning of his distress; Ampersand Lake lies at the foot of Mount Seward, of which in 1870 Colvin and a local guide had made the first recorded ascent, and which was therefore a special place to Colvin. On the day he discovered the dead trees at Ampersand Lake, he was told by the agent of the guilty lumber company that "they proposed to strip the forests from the slopes and ridges of Mt. Seward." Worse, learned Colvin:

> The agent informed me that not only was the timber in the valley to be cut and removed, but chutes were to be constructed, far up towards the summit of the high peaks, so that not only logs fit for lumber could be sent down to the skidways, but even the small softwood spruce timber would be thoroughly cut for pulpwood, as the company did not consider it desirable to keep and pay taxes upon these high uplands, where the trees are of very slow growth. The summit of Mt. Seward reaches almost to the timber-line, being over 4,000 feet above the sea. Of course the owners of the property have a perfect right to remove forests upon their land, or to manage their property in any way they desire, but it was sad to think that this last of the remote peaks of the Adirondacks, whose forests had never been touched by the axe of the lumberman, was now to be cut over in so ruthless a manner.

Thus did Colvin express his regret over the violation of what was to him a sacred province. Despite his profound experience in the wilderness and his acceptance of the value of wilderness, he was unable to condemn its destruction on the slopes of Seward. But he could not put the thought out of his mind; the next day, working in the same vicinity, he looked up at Seward and was again struck by the sadness of the situation:

> Southeasterly almost, as it seemed, under the sun, the great mass of Mt. Seward, dark and still, arose majestically, deep with the rich green color of its evergreen forest, which the axe of the lumberman threatened to destroy. There lurked the deer and bear; perhaps panther also; in that wild desolate forest, living as they had lived since the dawn of creation; but now the march of civilization had reached even the flanks of this great mountain, the lumber roads and skidways crossed and extended over the trails of the wild game.

He went on to predict hopefully that once the damage was done, "unless the demon of fire should sweep up the cliffs and reduce all to a dreary desert," nature would be able to restore the mountain to its original glory.[38]

Colvin's retreat from the implications of his own wilderness aesthetic represents his ultimate failure—or refusal—fully to accept and appreciate the wilderness. Colvin was finally bound to pay homage more to the gods of progress, civilization, and private property than to the wonders of process and the wilderness experience. In this respect, he was more representative of his age than were men who have received scholarly attention in the analysis of the eventual accommodation between certain Americans and the wilderness. While John Muir, for example, may have exercised considerable influence on American environmental attitudes as they developed in the twentieth century, the ambivalence of Verplanck Colvin more accurately reflects the dilemma of the late nineteenth-century mind which appreciated the joys of the wilderness experience while clinging tenaciously to the dominant culture's faith in the virtues of progress. For Colvin to have advocated the protection of wilderness would have meant restraining the forces of human progress and this was something that he—like most other Americans—was not ready to do.

Nevertheless, although Colvin did not support wilderness preservation and although he faded from the Adirondack scene after 1900, his wilderness aesthetic, living on in his reports, has had a marked influence on the twentieth-century wilderness movement. Robert Marshall, one of the most important conservationists of this century and a founder of the Wilderness Society, spent the summers of his youth at his family's camp on Upper Saranac Lake, where the Colvin reports constituted part of his father's library. Robert and his brother George read assiduously in these volumes and were inspired to set out on their own expeditions to the high peaks. Robert Marshall went on to explore in the Rockies and Alaska; earned a Ph.D. in plant physiology from Johns Hopkins; wrote extensively on recreation, land management, and wilderness; and at the time of his early death was Chief of the Division of Recreation and Lands of the United States Forest Service. As much as any other man in this century, Robert Marshall helped preserve a part of what remained of the American wilderness. And one of the earliest and most significant influences on his attitudes toward wilderness was the collection of the Colvin reports he read as a young boy.[39]

# V

# Wilderness Preserved:
## *The Forest Preserve and the Irony of Forever Wild*

Given the absence of genuine preservationist sentiment in the nineteenth century, how do we explain the legislative and constitutional steps adopted in the 1880s and 1890s? Romantics and explorers alike remained unsympathetic to wilderness preservation, yet a preserved wilderness is what New Yorkers had in the Adirondacks by 1895. In 1885 the legislature created the Forest Preserve out of what was left of the public domain in the Adirondacks; in 1894 a constitutional convention drafted a provision (adopted that year, becoming effective on January 1, 1895) guaranteeing that the Forest Preserve would "be forever kept as wild forest lands." This provision went on to declare that the timber on the Forest Preserve could not be cut, that the forest was to be left alone. In other words, what little wilderness remained was protected. But wilderness was not the concern of either politicians or voters, although it was apparently a necessary means toward achieving a certain end. The subject of this chapter is the explanation of this ostensible paradox.

Some sentiment for conservation in the Adirondacks had appeared over the years. In the 1830s, geologist Ebenezer Emmons called for wise use of Adirondack natural resources. In 1860, W. W. Ely described the scenery and wildlife of the region, pointed out its uselessness for agriculture, and warned that the lumberman would "desecrate the New York Wilderness" unless prevented by public interest in preservation. Four years later a *New York Times* editorial approved the construction of a railroad into the Adirondacks and predicted that it would make the region "a Central Park for the World." The *Times* supported conservation that would prevent the mountains from being "despoiled of their forests," but believed that such conservation as was necessary could easily be effected by private interests. It had no wish to prohibit lumbering, predicting that recreation and exploitation could exist side by side. This attitude prevailed for most of the rest of the century, changing only slowly as the public became aware of the ruthlessly wasteful practices of Adirondack lumbermen.[1]

After the Civil War, lumbermen began reaching farther and farther into the interior of the Adirondacks. Before 1883, any land owned by the state could be purchased by any person or corporation who bid for it, and prices were always low. Typically, a logger would purchase timberland, cut all the marketable pine and spruce, and abandon the site—which then became the property of the state again when its owner failed to pay taxes. The damage to the landscape caused by the removal of spruce and pine logs alone was not especially great, but the piles of brush and branches left on the ground soon became tinder for forest fires.

After the introduction of paper made from wood pulp, the smaller trees and more species were then cut, making the effects of logging more severe. In addition, many hemlocks were destroyed for their bark, which was used by tanneries in curing hides. By the time conservation measures were being considered, just about any softwood of any size was being harvested. Hardwoods were usually spared because they do not float well, and the most efficient method of getting felled timber to sawmills or pulp mills was by floating it down rivers. The use of railroads to move logs out of the forest did not become widespread until the early twentieth century.[2]

Publicity about logging abuse reached the public just as people were coming under the influence of the environmental ideas of George Perkins Marsh.[3] In 1864, the year in which the *Times* referred to the Adirondacks as a potential "Central Park for the World," Marsh published *Man and Nature*, which dealt with the ability of humans to alter the landscape, usually to their eventual loss. While the aesthetic implications of *Man and Nature* (discussed in the last chapter) were important and have been generally overlooked or minimized by scholars, Marsh's real significance lies in his warnings about the practical consequences of disrupting nature's harmonies. A scholar and businessman from Vermont, Marsh spent many years in the United States Foreign Service. He observed environmental problems in the eastern Mediterranean region and concluded that various cultures had, through prodigal cutting of the original forests, damaged watersheds and diminished the agricultural productivity of once fertile lands. He went so far as to argue that the fall of powerful civilizations derived from the abuse of forests.

The "destruction of the woods . . . was man's first physical conquest, his first violation of the harmonies of inanimate nature," Marsh argued; the indiscriminate cutting of trees had done more to alter the landscape "with momentous consequences to the drainage of the soil" than had any other human activity. By "momentous consequences," Marsh was not suggesting minor flooding or occasional drought. He believed that continued thoughtless exploitation of nature threatened the very future of mankind: "There are parts of Asia Minor, of Northern Africa, of Greece, and even of Alpine Europe, where the operation of causes set in action by man has brought the face of the earth to a desolation almost as complete as that of the moon."

Other forerunners of the conservation movement had urged the wise use of nature, but Marsh envisioned apocalyptic catastrophe as the direct result of abusing the earth's forests:

> The earth is fast becoming an unfit home for its noblest inhabitant, and another era of equal human crime and human improvidence . . . would reduce it to such a condition of impoverished productiveness, of shattered surface, of climatic excess, as to threaten the deprivation, barbarism, and perhaps even extinction of the species.[4]

Although direct citations of Marsh and his *Man and Nature* are not to be found in the nineteenth-century literature of Adirondack conservation, his influence is obvious. Throughout the periodically feverish conservation activity of the 1870s, 1880s, and 1890s, there is a continuing concern, often verging upon the hysterical, with the threat to the Adirondack watershed posed by uncontrolled logging. Before Marsh suggested that humankind could permanently alter the landscape, those apprehensive about the growth of the Adirondack lumber industry protested on aesthetic grounds or, more often, because prodigal exploitation of the forest might simply result in a scarcity of lumber. But armed with Marsh's predictions of environmental catastrophe, some observers warned that further destruction of the Adirondack forests would lead to a diminished supply of water for the Erie Canal, the Hudson River, and other commercial arteries, and that the eventual product of bared Adirondack slopes would be an endless cycle of flood and drought.

In 1872 the New York Assembly created a State Park Commission to inquire into the expediency of giving New York State title to the timbered regions lying within seven Adirondack counties and converting them into a public park. Among the members of this commission were Dr. B. Franklin Hough, who later was instrumental in the establishment of the United States Forest Reserves, and Verplanck Colvin, who was appointed Secretary. The commission recommended establishing an Adirondack park of approximately 1,730,000 acres, of which the state at the time owned only about 40,000 acres. The chief reason given was the protection of the watershed and

> the maintenance of that quantity of water in the navigable rivers, in the streams that supply the canals and afford power to mills and manufactures, which from time immemorial has flowed in undiminished volume in their channels, and which only in these later days begins to slowly fail and disappear.

Thus, although the use of the word "park" may appear to indicate a primarily recreational function, it was to avoid the kind of catastrophe Marsh had warned against that the commissioners advocated state ownership and supervision of Adirondack lands. In terms similar to those used by Marsh, their report discussed the effect on the Hudson and the Erie Canal of the destruction of Adirondack forests. The commissioners argued that since profligate cutting would have such a deleterious effect on populations and industries downstream, it was "the duty of the State to interfere and provide a remedy."[5]

Support in the press for the park proposal revolved almost exclusively around watershed protection. Even *Forest and Stream* (which was interested primarily, one might assume, in recreational benefits) maintained that such protection was the most important reason for establishing the park, and the *New York Times* also supported the prevention of watershed destruction. Both publications observed the recreational usefulness of such a public park, but this concern was secondary.[6] Still, despite generally favorable reaction to the proposal, no legislative action was taken.

The watershed argument attracted increasing numbers of advocates in the remaining years of the century. In 1882, Governor Alonzo B. Cornell warned ominously that if current trends in the removal of timber continued, "imminent danger will threaten. . . . The rain-falls will diminish, the springs and streams fail and unaccountable loss ensue." *Forest and Stream* also advanced this argument, editorializing repeatedly that legislative action was needed to stop "the foolish and ruthless destruction of these timber lands which has very materially affected the great and important water supplies of the State." The magazine underscored the utilitarian nature of its position when it insisted that "the reasons why the forests should be preserved are not sentimental, but very practical. If the Adirondacks are cleared the Hudson River will dry up."[7]

In 1883, following increased agitation for the state to take some action, the legislature voted to withdraw from further sale all state-owned lands in the Adirondacks—which by that time, because of the reversion of land to the state for unpaid taxes, totaled about 600,000 acres. Although much of this land had been logged or burned and was useless to the lumber industry, removing it from the market was the first step toward creating a permanent public domain in the Adirondacks.[8]

In the following year, the legislature appointed a committee of "experts . . . to investigate and report a system of forest preservation." The report of this body (known as the Sargent Commission, after one of its most prominent members, Charles Sprague Sargent, professor of arboriculture at Harvard) recommended the establishment of a Forest Preserve, which "shall be forever kept as wild forest lands." The legislature largely adopted the Sargent Commission's proposals; it declared that state-owned lands in the Adirondacks would be the state's "Forest Preserve," that they would be forever part of the public domain, and that a newly created Forestry Commission would oversee their maintenance. It was expected that the Forestry Commission would support itself and contribute surplus revenues to the state treasury by contracting with lumbermen for the timber in the Forest Preserve; the action reflected the legislature's hope that it could both protect the watershed and allow for continued timber harvest, since it was assumed that the Forestry Commission would be applying the principles of scientific forest management. The law establishing the Forest Preserve emphasized the protection of the land, not the timber: "The lands now or hereafter constituting the forest preserve shall be forever kept as wild forest lands. They shall not be sold, nor shall they be leased or taken by any person or corporation public or private." The Sargent Commission Report and the resulting Forest Preserve Law of 1885 were the source of the expression "forever wild," which has been used ever since in connection with the Forest Preserve.[9] Some of the language of the law was written into the 1895 constitution. But a crucial point of the 1885 law, worth repeating, was that while the land would be forever part of the public domain, the timber could be sold and harvested.

Protection of watershed and harvesting of timber were seen as compatible pursuits. And the advocates of scientific forestry expressed again and again their concern for watershed protection. In 1888, Sargent and others founded *Garden and Forest*, a journal devoted to promulgating landscape architecture, horticulture, and forestry. Sargent, one of the leading American proponents of scientific forestry, had been active at least since 1883 in trying to save the Adirondack forests from ruthless lumbermen; he may have been the author of the crucial language of the Forest Preserve Law.[10] During the six years of its existence, his magazine paid constant attention to Adirondack issues, editorialized for conservation legislation, and asserted that the only important reason for effecting conservation in the Adirondacks was to protect the watershed. In 1890, for example, it observed:

> No legislation will be satisfactory unless it is based on the principle that the first and only sufficient reason why the state should hold a tract of land within its borders is that it is essential that this particular region should remain forest-covered always so that the flow of the great water-ways of the state need not be impaired. . . . It is very well to have a sanitarium, and

it is proper that people should be able to enjoy the refreshing contact with wild nature, but, after all, these are secondary considerations.[11]

It apparently never occurred to the editors of *Garden and Forest* or to the advocates of scientific forestry that the outcome of growing public concern over watershed would be total preservation for state-owned lands, prohibiting even the scientific forester from pursuing his profession in the Adirondack Forest Preserve. Defenders of scientific forestry seemed unaware that they were failing in two ways: first, they were not selling the usefulness of their skills to the owners of Adirondack timberlands; second, they seemed unable to improve the image of the lumberman in the eyes of the New York canal interests.

Throughout this period, Adirondack writers established a picture in the public mind of a landscape being utterly destroyed by the ravages of irresponsible lumbering. The specter of imminent disaster was constantly raised. One of the most dramatic efforts to convince the public of the rape of the Adirondack landscape was a series of engravings by Julian Rix, published in *Harper's Weekly*. In one issue Rix proffered a before-and-after depiction. On the left he showed "A Feeder of the Hudson—As it Was." There the reader beheld a rushing mountain stream, tumbling over boulders protected from the sun by towering, ancient trees. On the right was "A Feeder of the Hudson—As it Is." There the reader saw a dry streambed between slopes covered with charred stumps stretching all the way to the horizon. Accompanying these pictures was an article by Sargent, arguing that continued abuse of the landscape by loggers would reduce the Adirondacks "to the condition of a desert."[12]

Such graphic presentations helped to establish in the public mind an image of the Adirondack landscape as an important but fragile guardian of the state's prosperity and future. The pictures outraged the reader for two reasons—the violation of the aesthetic integrity of a peaceful natural scene, and the threat posed to New York commerce by such continued abuse. The villain in the drama, of course, was the lumberman. The journals and newspapers that described the ongoing story of the rape of the Adirondacks insisted that the lumberman, almost without exception, was a ruthless, arrogant, greedy destroyer of the bounty of nature. This campaign made it impossible for the proponents of scientific forestry to defend their advocacy of forest management for state lands in the Adirondacks. The public perception of lumbering changed from that of an essentially harmless activity not inconsistent with wilderness recreation to one that threatened to destroy both recreation and commerce.

The romantic traveler had seen the lumberjack as a colorful native of the wilderness whose felling and driving of timber added a touch of the picturesque to the Adirondack backcountry. By the close of the pre-Civil War period a few travelers had become disenchanted with lumbering, and several writers after the war were especially upset by the damage to the aesthetics of the landscape caused by lumber dams.[13] But as long as the product of lumbering exceeded in value the watershed it ostensibly threatened, the public had generally assumed a hands-off attitude. Only when lumbering activities appeared to offer a net loss to society did the image of the lumberman suddenly deteriorate to the point where the efforts of Sargent and other foresters could not revive it.

▲▲▲▲▲▲▲

Before that happened, however, many people hoped that the professional forester, trained in the nascent science of silviculture, would replace the ruthless lumberman and thus provide New York with the opportunity to preserve its watershed and yet continue to exploit its timber resources.[14] Few people wished to eliminate lumbering altogether from the Adirondacks or even from the Forest Preserve, once it was created. The concept of multiple use enjoyed wide currency even while the press was denigrating the lumberman. Although the 1873 report of the Park Commission insisted that "protection of a great portion of that forest from wanton destruction is absolutely and immediately required," it went on in some detail to show how forests in Europe were managed by trained foresters: "In France and Germany, there are natural forests which are preserved and properly cared for, affording supplies of valuable timber for house and ship building. Should an Adirondack Park be created, careful consideration should be given to the utilization of the forest."[15] The first major conservation document relative to the Adirondacks, this 1873 report reflected the growing faith in scientific forestry as well as the refusal to commit public lands to wilderness.

The 1883 law that withdrew all state lands from public sale and the 1885 Forest Preserve Law represented efforts by the legislature to remove irresponsible, cut-and-run loggers from the Adirondacks and replace them with state-supervised silviculturists. Although the Forest Preserve Law spoke of protecting "wild forest lands," it did not intend that these lands be kept as wilderness as such. Indeed, the report of a senate committee created to investigate the proper use of state lands showed that the legislature was greatly concerned lest it be perceived as catering to proponents of a nonutilitarian approach. The committee insisted that it had no wish "to interfere with the great business interests of northern New York for the gratification of the aesthetic and sporting classes merely."[16]

The concept of scientific timber harvesting found continuing approval in the press. *Harper's Weekly* observed that silviculturists could extract just as much profit from a piece of timberland as the untrained lumberman could, but without threatening the watershed; *Forest and Stream* was eloquent about multiple-use management of the forest, maintaining that the axe was a fundamental tool of conservation; the *Times* foresaw a promising future for forestry in the Adirondacks. But some observers were troubled: although *Harper's Weekly* professed continuing faith in the concept of scientific forestry, it doubted the capacity of the state to manage its own lands and oversee the cutting of its timber competently. Neither that journal nor *Forest and Stream* was pleased, moreover, when one of the first appointments to the newly created Forestry Commission was Theodore Basselin, a Lewis County lumber baron. Basselin's appointment immediately raised the specter of collusion between the public commission and the lumber industry.[17] Exploitation of this possibility by the press was to play an important role in the further decline of the lumberman's image and of the concomitant perception that the state was unable either to work with or to control the lumber industry's appetite.

The inadequacies of the Forestry Commission and the continued irresponsibility of lumbermen were the focus of a series of articles in the *New York Times* in the fall of 1889. This eleven-part series dealt with all the apparently negative features of lumbering, from watershed destruction to the alleged trespass of some lumbermen on state land. The first article, appearing on the front page, announced the tone of the series in a strongly worded accusatory headline: "Despoiling the Forests—Shameful Work Going on in Adirondacks—Everything Being Ruined by the Rapacious Lumberman—State Employees Engaged in the Business." The article listed logging abuses and accused the Forestry Commission of collusion. It utterly condemned lumbermen as unscrupulous rapers of the landscape who were driven by an arrogant "commercial instinct."

The major point of this series was that the Forestry Commission was either unable to control the lumbermen or, worse, was actually conspiring with them to destroy the Adirondack landscape. Although the Forestry Commission maintained from the first year of its existence that it was vigorously prosecuting loggers caught trespassing on state land, the *Times* reporter described one incident after another of the theft of timber from the Forest Preserve. He named the transgressors as well as the state officials who failed to prosecute, and labeled the timber barons of the region "rapacious lumbermen," "pirates of the forest, lumber thieves and poachers." All of this led to the conclusion that the public domain in the Adirondacks was suffering under "useless forestry laws" and that "radical reforms [were] urgently needed."[18]

But neither the *Times* nor any other observer was yet willing to call for total preservation, including a ban on all cutting. The reforms that most people had in mind were simply to overhaul the Forestry Commission and to insist that the principles of scientific forestry be properly implemented. The *Times*, the *Tribune*, *Forest and Stream*, and *Garden and Forest* were consistent in stating that the villain in the Adirondacks was the uninformed lumberman; the answer to the problem was to hand the forest over to experts. Thus the response to the issue of lumbering in the Adirondacks reflected the prototypical progressive approach. The conflict here, like other conservation battles of the day, as Samuel Hays has shown, was not between the proponents of ruthless exploitation and the advocates of wilderness but between different brands of exploiters.[19] The series in the *Times* attacked the lumbermen on aesthetic grounds, but the aesthetic argument alone could never have led to preservation in the Adirondacks. Rather, it became just one more weapon in the arsenal of the utilitarian protectors of the watershed.

While the Forestry Commission remained under fire and while lumbering continued to be described as a destructive assault on the landscape, most observers resisted total preservation as wasteful. "Nothing," wrote a correspondent to *Garden and Forest* in a letter calling for state ownership and management of Adirondack lands, "could be more absurd than the notion that trees should never be utilized or removed." *Garden and Forest* repeated the position of the professional forester when it editorialized, "Of course we appreciate the truth that there should be steady income from a permanent forest; that such utilization of its products will not depreciate the value of the forest as a reservation; that, indeed, the forest will be safer for yielding an income."[20]

▲▲▲▲▲▲▲

Since the state-owned Forest Preserve constituted but a small part of the total area of the Adirondacks, the legislature began to take a new look at the proposition that the state should acquire title to a large contiguous park in order to protect watershed and—secondarily—to serve the needs of recreation. The legislature instructed the Forestry Commission to investigate the situation and, after receiving its report, voted in 1892 to establish the Adirondack Park. The park was defined by a line drawn around some 2,800,000 acres, of which the state owned just over 550,000 (some of the state-owned Forest Preserve was outside the proposed boundary). The border was drawn in blue on the official state map, and ever since then the boundary of the Adirondack Park has been known as the "Blue Line." It was intended that the state would gradually acquire, through either default of unpaid taxes or condemnation, all of the private land within the park; the legislation creating the Adirondack Park however, foresaw the continued existence of lumbering operations on state land.[21]

When the Forestry Commission discussed the establishment of the park, it maintained that foresters and those who wanted the acquisition of public lands for recreation agreed that "acquiring possession of the Adirondack wilderness for a public domain" was essential to the welfare of the state. It discussed the virtues of multiple use and affirmed that the utilization of the park

> as a pleasure or sanitary resort need not interfere with its management for forestry purposes. The friends of the forestry movement, therefore, view with pleasure the agitation in favor of the Adirondack Park, and welcome the prompters of that enterprise as needed allies in the work of acquiring the necessary land.[22]

Thus, while considerations of watershed and timber supply dominated conservation activity, there was a growing movement to include recreation within the sanctioned functions of the state domain in the Adirondacks. The 1873 Park Commission report had noted that a welcome side benefit of protecting watershed would be protection of lands for recreation. *Forest and Stream* and *Garden and Forest* both made the same point, the former emphasizing the middle-class origins of this position:

> The high pressure at which business generally is now carried on demands recreation and recuperation for our business men. Only those who have visited the Adirondacks for a few weeks' vacation can realize or appreciate the renewed life and increased vigor which its high pure air so generally bestows upon its frequenters.[23]

The legislation of 1892 recognized the need to acquire title to a contiguous public domain in the Adirondacks, and the governing management policy was to be multiple use, not preservation of wilderness. On state land inside the park and in the Forest Preserve counties outside the park, and on state land yet to be acquired, New York was committed to a policy of scientific forestry.[24] Nearly all conservation interests were united in their still-surviving faith in the eventual ability of the state to manage such lands competently. For the time being, the idea of an Adirondack Park in which both recreational and utilitarian interests were accommodated seemed to be the perfect solution to the problems of the region.

Any criticism of timber harvest on state lands was usually aimed at specific features; the concept itself enjoyed general approval. For example, the Adirondack Park Association, a conservation lobby supporting the establishment of the park, indicated its agreement and supported a bill passed in 1893 that formally expressed the intentions of the state to realize revenues from timber harvest in the park. The *New York Times* also backed the principle of cutting on state lands but was wary of both the scruples and competence of the responsible officials. *Garden and Forest* maintained the same position as that of the *Times*; it was suspicious of specific provisions of the 1893 cutting law, but it continued to uphold the principle of scientific forestry, pointing out yet again the virtues of proper management and its capacity to "improve" a forest.[25]

By the beginning of 1894, then, there was some controversy about the manner in which state lands were to be managed but little objection to timber harvesting. Within a year, however, a radical change occurred. During the New York State Constitutional Convention of 1894, which dealt with a variety of matters that had arisen since the 1867 convention, the question of forest preservation was introduced. Late in the session, David McClure, a New York City lawyer and convention delegate, proposed that the constitution include an article affecting not only the lands in the Forest Preserve but also the timber. As finally approved, Article VII, Section 7 read:

> The lands of the State, now owned or hereafter acquired, constituting the forest preserve, as now fixed by law, shall be forever kept as wild forest lands. They shall not be leased, sold, or exchanged, *nor shall the timber thereon be sold, removed or destroyed.*[26]

With the adoption of this provision, the state reversed its policy concerning the harvest of timber on state lands. The language abandoned faith in the lumberman and reflected apocalyptic fears concerning man's capacity to alter the landscape and threaten his own well being.

McClure was persuaded to introduce the amendment by the New York Board of Trade and Transportation. Though it had had serious reservations about the 1893 law and objected to the size of the trees that the law permitted to be cut, the board had not opposed the principle of cutting. But it soon decided that the old fears about the threat to the Adirondack watershed and thus to important commercial waterways were still justified. For the time being, the only reliable resolution of the issue of logging in the Adirondacks was to prohibit it entirely, at least on state lands (and at this time it was expected that the state would eventually acquire title to a large contiguous domain). Acting through McClure, it therefore introduced the amendment.[27]

Much of the anti-lumbering sentiment continued to derive from distrust of the Forestry Commission. In the spring of 1894, State Engineer and Surveyor Campbell W. Adams reported to the State Land Office that serious damage would result if lumbermen were allowed to continue harvesting timber under the current law.

He believed that the regulations by which the Forestry Commission proposed to supervise cutting on state land were entirely unsatisfactory, giving the contracting lumber interests a virtual free hand. The *Times* declared that the answer to this problem was for the state not to contract the logging to private lumbermen but to have its trees cut "by its own agents and under its own direction." Bernhard Fernow, one of the leading advocates of scientific forestry in America, agreed, insisting that the only way to stop the destruction of the forests and watershed of the Adirondacks was public ownership and management.[28] One of the ironies of Article VII, Section 7 is that its inclusion largely resulted from the charges of incompetence leveled at the Forestry Commission, and one of the most influential sources of such criticism was the community of professional foresters—men like Fernow and the editors and correspondents of *Garden and Forest*. Unknowingly, by dwelling on the inadequacies of the Forestry Commission, foresters were helping remove themselves from the public forests of New York.

Attacks on the Forestry Commission were not the only encouragement for altogether prohibiting lumbering on state land. In 1893 and 1894, New York and New England suffered from dry weather and low water levels, and forest fires were frighteningly common.[29] Marsh's vision of apocalyptic changes in climate and landscape caused by interference in the environment—especially by profligate tree cutting—seemed real and imminent. Irreversible drought and disaster appeared to be at hand, and the only course was to take the most drastic action.

After McClure introduced the amendment to the convention, debate was delayed for several weeks, during which time the American Forestry Association condemned the amendment as a waste of resources. But when debate opened, on September 7, 1894, McClure invoked watershed protection as the primary reason for taking such drastic measures. Pursuing this utilitarian line, he further argued that since the Adirondacks was worthless for agriculture, there was no harm in setting the region aside to protect the source of water for the Hudson and other commercial arteries. Almost as an afterthought, he paid passing notice to the benefits of a state preserve as a "great resort for people of this State"; clearly McClure's chief concern was watershed.[30]

In the debate that followed, no one expressed serious opposition to the concept of McClure's proposal, and one delegate gave dramatic evidence of the need for it when he reported that only a few days earlier he had walked across the Hudson at Fort Edward without getting his feet wet. This same man articulated perfectly the spirit of the backers of this provision:

> Now if you wish to preserve the waters of this State, if you wish to preserve the waters of the Hudson River, and if there are any friends of the canal system of this State in this Convention, if they wish to preserve the canals, it seems to me they must vote for this amendment, which may eternally preserve the Adirondacks.[31]

As statements like this demonstrate, without the watershed argument there would never have been protection for wilderness in the Adirondacks, even though protecting wilderness as such was obviously not what the speaker had in mind.

Nor did most observers think of the McClure amendment as permanent protection; it was generally felt to be necessary simply because the state and its Forestry Commission were for the present unable to manage state lands properly. As one delegate at the convention pointed out, as soon as the state found itself in need of timber, the prohibition clause could be dropped from subsequent constitutions. This sentiment was endorsed by both the *Times* and the *Tribune*, and the belief that the amendment could be changed when the need arose undoubtedly persuaded many delegates to support it. Defenders of forestry, however, howled with disapproval and, in the days before the statewide vote, sternly expressed their dismay. As *Garden and Forest* put it, "The absolute prohibition of cutting of any wood from the State preserve means actual and reprehensible waste."[32]

Among those professional foresters upset by the implications of the forever wild clause was Gifford Pinchot, who was then becoming one of the foremost advocates of forest management. Pinchot had a special fondness for the Adirondacks, having first visited the region in the summer of 1879 as a boy of thirteen. His father gave him his first fishing rod; he enjoyed camping in the wilderness; and his concern for American forests, according to one biographer, may be said to have originated at that time. But his concern was always utilitarian: Pinchot condemned any plan for a forest that emphasized recreation at the expense of wise exploitation of natural resources. In 1892, when he was invited to survey a large private tract in the western Adirondacks and prepare a management proposal, Pinchot studied the timber and submitted what he hoped would be a model plan for all Adirondack landowners, including the state. Its essential ingredient was a program of sustained yield, which, its author maintained, would both improve the forest and enrich its owner.³³

It is not surprising, therefore, that Pinchot was bitterly opposed to Article VII, Section 7. Early in 1894, speaking at a meeting called in Albany to address the subject of forestry in the Adirondacks, he had argued for a comprehensive management plan for all state lands. And after it was clear that the McClure amendment would pass the convention and go to the people, Pinchot lobbied against it. The prohibition on timber harvest struck him as the antithesis of progressive and enlightened use of natural resources; it was an example of the "sentimental horror" that arose when people with good intentions but a dearth of knowledge controlled public policy. To Pinchot, the McClure amendment was simply irrational: it was like "the case of a farmer who should refuse to cultivate his farm on the ground that he distrusted his own fitness and integrity."³⁴

But when, on the same day, the *Times* and the *Tribune* reported an investigation of collusion between state officials and unscrupulous lumbermen to rob the state of title to public lands, there were few left to argue for forest management in the Forest Preserve. Most people probably agreed with the middle-of-the-road position adopted by *Forest and Stream*: Article VII, Section 7 was "not an ideal disposition of the public forestry question; but it is perhaps the wisest one under existing circumstances." Like most observers of Adirondack issues, the magazine's editors hoped that the Forest Preserve could eventually be managed according to the principles of scientific forestry but feared that the time when the state could be trusted to apply those principles efficiently and honestly lay somewhere in the future.³⁵

Although the people of New York adopted the new constitution, including the Board of Trade and Transportation's Forest Preserve amendment, it is impossible to say how much attention the voters paid to Article VII, Section 7, and how much to the many other issues before them. One cannot interpret the popular vote as a statement one way or the other on matters of forestry or wilderness. The important thing was that the provision's presence in the new constitution represented a rejection (although regarded at the time as temporary) of scientific and managerial skills. It testified to the failure of professional foresters to persuade the representatives of the public—the delegates to the Constitutional Convention—that new techniques in forestry could protect the watershed of the Adirondacks. The efforts of professional foresters to alert the public to the need for the implementation of their nascent science were themselves largely responsible for the fashion in which the public turned against timber harvest altogether.

The introduction and approval of this amendment involved no little irony. The idea of total prohibition of timber cutting flew in the face of the spirit of the age, which insisted on efficient use of natural resources; more specifically, it ran counter to the wishes of virtually everyone expressing interest in the future of the Adirondack forests. That the Board of Trade and Transportation managed to get it approved indicates the persuasiveness of their argument that the Hudson watershed was threatened with cataclysm and that the utilitarian needs of the state's waterways were more important than the timber harvest in the Adirondacks.

If Samuel Hays is correct in arguing that the story of conservation in the progressive era involved chiefly the efforts of "experts" to supervise the exploitation of the nation's natural resources, then the imposition of such tight strictures on the New York State Forest Preserve provides an interesting exception to his generalization, for the approval of the McClure amendment represents the inability of the community of professional foresters to gain control of New York's publicly owned timber resources. Nor was it a case of one school of experts winning out over another; the arguments of geologists and hydrologists about the supposed deterioration of the Adirondack watershed are noticeably absent from the debates leading up to the popular vote. The perception of the threat to New York rivers and canals was largely produced by articles in popular newspapers and journals. While aesthetic or recreational issues were secondary, the popular press promulgated a picture of Adirondack logging and watershed problems as one in which the interests of the "people" were opposed by the commercial greed of private enterprise and the incompetence or corruption of public officials. The forests and waters of the Adirondacks emerged in the public mind as a landscape in which the people of New York had common concerns, and the adoption of Article VII, Section 7 represented the reluctance of the people to turn that landscape over to the lumber barons, the state bureaucracy, or the scientific foresters.

# VI
# Wilderness and the Conservation Bureaucracy, 1895–1940

▲▲▲▲▲▲▲

In the same year that Article VII, Section 7 went into effect, prohibiting the state from cutting the timber on its Forest Preserve, a new state bureaucracy was created to supervise the public domain in the Adirondacks. This was the Fisheries, Game and Forests Commission, charged with guarding the Forest Preserve, enforcing fish and game laws, and overseeing and monitering logging operations on private land.[1] Over the years this agency has undergone several name changes and its duties have been expanded, but the most significant development has been a profound shift in philosophy relative to the proper use of the Forest Preserve.

When the Fisheries, Game and Forests Commission began its work, its attitude to the forever-wild provision was one of nearly unqualified hostility. The men who worked for this agency adhered to the conservation ideas of Gifford Pinchot, who saw Article VII, Section 7 as wasteful and unnecessarily rigid. The early reports of this commission and its immediate successors contain repeated calls for constitutional amendments to relax the ban on lumbering in the Forest Preserve. These early agencies were also enthusiastic about harnessing Adirondack rivers to generate power, which would have required dams and reservoirs and the flooding of parts of the Forest Preserve.

There is a substantial secondary literature on the judicial and political history of the Forest Preserve in the twentieth century.

Frank Graham, Jr., Norman VanValkenburgh, and Roger Thompson have made significant contributions to our understanding of how policies were established, how the courts have interpreted the state constitution, and how the New York legislature has dealt with Adirondack issues. My aim here is not to write another political or judicial history of the Adirondacks; rather, I want to look at changing attitudes toward the idea of wilderness itself, for such a change did occur. Within the state agencies charged with overseeing the Adirondacks, it was nothing short of astounding. From a position of hostility or at best indifference to wilderness per se at the end of the nineteenth century, the official view evolved to the conviction that the chief value of the Forest Preserve lay in its recreational, aesthetic, and ecological value.[2]

▲▲▲▲▲▲▲

·Throughout the early years of the state agencies administering the Forest Preserve, we find predictable concerns—the problem of forest fires, the need for further acquisitions, the difficulty of enforcing the deer laws (which had existed in one form or another since colonial times) without enough game wardens, the ongoing litigation to have squatters evicted from state lands, and the continuing battle to prevent loggers from trespassing on state land and cutting timber. But a year seldom passed without an attack on the restrictions of Article VII, Section 7. Usually, the thrust of the argument was that the state was missing out on an opportunity to improve the forest and realize revenue from its holdings.[3]

In the report for 1897, Superintendent of State Forests William F. Fox began a series of "Short Talks on Forestry and Kindred Subjects," the first of which was "Why Our Forests Should Be Preserved and Protected." Fox is a paradigmatic figure; his views typify those of the state conservation bureaucracy at the end of the nineteenth century and the beginning of the twentieth. Born in Ballston Spa, New York, in 1840 (he was thus seven years older than Colvin), he graduated from Union College with a degree in engineering in 1860. After military service during the Civil War, he worked in his family's lumber business and acquired considerable knowledge in the developing science of forestry; he also studied in Germany, where the most advanced work in silviculture was being done. Between 1875 and 1882 he managed a private forest in Pennsylvania. By 1885 he was working for New York State as a forester and was employed by the State thereafter until his death in 1909. His entire public career was devoted to his concern for the proper care of forests in New York. The reports he submitted to the legislature and his superiors in various state agencies demonstrate his command of what was then known about the efficient, scientific administration of large forests.[4]

In 1895, when the Fisheries, Game and Forests Commission was established, Fox was named the first Superintendent of Forests. During his tenure in this and similar posts, Fox published many papers on forestry issues, including *The Adirondack Black Spruce* and *A History of the Lumber Industry in New York*. He was an early member of both the American Forestry Association and the Society of American Foresters. Although his views on the proper function of state-owned forests did not include the dedication of public land to wilderness, the extent and generally good condition of the Forest Preserve at the time of his death were largely due to his care. He oversaw the implementation of effective fire control and worked assiduously to expand and consolidate the Forest Preserve. A utilitarian to the tips of his toes, he pursued these tasks with the assumption that he was establishing a healthy forest that the state would eventually harvest. But when the state agencies finally abandoned the notion of timber harvest on state land, the existence of a sound, extensive forest testified to Fox's great accomplishments.[5]

Fox began his series of essays with a history of the abuses of nonscientific forestry—the waste of the resource, the frequency of fires, the failure to replant, and a host of other consequences of cut-and-run logging. He then moved to the now familiar watershed argument for conservation, citing instances where feeders to the Erie Canal had dried up because of poorly managed lumbering on their headwaters. In addition to watershed control, Fox continued, forests exercise many other beneficial functions; they moderate the weather, house fish and game, and provide relief for consumptives. His first essay ended with a call for reforesting bared lands throughout New York State. Fox's quarrel, up to this point, was only with the cut-and-run loggers who had ravaged so much of the Adirondacks and other parts of the state.[6]

His second essay promoted the need for humans to assist nature in managing forests; it thus began Fox's attack on forever wild. In his first sentence he declared, "Forestry is that business or industry which consists in the maintenance of forests, and the gathering of their products. It is the most successful when it yields the largest possible income annually and perpetually." There were, he said, two reasons for keeping forests on the earth. The first was to insure a present and future supply of wood; the second to protect those features of the earth's geography upon which depend the health and prosperity of mankind. To Fox, forestry meant forest preservation, but to him this often confusing term involved not a hands-off approach to individual trees but simply the continuing existence of the forest itself; his notion of preservation included cutting certain trees and making a profit from them.[7] In modern parlance, this would be conservation, not preservation.

In Fox's view, nature left alone is an inefficient producer of trees:

> Nature will supply the wants of man much better when assisted or placed under intelligent control. . . . Unfortunately, Nature takes little heed of our ideas or wants in raising her forests. She furnishes in profusion the species for which we have little need, and yields only a scanty supply of the kinds we want most.

The function of the forester, then, is

> to control and regulate the forces of Nature, that in a growing forest, or in the conversion of one already grown, the product shall conform closely to our needs and demands; and, that worthless and undesirable species shall be gradually removed to make room for the kind people want.

Finally, making as explicit as possible his utilitarian point, Fox insisted that "the wild or natural forest is as different from the cultivated one in valuable species and amount of production as the waste lands of the farmer is [sic] from his wheat fields."[8]

Obviously, the intent of Fox's essays was to convince the legislature, to whom the report in which they appeared was directed, that the Forest Preserve contained valuable timber and that the state was failing to take advantage of an opportunity to make money. As Fox insisted, "When a forest tree has ceased growing it should be converted into money, and its timber used to supply some of the many purposes for which wood is needed." He concluded his essay with the hope that "when our State is ready to withdraw the present constitutional restrictions relating to timber cutting and other forest revenues . . . our great woodland areas will be managed under the best approved forestry system." To a trained forester like Fox—as to his apparent inspiration, Gifford

Fig. 1 Fig. 2

Fig. 3 Fig. 4

**Fig. 1:** Joel T. Headley. A popular historian, Headley wrote *The Adirondack; Or, Life in the Woods* (1849), one of the earliest romantic and travel and sporting narratives.

**Fig. 2:** Verplanck Colvin. Colvin was an Adirondack explorer, surveyor, and conservationist of the late nineteenth century.

**Fig. 3:** Ebenezer Emmons. A geologist, Emmons proposed the name "Adirondacks" for the wilderness he explored in the 1830s.

**Fig. 4:** The Reverend W. H. H. Murray, 1871. Author of *Adventures in the Wilderness; Or, Camp-Life in the Adirondacks* (published in 1869), Murray popularized wilderness camping.

Fig. 5

Fig. 6

**Fig. 5:** "A Good Time Coming," 1862, painting by Arthur Fitzwilliam Tait. Symbols of civilization, such as champagne and neckties, made the gentleman's stay in the wilderness seem less distant from his life in the city.

**Fig. 6:** "In the Adirondacks," 1889. Although sportmen usually wanted the wilderness protected only for their own special interests, their concern about recreation and hunting contributed to the conservationist sentiment that developed at the end of the century. Photograph by Seneca Ray Stoddard.

Fig. 7

Fig. 8

**Fig. 7:** "Blue Mountain Lake House, Adirondacks," 1889. This popular hostel, which burned in 1904, and others catering to genteel tourists made Blue Mountain Lake one of the nation's most popular resorts between 1880 and the turn of the century.

**Fig. 8:** "William West Durant. Camp Pine Knot," no date. Durant designed many camps in the Raquette Lake region. Intended for Gilded Age millionaires who wanted wilderness without the discomforts of camping out, cabins such as this one combined rustic exteriors with lavishly appointed interior spaces. Photograph by Seneca Ray Stoddard.

Fig. 9

Fig. 10

**Fig. 9:** "Lumbering in the Adirondacks: The Choppers," 1888. By the 1880s concern about the abuses of Adirondack loggers persuaded many New Yorkers that the forests of the region had to be protected by the state. Photograph by Seneca Ray Stoddard.

**Fig. 10:** "Upper Ausable Lake from Boreas Bay," 1887. The photographer of these mountains and lakes in the high peaks drew on the traditional aesthetic of the romantic sublime, but also, influenced by luminist painters, emphasized light and horizontal line. Photograph by Seneca Ray Stoddard.

Fig. 11

Fig. 12

**Fig. 11:** "High Art, Blue Mountain," 1879. Seneca Ray Stoddard, shown here with his portable darkroom, was a prolific photographer and publisher of guidebooks between 1873 and 1910.

**Fig. 12:** "Horicon Sketching Club," 1882. For most women in the nineteenth century, experience of wilderness was limited to activities demanding little exercise. Photograph by Seneca Ray Stoddard.

Fig. 13

**Fig. 13:** "A Feeder of the Hudson—As It Was," engraving by Julian Rix, *Harper's Weekly*, January 24, 1885. This engraving and its companion provided a powerful aesthetic argument against the depredations of lumberjacks on the Adirondack landscape.

Fig. 14

**Fig. 14:** "A Feeder of the Hudson—As It Is," engraving by Julian Rix, *Harper's Weekly*, January 24, 1885.

Fig. 15

**Fig. 15:** "Avalanche Lake," 1888. Nature's grandeur in contrast to human insignificance was a traditional theme in romantic art and literature, and persisted throughout the nineteenth century. Photograph by Seneca Ray Stoddard.

Pinchot—the language of Article VII, Section 7 involved a colossal human error. He recognized it as a response to the depredations of nonscientific loggers, but it prevented him, a professional in an age when the professional expert was coming to exercise considerable influence in nearly every domain of American affairs (especially the management of publicly owned natural resources), from plying his chosen trade.[9]

The mind of William Fox was incapable of accepting Article VII, Section 7 as anything other than temporary. Fox believed that the constitutional provision was no more than an emergency ad hoc response to a pressing need for immediate action. He subscribed to the George Perkins Marsh position that abuse of nature could result in catastrophe, but he also represented the growing class of American technocrats, to whom wilderness was an affront. To John Todd, the thick forests on the hills around Long Lake in the 1840s had suggested an insult to God, evidence of a failure to follow the divine admonition to subdue nature and have dominion over it.[10] Fox's abhorrence for forever wild was a late-nineteenth-century translation of Todd's credo into the secular terms of profit and utility.

In the report of the Fisheries, Game and Forests Commission for 1898, another distinguished forester, Bernhard Fernow, added his opposition to forever wild. Fernow, one of the first European-trained foresters to work extensively in the United States, had just been appointed director of the New York State College of Forestry at Cornell University. Convinced that if professional foresters were to contribute to the New York economy, they must be allowed to work in the Forest Preserve, Fernow pointed out that the forever-wild provision "was intended, not to establish a policy of non-use, and to exclude forever the application of such forestry work as requires the use of the ax, but rather to delay it until conditions should be more favorable for the employment of technical forestry management." To Fernow the very establishment of his new college was evidence of the state's intent to remove the restrictions of Article VII, Section 7.[11]

Fernow acknowledged that not everyone saw the Forest Preserve in terms of its capacity to fill the state's treasury; he listed the watershed argument and even recreation as other possible reasons for protecting the Adirondacks. His vision of the future for the region was one of multiple use: scientific forestry and professional management would protect the watershed essential to commercial arteries and also permit the use of the woods by campers, sportsmen, and seekers of natural scenery. "Forest preservation," he said, was his goal; to him, as to Fox, the term meant maintaining the forest within established boundaries and improving its productivity by selective cutting:

> Forest preservation is attained in the same way as the preservation of mankind, by reproduction, by removing the old and giving a chance to the young crop. This involves the cutting of trees, to be sure; but if this is done with regard to securing a new growth of better composition, it is the rational method of forest preservation.[12]

The state's conservation agencies (in 1900 the Fisheries, Game and Forests Commission was reorganized into the Forest, Fish and Game Commission, which in 1911 became the Conservation Commission) continued their attacks on Article VII, Section 7 with routine frequency until World War I. In 1900 the Forest, Fish and Game Commission enlisted the additional persuasive powers of the United States government. With its recommendation that the constitution be amended to "provide for the practice of conservative forestry on State lands," the commission introduced a lengthy report prepared by two professional foresters working for the recently established Division of Forestry of the U.S. Department of Agriculture. "A Working Forest Plan for Township 40" showed how a program of planned management of the state-owned forests in the township that included Raquette Lake could protect both the watershed and the aesthetic appeal of the region, while generating a constant flow of revenue. The report was accompanied by a letter from Gifford Pinchot, chief of the U.S. Division of Forestry. Pinchot, who had opposed the institution of the forever-wild provision from the outset, hoped that the invitation from the New York commissioners to prepare this working plan indicated that New York would soon ease the restrictions of Article VII, Section 7.[13]

The following year a similar survey was made of three further Adirondack townships, all in Hamilton County. In urging the state to proceed with timber harvest on the contiguous four townships surveyed so far, William Fox asserted that the immediately realizable revenue was a half-million dollars. He maintained that the merchantable timber constituted only 8 percent of the standing trees and that to harvest it posed no threat to the watershed or the remaining forest. Extrapolating from the figures provided by the federal foresters, he averred that in spruce alone the Adirondack Forest Preserve held over $2,700,000 worth of timber, which, "whenever the law will permit . . . can be sold for that amount and removed without any injury to existing forest conditions."[14]

In 1914 the Conservation Commission was again lamenting the restrictiveness of the constitution. The framers of Article VII, Section 7, the commissioners wrote, were "wise men in their day and generation, prudent and foreseeing. . . . The time has come, however, when modification of this drastic policy may safely be considered." Arguing that the state could realize a million dollars a year, the commissioners repeated their position that "selective cutting and removal of ripe timber is beneficial to the forest."[15]

Even as these hopes for timber harvest on the Forest Preserve persisted, a new utilitarian threat emerged: the prospect of damming Adirondack rivers for water storage and the generation of electric power. In 1913 the Conservation Commission advocated a massive involvement of the state in the production of hydroelectric power. Much of the opposition to this plan stemmed from fears that it was a step toward socialism, but the important implication for the Adirondacks was that it required an amendment to the constitution permitting flooding of timbered lands in the Forest Preserve. On this issue the Pinchot-oriented conservationists in the state bureaucracy eventually had at least part of their way; the constitution was indeed amended to provide for limited flooding. The significant feature of this story is that the Conservation Commission, the agency charged with protecting the Forest Preserve and administering the laws concerning it, consistently held a position inimical to the preservation of wilderness. The complaints of the commissioners about the annoying interference of Article VII, Section 7 with the efficient management of the state's water resources were very similar to their protests about unnecessary prohibitions on cutting timber.[16]

The agency rationale for building dams in the Forest Preserve contained an interesting variation of the old watershed argument. The same damage to the headwaters of important rivers that had necessitated the establishment and protection of the Forest Preserve, according to this rationale, also demanded that the flow of these rivers be controlled by dams and reservoirs: "The removal of the forests along the headwaters of these streams has resulted in a rapid run-off of water during the spring and autumn seasons." The same document recommended construction of a dam on the Raquette River at the Oxbow just above Tupper Lake; such a dam would have flooded the Raquette, one of the best canoeing rivers in the Adirondacks, all the way to the foot of Raquette Falls. The justification given for this dam was that it was needed to regulate flow, not to generate power. The watershed argument, without which there would never have been a Forest Preserve or state-protected wilderness in the Adirondacks, was thus called upon to justify the elimination of much of the wilderness that had been inadvertently saved.[17]

In 1914 the Conservation Commission released an elaborate plan for regulating the Saranac River by means of several dams and reservoirs. The project was, according to the commissioners, "highly desirable for summer resort, health and pleasure purposes, as well as for power." Accompanying the descriptions and maps outlining the proposal was a series of black-and-white photographs of the Saranac River, prominently displaying the swamps and flooded lands that typically appear in low spots along Adirondack rivers. A further advantage of the dams, suggested the pictures and their captions, would be the elimination of such unsightly marshes.[18] An aesthetic argument was thus added to the utilitarian in advocating these water projects, and it shows how the aesthetic response to nature, at least in the minds of the Conservation Commission, continued to adhere to conventional standards. The swamp, the portion of the landscape that failed to be pretty or scenic, was still seen as expendable, something to be changed in order to make better use of the land. The reluctance to accept the swamp as an integral part of the landscape derived from a conventional set of aesthetics, which in turn was at least partially informed by the utilitarian conviction that whatever was not useful could not be aesthetically appealing.

▲▲▲▲▲▲▲

But the utilitarian position was also essential to a gradual shift in the stance of the Conservation Commission. Even in the earliest years of the state's conservation bureaucracy, there was some admission—slim at first—that certain recreational functions might be suitable, in addition to forest management and the hoped-for harvest of mature trees on the Forest Preserve. The chief recreational pursuits that the bureaucracy saw fit to promote were field sports—hunting and fishing. Popular activities since the time of the first European contact with the region, these were essential parts of the popular image of the Adirondacks. They also appealed to the elite class that still dominated New York politics. The Fisheries, Game and Forests Commission, whose very name indicates the importance of field sports, advocated changes in the deer laws that would, it declared, guarantee a permanent deer herd, and it also investigated a number of ways to improve the fishing in the Adirondacks. It saw no reason, of course, why these activities should suffer once logging returned to the Forest Preserve. Moreover, the relative number of printed pages devoted to forest management and field sports makes it clear that the early conservation agencies saw forest management as their chief function.[19]

That the bureaucracy was willing to entertain other points of view, however, is suggested by its agreeing to print an essay by A. Judd Northrup, a gentleman field-sports writer whose 1880 book, *Camps and Tramps in the Adirondacks*, described his fishing adventures in the region. In 1903 his "Fishes and Fishing in the Adirondacks: From the Sportsman's Point of View" appeared in the annual report of the Forest, Fish and Game Commission. A large portion of this essay was devoted to descriptions of native and imported fish and advice to would-be anglers on how to catch them, but Northrup also expressed his own opinions on what the Forest Preserve was good for. These diverged, but not radically, from those of the commission.[20]

Northrup outlined the history of sport fishing in the Adirondacks and nostalgically recalled the golden age before Murray with its putatively fabulous abundance of trout. He then rehearsed the familiar lament about the decline of fishing and the appearance in the woods of hunters and anglers not properly versed in the gentlemanly arts of killing deer and catching trout. The answer to these problems, suggested Northrup, was for the state to add all remaining Adirondack wild lands to the Adirondack Park and care for its lands as if being a park were their most important function: "This wilderness ought to belong to the people of the State"; it ought to be protected as New York's "great vacation park, and 'play ground' of grown up men and women." Then because he recognized the political difficulty of having the state reserve a huge region like the Adirondacks for the pleasures of a relatively small portion of the population, Northrup suggested lumbering as a source of revenue to support the park; otherwise, it would seem as if downstate taxpayers were subsidizing the fishing trips of wealthy businessmen. In this way Northrup arrived at an argument for amending the constitution:

> The revenue that might be derived from utilizing the surplus timber would go far toward relieving the state treasury of much of the burden of administering the State's supervision of the Adirondack Park, and enabling the State eventually to acquire substantially all the lands within the borders of the Preserve.[21]

In his account of what made a fishing trip into the Adirondacks meaningful, Northrup invoked most of the tenets of the romantic credo: he spoke of hidden "enchantment," the "sublime secret of life," and scenery "of such imposing majesty as to move you, if you have the reverent soul, to lift your eyes to the heavens over you and feel in your heart of hearts a new reverence and worship of the power of which this majestic grandeur is an expression." (Although the precise vocabulary of Burke has been a bit watered down, the inclination to see grand scenery as evidence of the omnipotence of God persists.) Still, like most participants in the patrician romantic tradition, of which he was one of the last major exponents, he did not wish to see the Forest Preserve dedicated to wilderness alone. He was enough of a utilitarian to approve of continued lumbering in the Adirondacks—on both public and private land. No less than Street or Headley, Northrup was uncomfortable with the notion of preserving wilderness per se.[22]

---

▲▲▲▲▲▲▲

---

Meanwhile, the recreational potential of the Forest Preserve was beginning to achieve genuine currency within the conservation bureaucracy. In 1908, Forest, Fish and Game Commissioner James S. Whipple, besides presenting the familiar recommendation that Article VII, Section 7 be changed to permit timber harvest, emphasized the need for the state to publicize the existence of the Adirondacks. In Whipple's view, the forever-wild clause itself was responsible for keeping people out of the Adirondacks and should be changed so that more roads could be built to and through the Forest Preserve. Then "more of our people may visit the Adirondack and Catskill regions and have a chance to see and enjoy their great beauty." The idea that improved transportation arteries will bring more tourists to the Adirondacks is still current; it is the final manifestation of the antebellum conviction of Ebenezer Emmons and others that the absence of roads was responsible for keeping the region out of the mainstream of American life. The idea that wilderness protection is antagonistic to legitimate recreation also persists. One of the most often heard complaints, both inside and outside the state's conservation agencies, about forever wild is that it locks up land away from hunters, anglers, and others in search of recreation but unable or unwilling to endure wilderness travel.[23]

The introduction of better transportation arteries was part of Whipple's grand vision of multiple use for both the Adirondacks and the Catskills. Whipple foresaw the state administering a "forest preserve in its truest sense." To him, this meant providing recreational facilities and opportunities for "the rich, the well-to-do and the poor," utilizing "water horsepower for legitimate purposes," leasing small lots to private individuals, and encouraging the state or its agents to harvest mature timber. All of this, of course, required a constitutional amendment, and Whipple both admonished the legislature to begin the process and offered his own version of such an amendment.[24]

In spelling out his views, Whipple explicitly showed what he thought of wilderness as such. Discussing the precise language of Article VII, Section 7, he correctly noted that the word "wild" is ambiguous; perhaps the original wishes of the authors of the forever-wild clause could be misinterpreted.

> To the forester, it [the word "wild"] conveys an idea that is pleasing or the reverse, according to the association in which it is used. Wilderness in a sense that a country is too distant, rough or inclement for civilized men to occupy permanently is an idea that has standing, that appeals to all active and sturdy men. But wilderness that is merely sentimental, the withdrawal of great areas of land from the common and natural uses to maintain a wilderness that is merely romantic is an idea which, to professional foresters, makes no appeal.

These ideas about wilderness are interesting. They suggest a mixture of the utilitarian outlook and the masculine sense of adventure associated with Whipple's contemporary and fellow New Yorker, Theodore Roosevelt. Wilderness should exist, but only in places suited for absolutely nothing else; there the outdoor-oriented American male may pursue his rites of manhood. But wilderness should not be allowed to persist where improvements seem beneficial or there is money to be made. When Roosevelt himself was faced with the choice between saving wilderness for "merely sentimental" reasons or eliminating it in the name of progress and utility (as in the controversy over flooding the Hetch Hetchy Valley near Yosemite), he opted for utility.[25]

But Whipple's objection to the protection of wilderness in the Adirondacks for its own sake was really only a matter of degree. By acknowledging the value of wilderness somewhere, he granted, perhaps without intending to, the intrinsic value of wilderness itself. To his professional forester's mind, the utility of the timber in the Forest Preserve seemed more valuable to society, in whatever terms such value was to be measured, than the wilderness experience obtained in "a wilderness that is merely romantic." It was only a short step to someone else's conclusion that the wilderness experience available in the Adirondacks was sufficiently valuable to exclude nonwilderness functions. The very language of Whipple's objection to Article VII, Section 7 suggested that even within the state's conservation agencies the nonutilitarian potential of the Forest Preserve might soon be more fully acknowledged.

▲▲▲▲▲▲▲

Such an acknowledgment was not far off. The report of the Conservation Commission for 1919 contains a startling shift. After more than two decades of complaint about the wasteful rigidity of Article VII, Section 7, the conservation bureaucracy admitted that it had been remiss in failing to cultivate the recreational potential of the Forest Preserve:

> It is . . . surprising that in more than thirty years of continuous development of the Forest Preserve . . . not a single vacationist's trail was ever built or marked on State property at State expense, not an open camp or fireplace was constructed by the State, nor any vacation map or guide book published by the State, nor in fact much else done by the State itself to make this big vacation country more accessible, more usable, and better known to those whose property it is.

Because the Forest Preserve was so close to such a large portion of the country's population, the report went on to say, it constituted "the most important public vacation grounds in the United States."[26]

Accordingly, the commission declared itself dedicated to new duties in the Forest Preserve: "The work of improving and marking trails, the building of open camps and the construction of fireplaces throughout the Forest Preserve should now be undertaken on a scale commensurate with the great use that the people are making of this public property." A special appropriation of $5,000 with which to begin trail construction was requested. Ominously, the establishment of these trails would itself involve a violation of Article VII, Section 7: the commission planned, "by bending the trail to one side, or by a little lopping of branches or trees, to open vistas of entrancing beauty."[27] Thus the shift of emphasis from timber harvest to recreation did not eliminate the hostility either to forever wild or to the idea of wilderness as such. The efforts of the conservation bureaucracy to "improve" the Forest Preserve for recreation would become increasingly controversial in the next several decades. An impoundment dam, even if only a few feet high, or an interior ranger station violates a wilderness aesthetic nearly as much as does logging or a dam built to generate power.

That the scenic appeal of the Adirondacks was becoming more important to the bureaucracy was clear in a statement on lumbering in the high peaks. Accompanying this were several photographs, the first showing the summit of Mount Marcy from the top of Haystack—always one of the best views in the Adirondacks. A few pages later appeared two photographs of current lumbering operations on the high slopes of Marcy. Their shock value, as with the Rix engravings of logging depredations in the 1880s, was enormous: in striking contrast to the distance shot, they showed a scene of devastation, marked by piles of cordwood destined for a pulp mill and masses of brush. In the text, the commissioners declared one of their most pressing priorities to be the acquisition of the high slopes still in private hands. Once added to the Forest Preserve, these lands "should be forever maintained as protection areas . . . upon which no lumbering should ever be permitted."[28] The critical argument for thus setting part of the Forest Preserve forever off bounds to even the most scientific of lumbering continued to be watershed protection, but for the Conservation Commission to temper, even to this relatively minor extent, its hopes for timber management represented a crucial step toward accepting wilderness.

The future and use of the high peaks was particularly on the minds of the commission, partly because much of the Mount Marcy region had recently been added to the Forest Preserve, but also because of the obvious grandeur of that part of the Adirondacks. In a section on "Public Use," the report compared the recreational possibilities of the Adirondacks to those of the national parks. Illustrating the text were photographs of Mount Seward, Avalanche Lake, Indian Pass, Hanging Spear Falls on the Opalescent, and Lake Colden. The Forest Preserve, the report asserted,

> in size and beauty is comparable to any of the national parks. . . . One need not go to the west for rugged mountains to climb or deep passes to thread. Mt. Marcy . . . rises 5,344 feet above sea level, high enough to cleave the clouds on all but the most perfect days. . . . Immediately under the eastern foot of Marcy is Panther Gorge, of wild and rugged beauty. A little to the west, between Mt. Colden and Mt. McIntyre, is the deep cleft of Avalanche Pass, with the precipitous sides of the mountains rising on either hand, so that the only passage is over the water of Avalanche Lake itself. Avalanche Lake is the highest lake of any size in New York State, and its deep mountain setting is one of the most secluded and inspiring pictures of the wilderness.[29]

Although this passage does find something positive in wilderness, the nature of the discovery still involves the scenic (note the word "pictures") at the expense of wilderness for its own sake. Like the searchers for sublime scenery during the romantic era, the author of this passage describing the glories of the high peaks was attracted to landscape that satisified his culturally predetermined inclination for the picturesque. One wonders whether he could have been quite so eloquent about an untouched swamp. That scenery, not wilderness, was the emphasis is clear; the goal of the Conservation Commission was to make the high peaks "accessible to [the public] to the fullest possible extent." In other words, the high peaks constituted a landscape to be seen, not an environment to be experienced in its totality.[30]

Still, the conservation bureaucracy was slowly changing its stance relative to the Forest Preserve. Its reasons for doing so reflected a combination of popular romanticism and utilitarianism.

On the one hand, the commission went on at great length about the hardships of life in an urban, industrial, commercial nation. Perhaps because of the recently ended World War, the report of the Conservation Commission for 1919—for the first time since the establishment of the state conservation bureaucracy—ran through a litany of the shortcomings of modern life, which involved great "nervous strain," "radically changed industrial and living conditions," "monotony of occupation," and "high tension machine work." The solution to these probelems, which, collectively, "threaten an actual break-down of society," was relaxation—particularly relaxation in the bosom of nature. The efforts of New York State to respond to the crisis of modern life "is work of vital importance to the people, as an off-set to the nervous strain of our modern highly organized industrial and social life." To confirm the intellectual roots of this romantic position, the report quoted from Emerson's "The Adirondacs"; the passage chosen emphasized the powers of nature to relieve modern man of his "pack of duties."[31]

In addition to this rather routine brand of twentieth-century anti-modernism, however, there was a more telling reason for such a shift of attitude: all those businessmen and factory operatives seeking solace in nature brought money with them and left a good bit of it with local merchants. In further justifying its nascent concern with building trails, the commission noted that the tourist trade had become a major industry in the area:

> Everywhere throughout the Forest Preserve region in both Adirondacks and Catskills, the use of this great vacation ground is increasing at a tremendous rate, until now the most important business of the whole region is that of caring for vacationists. More money is invested in hotel and other properties, more people are employed, more wages are paid, and the annual turnover is greater, than in the entire lumber business, which once figured as the most important activity of the mountains.[32]

The key to this dramatic increase in recreational use of the Forest Preserve was the automobile. As long as transportation to the Adirondacks was limited to trains, the number of people who could or would reach the region was necessarily small. Although the attacks on Murray after publication of his *Adventures in the Wilderness* implied that the woods were literally swarming with campers, hunters, and anglers, it was not until after World War I, when the widespread use of automobiles for family travel truly opened up the Adirondacks, that the "rush to the wilderness" began in earnest. As the commission report observed, "State roads and automobiles are largely responsible for this increase in the number of vacationists."[33] Thus, as with the watershed argument of the 1880s and 1890s, it was economics that motivated steps toward wilderness protection.

One of the immediate consequences of the changing attitude was an enlargement of the rationale for further additions to the Forest Preserve. As late as 1918, the Conservation Commission's three reasons for acquiring more land were the familiar ones: watershed protection, more efficient administration of consolidated parcels, and the consequently diminished fire hazard. Four years later the Conservation Commission supplied four reasons for adding to the Forest Preserve: after watershed protection (presumably still the most important) came the need to enlarge state holdings for recreational and aesthetic purposes. This commitment to recreation still fell within the framework of multiple use, however, since the same report also insisted that one of the main functions of the Forest Preserve was to protect a future timber supply.[34]

▲▲▲▲▲▲▲

One further rationale behind the new interest in recreation should be noted. In 1916, President Woodrow Wilson signed legislation creating the National Park Service, an agency that would administer federal lands dedicated exclusively to scenic and recreational purposes: this was sure evidence that the idea of recreational use of public lands had achieved national legitimacy. It also suggested to the United States Forest Service and other advocates of the resource-management approach to public lands that the growing interest in recreation could no longer be ignored. Only one year after the Park Service legislation, the Forest Service showed a sudden, intensive interest in encouraging recreation on its lands; one reason was probably its fear that if it failed to acknowledge recreation as a legitimate use of the lands under its jurisdiction, then large parcels would be transferred to the care of the Park Service.[35] It is not improbable that the New York State Conservation Commission, still hoping that it might eventually be permitted to harvest timber in the Adirondacks, saw the promotion of recreation as good public relations: if recreation were minimized despite public interest in it, the commission may have reasoned, the Forest Preserve might be wrested from its control altogether.

During the 1920s the Conservation Commission devoted more and more of its resources to administering and protecting a forest whose chief purpose was to provide recreational and aesthetic outlets for the people of New York. Its annual report settled into routine discussions of miles of trail maintained, leantos constructed, number of visitor-days at various state campsites, and the ever present need for more money. By 1931 the Conservation Department (in 1927 "Commission" became "Department") could declare, "Realizing that in their recreational use to the public lies probably the greatest present value of the State lands which constitute the forest preserve, the Department during the year has carried on an aggressive program of development to increase their availability to all."[36]

Three years later, as the Conservation Department contemplated how it would observe the fiftieth anniversary of the 1885 law establishing the Forest Preserve, it congratulated itself that in this half century "the preserve has been elaborately developed as a great recreation area, without interfering with its wild forest character."[37] Although the celebration of "Fifty Years of Conservation" did not so note, the most significant development of those fifty years was not trails or campsites but a radical shift in the thinking of the conservation bureaucracy.

To be sure, the Conservation Department had not suddenly declared itself to be the protector of wilderness as such. The impulse to encourage recreation was itself a threat to wilderness, as trails, cabins, and other human intrusions appeared in the midst of the hitherto benignly neglected Forest Preserve. Indeed, one of the bitterest battles between preservationists and the bureaucracy involved the state's intention to construct a bobsled run on state land for the 1932 Winter Olympics held in Lake Placid. The preservationist Association for the Protection of the Adirondacks took the Conservation Department to court and won; the appellate court in Albany ruled that the Forest Preserve "must always retain the character of a wilderness." Although this vague mandate hardly provided final safeguards, it suggested both that wilderness was important and that the conservation bureaucracy, even in its new dedication to recreation, was not universally seen as a protector of wilderness.[38]

From a mentality that had perceived the Forest Preserve almost exclusively in terms of the revenue someday to be realized from state-owned timber, the conservation agencies had moved to a different but still utilitarian position. As the primacy of recreation became more or less established policy, the Conservation Department interpreted its mission in terms of improvements like fireplaces and dams. These may have promoted recreation, but they were in de facto violation of whatever wilderness existed in the Forest Preserve. In 1940, for example, the department listed scores of improvement projects completed with labor provided by the Civilian Conservation Corps. Among these were impoundment dams on remote Adirondack rivers and streams, including the dam on the Cold River at Duck Hole, a remote pond in the western high peaks.[39] The enthusiasm with which the Conservation Department promoted these improvements measured the distance it still had to go before a wilderness aesthetic could be integrated into official policy.

Another issue on which the conservation bureaucracy showed its insensitivity to wilderness values occurred in the 1930s when it undertook the construction of firetruck roads in the Forest Preserve. These roads, also part of a Civilian Conservation Corps project, were designed to diminish the fire hazard on remote parcels of state land. That they appealed to Conservation Commissioner Lithgow Osborne shows again how the protection of trees (perhaps for eventual harvest) remained central to the bureaucracy's sense of mission. For although improved access might indeed reduce the acreage burned if a fire actually started, the very existence of the roads vitiated the quality of the wilderness. Preservationists were unsuccessful in their efforts to prevent the construction of these roads, although the Conservation Department was enjoined from ever opening them to the public.[40]

Throughout the next three or four decades, as the Conservation Department wrestled to define its duties in the Forest Preserve, the major problem lay in its ambivalence toward wilderness— which, in turn, reflected a wide range of attitudes among the people of New York. For a long time—until well into the 1960s—the bureaucracy continued to identify as its chief constituency that part of the population that wanted its woodland recreation assisted by human "improvements." And this group was undoubtedly large, including many hunters, fishermen, and campers. In the meantime, however, a wilderness aesthetic insisting on purity and absolute preservation was slowly developing in the minds of some New Yorkers.

# VII
# A Wilderness Aesthetic

Much has been written about the activities of citizen lobbies and organizations and their efforts to prevent various attempts to violate Article VII, Section 7. As noted earlier, this study does not intend to repeat or reinvestigate the judicial and political history of the Forest Preserve in the twentieth century. As Frank Graham, Jr., has effectively shown, many people have fought a number of efforts to dilute the protections provided by Article VII, Section 7; as early as the 1930s, men like Paul Schaefer, John S. Apperson, and Robert Marshall were going to court, lobbying the legislature, arousing public opinion, and doing everything they could to keep dams, truck trails, and highways from compromising wilderness in the Forest Preserve. We know that, in fact, it was wilderness they wanted to save, that they were thus working from assumptions entirely different from those of the New York Board of Trade and Transportation and David McClure, who were originally responsible for the forever-wild provision.[1]

In other words, beginning in the 1930s a wilderness lobby existed whose chief mission was the defense of wilderness in the Adirondacks, and whose chief tool in that defense was the language of Article VII, Section 7. The activities of this lobby have involved arguing before the legislature, convincing voters of the value of wilderness, and insuring that the protections of the forever-wild clause were written into subsequent constitutions. The important point is that a preservation lobby existed at all. Before the 1930s, it did not—at least not to any appreciable degree. Yet the existence of the preservationist philosophy is now taken for granted, both in the Adirondacks and nationally.[2] Its political skills have increased, its money-raising techniques have become more sophisticated (though preservationists seldom have more than a fraction of the financial resources available to developers and other anti-wilderness forces), and its ranks have grown. It has learned how to use the media and how to get out the vote. But its mission and rationale have remained essentially the same since the 1930s. As *Nature Magazine* editorialized in 1932, arguing against a proposed amendment to Article VII, Section 7, "The issue is fundamental. It involves a vital question—preservation of wilderness."[3] This statement would have seemed ridiculous to the constitutional convention of 1894, which was all for protecting forests but had no interest in wilderness.

Why does wilderness move people in the twentieth century in ways that would have been impossible in the nineteenth? As we have seen, both the romantic travelers and Colvin found much in the wilderness that stirred them deeply. But throughout the nineteenth century, the idea of protecting wilderness against the demands of utility and progress was inaccessible even to those who found genuine meaning for their lives in the wilderness. The framers of the forever-wild clause took great pains to insure that they would not appear to be preserving wilderness for its own sake; the purpose of Article VII, Section 7 was almost exclusively utilitarian. Yet in this century, a provision intended to protect watershed has been invoked to prevent a host of just the sort of progressive developments that would have appealed to both Emerson and Colvin, as well as the New York Board of Trade and Transportation.

Until roughly the 1920s, the main reason why Article VII, Section 7 both survived and was cited to prevent forestry and other developments in the Forest Preserve was negative, reflecting not a commitment to preserving wilderness but a continuing mistrust of the state bureaucracy's ability to administer public lands and forests properly. The poor image of the old Forestry Commission was a significant factor in the original passage of the article, and the people of New York continued to suspect chicanery or incompetence on the part of those appointed to guard the state's natural resources. In 1895, when New York voters overwhelmingly rejected the first of many attempts to weaken the restrictiveness of forever wild, they were expressing not an inclination to maintain the Adirondacks as wilderness but their conviction that the time was not yet right to trust politicians and their lackeys with the state forests.[4]

Similar mistrust persisted thereafter (and was confirmed by several ill-chosen appointments to important offices); at the 1915 Constitutional Convention, Article VII, Section 7 was incorporated—in precisely the same language—in a new constitution. This public apprehension about the competence of state foresters explains why their repeated requests that the constitution be amended were either ignored or rejected. It is not accurate to say, as do Graham and others who have discussed the early history of the Forest Preserve, that the concept of forever wild quickly acquired a "constituency" whose aim was to defend wilderness in the Adirondacks.[5]

Such a constituency, to be sure, did appear, but later; when it did, the disposition to protect wilderness in the Adirondacks for its own sake was something new. It occurred at roughly the same time that many other Americans were learning to look with new eyes on what remained of their wilderness. The high priest of this movement was undoubtedly John Muir of California; in articles, books, and speeches, Muir extolled the appeal and value of wilderness for its own sake. He was among the first to recognize the importance of forests in protecting watershed, but the essential message of his long career is that wilderness is aesthetically and spiritually satisfying and worth preserving simply because it is in fact wilderness.[6]

The point of this chapter is to ask how and why this wilderness aesthetic first appeared in and for the Adirondacks. To answer this question, I want to look not at the arguments used in the media, the courts, the legislature, or constitutional conventions to prohibit the construction of dams or firetruck trails in the Forest Preserve, but—as in the chapters on Colvin and the romantic travelers—at an actual response to the wilderness.

In the twentieth century, unfortunately, we do not have the wealth of travel narratives that make studying the nineteenth-century response to the Adirondacks such a pleasure. There is no Headley, no Murray; because of changes in the tastes of the American reading public—changes perhaps due to the dramatically improving quality of cinematography—popular travel narratives have not been nearly so common or articulate in our age. There have been good additions to the American tradition of contemplative literature—Aldo Leopold, Edward Abbey, and Annie

Dillard come to mind—but a look at the table of contents of Paul Jamieson's *Adirondack Reader* shows how relatively slight is the literature of travel and contemplation in the twentieth century in comparison with that of the nineteenth, at least in the Adirondacks.[7]

Nevertheless, in what there is of modern Adirondack literature, we can find evidence of a new way of perceiving nature. This new perception arises from a confluence of two trends already extant in the aesthetics of nature in the Adirondacks. From the romantic tradition the twentieth-century wilderness advocate has accepted the spirituality of nature. The accounts of backpackers and others give modern expression to an old idea: that nature, particularly where human influence is least noticeable, is spiritually edifying. Although contemporary wilderness enthusiasts use a vocabulary less elevated than that of the romantic travelers, the philosophical content of their response to the wilderness is often remarkably similar to what Street and Headley expressed in their pantheistic reveries.[8]

The other significant element in the modern wilderness aesthetic is the discovery implied in Colvin's narratives: that nature, when left alone, displays a perfect nexus of balance, process, and dynamism. Colvin's aesthetic was largely shaped by the work of George Perkins Marsh, and Marsh had a profound—if often indirect and unacknowledged—influence on the development of a twentieth-century wilderness aesthetic. Marsh pointed out the importance of *all* the details of nature, and Marsh's discoveries began a reorientation of nature aesthetics. Whereas the romantics had been most impressed by the grand prospect or the peaceful lakeside—those landscapes that fulfilled the expectations of the cult of the sublime and the beautiful—the new aesthetic responded appreciatively to processes as much as to views.

Magnificent scenery, of course, continues to appeal, and contemporary efforts to preserve wilderness have often emphasized the scenic values of wild places. But added to this has been the notion of nature as system, the understanding that nature is a complex combination of many processes, and the conviction that to interfere with any of these processes disturbs the dynamic harmony that previously existed. Only after the leap from nature-as-scenery to nature-as-process has been made do swamps, wetlands, a forest dark and cluttered with undergrowth and fallen trees (these are Adirondack examples; others would include deserts, tundra, etc.) appeal aesthetically. Only after the implications of the discoveries of the last century and a half of science are integrated into the response to nature does a genuine wilderness aesthetic emerge.

Obviously, there are other reasons that inspire some Americans to rally to the defense of wilderness. Robert Marshall, one of this century's most vigorous exponents of wilderness preservation, who first encountered wilderness near his family's summer home in the Adirondacks, often wrote of the virtues of strenuous exercise in a wilderness environment, of wilderness exploration as part of American history, of the independence of body and mind promoted by wilderness camping, and of how the sense of danger and the contrast between wilderness and civilization can ease the barely tolerable stresses of modern life. Roderick Nash and other historians of the wilderness movement have shown how these attributes have appealed to Americans. The lure of the wilderness and the inclination to wish it preserved undoubtedly depend, at least in part, on anti-modernism and the American ideal of independent individualism; I do not mean to argue that these have not been important in preservation struggles in the Adirondacks. I do think, however, that the aesthetic I am describing is a key element, but an element either ignored or misunderstood, in the story of the American wilderness in the twentieth century.[9]

Henry Abbott was a New York City watchmaker and inventor who began visiting the Adirondacks near the end of the nineteenth century. Like many others, he opted for the rugged life in the forest when city ways and business seemed onerous. Leaving his family in a cottage on Long Lake, he would set off with a local guide, Bige Smith, for an isolated spot in the woods and spend several days observing nature, resting, and contemplating the peace and beauty of the Adirondack environment. After a day or two back in the cottage, Abbott and Smith would be off again for the woods. None of this was unusual, nor was Abbott's inclination to write about what he saw and felt in the wilderness. But his narratives of experiences close to nature made an addition to the Adirondack canon that was at the time unique: in his *Birch Bark Books*, we find the first consistent or systematic Adirondack expression of a modern wilderness aesthetic.

Little in Abbott's background suggested that he would set off in a literary and intellectual direction so different from that of the scores of travelers who had preceded him in the Adirondacks. Born on a farm near Danbury, Connecticut, in 1850, he moved with his family through a number of towns in New York (including Lawrenceville north of the Adirondacks) and New Jersey. At sixteen he quit school and apprenticed himself to a Newark watchmaker. He was adept at his chosen trade: in 1876 he took out a patent on the first effective stem that could both wind a watch and move the hands. He also held patents on typewriters and a variety of other devices.

His first trips to the Adirondacks were brief, but by 1899 he was spending up to three months a year there. He was known around Long Lake for an obsession with planning and an unusual fastidiousness of dress; even when fishing at a pond as much as twenty miles from the nearest settlement, Abbott insisted on wearing a white shirt, jacket, and tie. Beginning in 1914, Abbott began to write up his wilderness adventures and have his narratives printed and bound between photographs of birch bark; these *Birch Bark Books*, as they have come to be called, he mailed to friends as Christmas greetings. He continued to write these books until 1932, producing nineteen in all.[10]

Except for an occasionally indulged tendency to anthropomorphize the animals he described, Abbott's accounts of his observations of nature are remarkably straightforward and well written. Gone are the rhetorical flourishes and the purple prose of the romantic travelers. The leanness of Abbott's style reflects his response to the nature he was observing. The romantics, by means of conventional rhetoric, were imposing their cultural preconceptions on the wilderness: Abbott, in the spirit of the scientific objectivity that helped to define the culture of his day, was trying not to impose himself on nature but merely to tell what it was really like. Though not himself a scientist, Abbott clearly had absorbed the conventions of scientific observation and description. Thus the bulk of his narratives involve not scenery but processes and occurrences. Where the romantics used most of their literary energy in trying to describe what nature looked like, Abbott's chief accomplishment was in lucid accounts of what was happening in the dynamic, always changing process of nature. To Headley, the glory of the Adirondacks was the view from Marcy; to Abbott, who appreciated the good view as much as anyone, the fascination of the wilderness lay in spending years observing the reforestation of a burned-over hillside.

Although Abbott's love of the wilderness was deeply felt, even he displayed occasional inconsistencies. Finding a beaver dam threatening "valuable" timber, he set about trying to destroy it, eventually resorting to dynamite. Like nearly all campers of his day, he removed the bark from live trees to construct temporary shelters. And, for a while, he saw predators only as destroyers of game. But in his attitude toward predation, Abbott began to recognize his own inconsistency; by the end of his series of books, he expressed regret that he had ever shot at a hawk and acknowledged that predators had as much—if not more—right to their prey as hunters. He also admitted that predation was important in keeping the numbers of the prey species in balance with *their* food supply. Such a discovery seems commonplace today, but in Abbott's time it was unusual for a sportsman to accept predators. It was part of Abbott's recognition of nature as dynamic system.[11]

Another difference between Abbott and his romantic predecessors was in his reaction to getting lost in the wilderness. With justifiable faith in his own skills as a woodsman, he considered himself "perfectly safe" even when alone. More important, he did not experience the fearful sense of psychological disorientation that so unnerved men like Todd and Street; rather, being lost offered yet another way to observe nature. One night he was paddling on South Pond when a thick fog settled, obscuring all landmarks and keeping him out on the lake, unable to reach shore, until dawn. This episode, which begins one entire *Birch Bark Book* devoted to the subject of being lost, allowed Abbott to listen to wildlife—herons, deer, fish, a loon, and other animals—in ways he had not been sensitive to before. (Of course, Abbott knew generally where he was, while Street and Todd, only too aware of their own incompetence in the woods, had genuine reason to be afraid should they become truly lost.) On another occasion, utterly lost and alone in the middle of the woods, Abbott noted that he could "still enjoy being in the forest," and that "night in the forest had no terrors for me."[12]

Abbott was very much aware of the tradition that the civilized man lost in the wilderness was likely to lose his sanity, and he described at length the steps one should take to avoid becoming "fear stricken." In his view, moreover, the psychological disorientation derived not from the inherent malignancy of the wilderness, as the romantics had thought, but from mere incompetence in the woods. Finally, he translated the traditional romantic hostility toward cities into evidence of the virtues of the wilderness; even though one could get lost there, "trees do not fall on and kill people one percent as often as bricks or stones from tall buildings on pedestrians in cities. People lost in forests do not starve as often as those lost in cities without money."[13] This was meant ironically, of course, but it suggests the extent to which Abbott was both aware of and rejected old fears about the wilderness.

▲▲▲▲▲▲▲

To Abbott the wilderness was alluring for many reasons. An unlumbered forest, he noted, was easier to walk in than one that had been logged. Even when wilderness hiking demanded scrambling through tangled underbrush, climbing over rocky ledges, negotiating swamps, or fighting through blackberry bushes "as high as one's head," it always had the "charm of variety." Whereas Street, Headley, and other romantic travelers stayed either on or close to the lakes, Abbott took delight in cross-country bushwhacking, relying only on his compass. He thus described trekking alone across a varied terrain west of the inlet of Long Lake:

> So, frequently consulting my compass, I proceeded down the mountain, over hillocks, across ravines, through swamps, often following the beaten path of a deer's runway; again, forcing a passage through a briar patch or tangled witch-hopple. Then, there were long stretches of smooth forest floor carpeted with a Persian rug of Autumn leaves of brilliant and somber hues, woven into the most gorgeous and fantastic patterns. A soft October breeze rustled the tree tops and partially drowned the noise of rasping dry leaves under foot. It was an ideal day for wandering alone in the woods."[14]

To Abbott, the joy of intimacy with the wilderness was not in its scenery but just in being there.

Inevitably, Abbott had to consider the relationship between logging and what was left of wilderness in the Adirondacks. He often mentioned how logging changed the character of the woods, noting that in his day lumberjacks took out only softwoods and that forest fires all too often raged over recently logged lands. At the same time he, as had Headley and others, saw the lumberjacks and their camps as picturesque additions to the landscape. Log drives on Adirondack rivers were "thrilling and exciting events." The hard work and ingenuity involved in felling timber and getting it to the mills intrigued Abbott. But finally he acknowledged that logging constituted a threat to the future of wilderness in the Adirondacks. He hoped that even on private property—and this sets him off from virtually every wilderness enthusiast up to his day—logging would eventually decline and vanish, so that

> our forests which for a hundred years systematically have been robbed of their products with no thought of replanting or fertilizing, may be restored to the care and control of "Mother Nature," who, with true conservation, for thousands of years has nurtured and fertilized her growing trees with the decayed remains of earlier generations of similar trees.[15]

Abbott believed in the capacity of nature to recover from interference with natural processes, even when the disruption was as disastrous as the forest fires that often ravaged Adirondack lands after the lumberjacks had left. Just east of Forked Lake is Pine Brook, which Abbott and Bige Smith fished for the first time in 1899, a year after lumber operations had ceased there. The trout were plentiful, but Abbott noted that the loggers, following the practice of the day, had left piles of brush and branches wherever they had fallen. These soon dried and became highly inflammable. The inevitable occurred, and the area was swept by fire the following June. For the next thirty-two years Abbott watched with growing admiration as the forest was restored, not by any efforts of man, but by "the processes of Mother Nature in her efforts to heal the wounds inflicted in the year 1900."[16]

Abbott was particularly impressed by the succession of species, noting how each was suited to the changing environment for a while and then yielded to another. First came thickets of raspberries, then shade-intolerant trees like pin cherry, aspen, and white birch; next came more tolerant species like yellow birch, which were in turn succeeded by climax species—balsam fir, red spruce, hemlock, sugar maple, and beech. Observing the long sequence by which nature salvaged the landscape, Abbott was struck by the complexity and perfection of "Nature's reforestation process."[17] The key to this was the omnipresence of death and decay, which were critical in the natural process of thinning out the first and second growths:

> The weaker trees died. They died standing. . . . Only when decay had proceeded to the point where the weight of winter snows crushed to earth the unfit, were the fitter trees relieved of their burden of the dead, whose bodies now would soon be converted into fertilizing food for the living.[18]

This faith in the processes of nature, which depended on death, decay, and new growth, was Abbott's greatest leap forward from the conventions of the romantic travelers. And it allowed him—unlike the great majority of his contemporaries—to ignore the utilitarian value of a forest. The idea of a forest as one great complex system appealed to him, and the implication of this notion was that the Adirondacks should be dedicated to wilderness.

Abbott's acceptance of death and decay obviously derived at least in part from his subscription to a Darwinian conception of nature:

> The struggle for existence, the elbowing, pushing and crowding of individuals, and the final survival of the stronger, the more fortunately placed, or the one who arrived and got established first, is nowhere more marked or more conspicuous than among forest trees. The weaker ones die before they mature, because there is not "room in the sun" for the branches of all; and because, as the roots develop and increase in size, there is not enough room in the ground for the roots of all. Also, there is not enough plant food in the soil to sustain life in all the trees that get a start in the forest.[19]

To the forester, the discovery of the principles of succession and survival of the fittest suggested that humankind should take advantage of these processes to produce stronger, more plentiful trees—and it was precisely during the period that Abbott was composing his response to the wilderness that foresters were discovering the practical usefulness of these principles. The role of science, in this view, was to penetrate nature's secrets and bend nature's processes to the human will.[20] To Abbott, on the other hand (who, as an inventor, doubtless understood that science and progress were important and necessary to American civilization, and was interested in preserving wilderness only in those pockets where a bit of it remained), nature's processes were especially fascinating and appealing when they were left alone.

Exploring the mountains around Cold River, Abbott found a

landscape with no apparent signs of human activity and concluded that the absence of science and human manipulation was that country's chief aesthetic asset:

> On the higher slopes of these hills, the hand of man, certainly, never had wielded an axe. Nature's unhampered processes there, had developed a type of forest perhaps not scientific, but certainly wildly beautiful. There, the ripened, fallen monarch, decaying, fertilized roots of succeeding generations of trees, whose interlaced branches formed a canopy far above, through which only limited shafts of sunlight filtered. Mushrooms and other fungi in great variety of form and brilliant colors abounded. Mosses furnished soft, luxurious carpets for the floor of these temple aisles. . . . There, we found a wonderland, a playground. . . . Sounds of human industry never penetrated this remote region, but the quiet listener might hear the voices of forest inhabitants about their pleasures and their business of hunting each other.[21]

This passage illustrates well the confluence of romanticism and naturalism in the modern wilderness aesthetic. Abbott sees untouched nature as a "temple" of a pantheistic deity, but he adds to this tradition the acceptance of nature's processes: he acknowledges that the "ripened, fallen monarch" must die, decay, and return its elements to the soil for the nourishment of younger trees; he finds the "mushrooms and other fungi" to be significant features of the landscape; he even delights in knowing that among the sounds of the forest environment are those of animals hunting and killing each other. Such a comprehensive response to the wilderness implies that all the elements described are part of the total system, and that the whole is aesthetically appealing to the extent that all its parts are not interfered with.

When people admit, as Abbott did, the necessity of death in nature, they begin to think in terms of cycles. Western civilization—committed to a Judaeo-Christian orientation, devoted to progress and a sense of time that holds that one thing develops out of another and is an advancement compared to what preceded it—tends to think in linear time, beginning in the primitive, unknowable past and pushing ahead toward a distinct and ever-improving future. Meanwhile, our culture avoids or denies the physical realities of death and decay. To think in terms of cyclical time, on the other hand, is to believe, however unconsciously, that the obvious cycles of the day and year are mirrored in all of nature and especially in the cycle of life, death, decay, and new life. It is hard for the Western mind to perceive reality in terms of cyclical time: Thoreau occasionally could (and to the extent that he could, he was truly a radical), but most of us are programmed by our culture to deny the inevitability and necessity of death.[22] That may have been why romantic travelers in the Adirondacks were depressed by swamps surrounded by dead trees, and that is why a genuine wilderness aesthetic is so rarely expressed by Americans: it depends on accepting the entirety of nature's processes, including the cycles of life and death.

To Abbott, nature's cycles were everywhere. He knew that saplings depended on "the death and fall of some forest patriarch that now overshadows them." He also admired the cycles of the creeks and rainfall, wherein water flows down Adirondack streambeds and eventually to the ocean,

> where it is evaporated, formed into clouds, floated back, possibly over the same mountain, condensed, falls in rain washing leaves, fertilizing roots, percolating through soil and rocks back to the same spring to start the same trip over again; a cycle which, possibly, has consumed months of time; one is filled with admiration by this simplest of Nature's processes.[23]

All of nature, then, was a system of repeating processes. Colvin had been subliminally aware of this perfect system, but Abbott's sensitivity went a significant step further. He was not chained to the Western sense of progress that ultimately compromised Colvin's wilderness aesthetic.

It is important to remember, however, that both inside and outside the state bureaucracy, the old hostility to preservation of wilderness persisted. While Abbott was composing his *Birch Bark Books*, for example, A. B. Recknagel, professor of forest management at Cornell, published *The Forests of New York State* (1923). In addition to offering a survey of New York forests, outlining their history, and discussing their composition and commercial potential, this book showed that antagonism to the idea of forever wild remained strong, especially among professional foresters. Recknagel declared that the Forest Preserve was a "forest cemetery," that it would soon "become overcrowded, stagnate, and, finally, go to pieces for want of proper silviculture." He acknowledged the existence of "aesthetes" like Abbott, who wanted "the trees to mature, to die and fall," who valued "the dead tree and the rotten limb." But he argued that their position was meaningless in the face of the demonstrable economic benefits of efficient cutting, and he was sure that "ultimately the State Forest Preserve will be opened to conservative utilization."[24]

The importance of Henry Abbott is thus that he represents a turning point in attitudes toward wilderness in the Adirondacks; he reflects changes that were beginning to occur in the culture. His *Birch Bark Books* contain the earliest local expression of a modern wilderness aesthetic, which appeared at a time when it was radically different from mainstream thinking on the subject of forests and their proper care. Writers who preceded him had hinted at much of what he wrote, but no one else had effected the crucial combination of romanticism and naturalism. It would be difficult to prove his direct influence on wilderness advocates like Paul Schaefer and John Apperson, who took up the defense of Article VII, Section 7 during this same period.[25] Indeed, it is unlikely that either of them ever met Abbott or read any of his narratives. In other words, he did not invent this aesthetic; he showed that attitudes in his culture were changing.

One eventual consequence of the kind of discoveries Abbott and others were making about nature is the ultimate synthesis of romanticism and naturalism, wherein an awareness and appreciation of process leads to spiritual transcendence. In Abbott's own narratives this transcendence does not appear: perhaps he was too much the fastidious watchmaker to become an Emersonian "transparent eyeball." In the works of later writers responding to American nature, however, we do find evidence of just such a transcendence deriving from intimate, empirical appreciation of nature's details and processes. One of the best examples (although not an Adirondack example) is Rachel Carson's *The Edge of the Sea*, where the author, after describing with loving precision the tiny bits of life in a tidal pool, writes: "Contemplating the teeming life of the shore, we have an uneasy sense of the communication of some universal truth that lies just beyond our grasp. . . . The meaning haunts and ever eludes us, and in its very pursuit we approach the ultimate mystery of Life itself."[26]

We do not have a twentieth-century Adirondack writer of such talent or insight. But the spiritual message in Carson's account of a life spent close to nature suggests how her discoveries were in the same tradition as Abbott's. Her prose is more elegant, and her willingness to move from understanding process to a moment of transcendent awareness of the essence of life is far bolder, but to both writers, the origin of nature's meanings and lessons lay not in God's immanence in the landscape or in sublime grandeur but in the perfection, harmony, and interdependence of all of nature. The gradual acceptance of this possibility by at least part of the New York conservation bureaucracy is the most recent episode in the evolution of attitudes toward wilderness in the Adirondacks.

# VIII
# The Institutionalization of a Wilderness Aesthetic

On November 25, 1950, hundred-mile-per-hour winds swept through the Adirondacks. In some sections of the Forest Preserve, where mature trees were particularly vulnerable, vast expanses of forest were virtually leveled. The Conservation Department estimated that the effects of the blowdown, as the wind and its results came to be known, were especially severe on 255,000 acres of the Forest Preserve (which in 1950 consisted of 2,178,241 acres). Once the extent of the damage became known, the state had to decide what to do with its wind-thrown timber. One option was to do nothing, which would have meant allowing millions of board feet of lumber and pulp wood to rot on the ground, encouraging the proliferation of insects and other pests, and abandoning the downed trees to the fires which would certainly occur once the wood dried out.[1] That this line of action (or inaction) did not appeal to the Conservation Department shows how the old utilitarian philosophy remained strong in the conservation bureaucracy. For although it had committed itself and the Forest Preserve to recreation, it had by no means abandoned its reluctance to let natural processes govern the landscape.

Instead, the Conservation Department argued that the fire potential posed a threat to the surviving trees on the Forest Preserve. Since the forever-wild clause (known as Article XIV since the Constitutional Convention of 1938, where Article VII, Section 7 had been incorporated in a new constitution in precisely the same language) prohibited the removal of trees, dead or alive, from the Forest Preserve, any clean-up operation would be in technical violation of the constitution. Accordingly, the Conservation Department requested an opinion from the state attorney general on the legality of salvaging the timber in the blowdown areas. He agreed that the need to protect what remained of the state's forests in the Adirondacks outweighed the constitutional prohibition, and he decided to allow salvage operations. The Conservation Department was also permitted by the legislature to solicit bids from private companies, who would take out the merchantable trees, sell them, and clean up the areas devastated by the blowdown.[2]

Encouraged by the willingness of both the legislature and the attorney general to bend the forever-wild provision in the direction of utility, the Conservation Department proceeded to mount an assault on Article XIV. In its official magazine, the *Conservationist*, it posed four loaded questions on the proper management of the Forest Preserve:

1. If our objective is the preservation of the forest, are forests best preserved by prohibiting cutting?
2. What is meant by "forever wild"? Does it suggest an abundance of birds and animals and if so, does our present management policy promote that objective?
3. How does the present management policy, as prescribed by our constitution, contribute to the economic needs of state and nation?
4. Under this policy, are we making the most of the potential recreational values of the Forest Preserve?[3]

The first of these questions illustrated how the word "preservation" continued to suggest different meanings to different people. The author of these questions was using the word in the same way that William Fox and others had at the beginning of the century. In this sense, it does not mean allowing the forest to grow and mature by natural processes, but simply producing and protecting an abundance of trees. Answering its own questions, the Conservation Department declared that the forever-wild clause prevented the best use of the Forest Preserve: the prohibition on cutting kept the state forests from generating revenue, inhibited the department in its efforts to promote larger wildlife populations, and minimized the recreational potential of the Forest Preserve. Among other things, wrote *Conservationist* editor P. W. Fosburgh, we believe . . . that its forests could be made and kept healthier, and that in doing this a modest income might be realized that could be plowed back into our property; that wildlife in the Forest Preserve could be made more abundant than it is now; that provisions could be made so that more [New Yorkers], now unable to use and enjoy the Forest Preserve, might be able to do so in the future.[4]

The position of the Conservation Department was essentially that its mandate to encourage all sorts of recreation was unduly limited by forever wild. For the most part, it did not wish to see intensive logging in the Forest Preserve, but it felt hamstrung in its efforts to develop the Adirondacks for recreation. The willingness of the Conservation Department to attack Article XIV, moreover, stemmed from more than the urge to build more trails, public campsites, and interior ranger stations.[5] In the discussion of these four questions, officials of the department revealed their discomfort with the very idea that a forest could be left subject to natural processes alone and not be actively managed by trained foresters. Superintendent of Forests F. W. Littlefield argued that because they were not being harvested, the trees in the Adirondacks were suffering from "fungous and insect pests which are the concomitants of over-maturity." To Littlefield, a forest where "rotting beech, dying birch, and 'conky' maple" were allowed to stand simply was not being "preserved." He specifically insisted that he was not arguing for profit-oriented lumbering; he just could not tolerate the idea of diseased or infested trees. Like the romantic travelers who found swamps aesthetically repulsive, Littlefield was unwilling to accept the natural processes of death and decay. It was his mission, as well as his profession, to see that those processes did not operate in the Forest Preserve.[6]

Other conservation officials advanced further reasons for ending the prohibition on cutting. Two game managers correctly pointed out that the primordial Adirondacks had not been a "great wildlife reservoir," and that wherever the Forest Preserve approached original wilderness conditions, the wildlife populations—especially of white-tailed deer—diminished. Others, arguing that the status quo prevented most New Yorkers from using the state's forests, proposed that the entire Forest Preserve be zoned, some of it being devoted strictly to wilderness functions and the rest made available for more intensive management and recreation. (The notion of zoning eventually achieved legitimacy in the 1970s, though all of the Forest Preserve remained protected by Article XIV.) Finally, Deputy Conservation Department Commissioner J. Victor Skiff went so far as to raise the old issue of potential state revenue from timber harvest.[7] This episode was the most recent serious effort of the conservation bureaucracy to do away with the constitutional protection of the Forest Preserve.

▲▲▲▲▲▲▲

Opponents of any tinkering with the concept of forever wild responded in force; one immediate result was renewed interest in the Forest Preserve on the part of the legislature. At the request of Conservation Commissioner Perry Duryea, in 1953 a Joint Legislative Committee on Natural Resources began investigating the management and future of the Forest Preserve. This committee invited a number of prominent businessmen, journalists, and forestry experts to form a Special Advisory Committee on the State Forest Preserve. Among the members was Paul Schaefer of Schenectady, founder and chief officer of Friends of the Forest Preserve and one of the most articulate and active members of the wilderness preservation lobby.[8] The inclusion of Schaefer on this committee represented a turning point in the management of New York's wilderness. For the first time, someone expressing a wilderness aesthetic held an official position on a public body. Of course, the function of this committee was purely advisory; it had no power to enact laws or formulate official policy, but Schaefer's appointment was a significant first step in official acknowledgment of wilderness values.

At first, the reports of the Joint Legislative Committee suggested that the anti-forever-wild credo of the Conservation Department was predominant. The same arguments appeared as those advanced with the *Conservationist*'s controversial four questions. Sections of the reports observed that watershed protection could be enhanced by selective cutting, cited ornithologist Edwin Way Teale's statement that bird populations flourish and increase in forests where logging operations have opened up the canopy and encouraged new growth, and quoted the assertion of a forester working for the United States Forest Service that timber harvest improves wildlife habitat.[9]

A long statement from William M. Foss, director of the Division of Lands and Forests of the Conservation Department, outlined the major objection of the bureaucracy to Article XIV: the department was constructing and maintaining facilities in the Forest Preserve worth millions of dollars, yet their constitutionality was uncertain. Foss observed that although recreation had not been even mentioned in the provision of 1894, by his time it was "*the* major use of the Forest Preserve." He asked that the Joint Legislative Committee address the difficulty of administering the Forest Preserve under the constitutional strictures.[10]

The most important part of Foss's statement was his hope that the committee would recommend zoning the Forest Preserve. This scheme, part of the Conservation Department's strategy for weakening the grip of forever wild, nonetheless contained elements key to the eventual official acceptance of a wilderness aesthetic. One of the zones would be "Restricted Areas . . . to include scenic, wilderness and roadside areas with outstanding natural features. Development within these areas to be permitted only to the extent necessary for the construction of primitive facilities such as trails, lean-tos, fireplaces, etc." Although even this amount of interference still violated the purest definition of wilderness, the conservation bureaucracy was for the first time declaring its willingness to minimize the development of at least some part of the Forest Preserve. It was a major step toward admitting the legitimacy of wilderness. In a later report William Foss assured the Joint Legislative Committeee that "existing outstanding wilderness areas of substantial acreage will be maintained in their present state without any development whatsoever." And still later, in 1959, the committee was again discussing the need to distinguish between those areas in the Forest Preserve where wilderness of "superior or superlative characteristics" prevailed and areas where substantial interference in the environment was obvious. Under the aegis of the committee, specific parts of the Forest Preserve began to be mapped, named, and identified as possessing especially valuable wilderness characteristics.[11]

Finally, in 1960, the Joint Legislative Committee on Natural Resources released its proposal for establishing eleven wilderness areas in the Adirondack Forest Preserve. Throughout the report containing this proposal, the committee begged the question of just why these areas deserved special consideration. It spoke often of "wilderness values" and "wilderness character," and it delineated a set of criteria, including size, absence of noticeable improvements or private inholdings, contiguity, and other easily measured features. But other than the potential of these areas for certain kinds of recreation, the report offered little in the way of a genuine aesthetic argument beyond the obvious concern to protect wild scenery. In any case, no official action was taken on the committee's zoning recommendations. But the research performed by the staff of this committee, to determine which parts of the Adirondacks were suitable for special wilderness classification, was useful several years later.[12]

▲▲▲▲▲▲▲

In 1968, New York Governor Nelson Rockefeller appointed a Temporary Study Commission on the Future of the Adirondacks. The creation of this commission was in response to a proposal, prepared under the aegis of Rockefeller's brother Laurence, that the central Adirondacks be turned over to the federal government and become the Adirondack Mountains National Park. Such a development would have required state cession to the Department of the Interior of some 1.2 million acres of the Forest Preserve and federal purchase of about 600,000 acres of private land. The national park idea, though it never moved beyond the original proposal, generated much controversy and discussion—which may have been the intent of its authors: it stimulated the state to think about what it should be doing with the Adirondacks and how it should be planning for the future.[13]

The members of the Temporary Study Commission were prominent conservationists and others concerned with Adirondack issues. The staff consisted of professional ecologists, wildlife experts, economic planners, and an attorney. The most significant of its final recommendations was that the state should create an Adirondack Park Agency, whose chief function would be to oversee the zoning and development of all private land in the park. The rationale for such a radical departure from the more or less laissez-faire attitude with which the state had for decades treated the millions of acres of privately owned land was the widely perceived threat of massive construction of vacation homes and the consequent elimination of the open-space character of the Adirondacks. Thus, for the first time, the state expanded its Forest Preserve orientation to include issues of parkwide significance. The political, economic, and philosophical ramifications of the Private Land Use and Development Plan that the Park Agency eventually produced are still being felt in the Adirondacks and are a continuing source of controversy and acrimony.[14] Although the institution of the plan largely derived from an urge to protect the character of the Forest Preserve land abutting potentially developable private land, the plan itself is not what I intend to discuss here. More useful to a study of changing attitudes toward wilderness are the recommendations of the Temporary Study Commission relative to the Forest Preserve, and the later State Land Master Plan produced by the Adirondack Park Agency before it began the more difficult task of preparing the Private Land Use and Development Plan.

The distinguishing characteristic of the study commission's recommendations was that they treated the Forest Preserve as a functioning ecological system rather than as land for recreation—indicating the extent to which the wilderness aesthetic had penetrated the culture. The makeup of the commission and its staff seemed calculated to produce documents leaning away from utilitarian thinking and toward a land ethic such as that promulgated by Aldo Leopold. Of course, the appointments reflected the predisposition of the governor and his advisors; as is the case with any politically created entity, it would be impossible to say that the views of the commission were exactly those of the New York electorate; indeed, during public hearings, many Adirondack natives argued that the commission's views were entirely out of step with public opinion.[15] But the very bias implied in the appointments indicates how the official notion of what was best for the Adirondacks had changed since the early part of the century.

The Temporary Study Commission noted that of all the public lands used for recreation in the United States, the Adirondack Forest Preserve was the only sizable parcel not subject to a management plan. As part of establishing and instituting such a plan, the commission—adopting the proposals advanced ten years earlier by the Joint Legislative Committee on Natural Resources—recommended that the Forest Preserve be administratively divided into several categories, according to the character of the forest and size of the parcel. Although all state lands were to continue to be protected under the forever-wild provision, the commission noted that Article XIV was not sufficient to protect wilderness as such; however strictly enforced, that provision resulted in "the maintenance of a wild forest environment, not wilderness."[16]

Acknowledging this distinction was a significant step, involving an insistence on a measure of purity in wilderness classification. In such a scheme, wilderness becomes a special kind of forest area; the degree of wilderness becomes the standard against which forest land is judged. The reason for designating certain lands within the Forest Preserve as wilderness was that since Article XIV was ambiguous, the conservation bureaucracy had not maintained all Forest Preserve land in a wilderness condition. In fact, one of the chief objectives of the commission was to curb the tendency of the Conservation Department to "improve" the Forest Preserve in the name of recreation. It acknowledged that this disposition to develop (with ranger stations, campsites, truck trails, and similar intrusions) rather than to preserve persisted in the conservation bureaucracy and that it was offensive to a wilderness aesthetic. To deal with this inclination, the commission insisted that "administrative personnel must develop totally new attitudes about their role and methods of work."[17] The recommendations of the Temporary Study Commission are thus doubly significant because they declared that a wilderness condition, for its own sake, was indeed a viable and valuable goal for at least part of the Forest Preserve, and because they identified the conservation bureaucracy as a major obstacle to wilderness values. It was the beginning of the institutionalization of a wilderness aesthetic for the Adirondacks.

Two of the proposed zoning categories were Wilderness and Primitive, the former being the least altered by human intrusions. Recommendation 36 stated, "In areas of the preserve classified as wilderness and primitive, the goal should be the perpetuation of natural plant and animal communities where the influence of man is not apparent."[18] These parcels of the Forest Preserve declared wilderness were those that already satisfied the commission's criteria. Primitive areas were pieces that nearly satisfied them but that contained one or more nonconforming characteristics; once these were eliminated, the primitive areas would be reclassifed as wilderness. In announcing a wilderness condition as the guide for classifying land, the commission offered its definition of the word "wilderness," basing it on the similar definition in the 1964 federal Wilderness Act:

> A wilderness, in contrast with those areas where man and his own works dominate the landscape, is hereby recognized as an area where the earth and its community of life are untrammeled by man—where man himself is a visitor who does not

remain. An area of wilderness is further defined to mean an area of undeveloped forest preserve land retaining its primeval character and influence, without permanent improvements or human habitation, which is protected and managed so as to preserve its natural conditions and which (1) generally appears to have been affected primarily by the forces of nature, with the imprint of man's work substantially unnoticeable; (2) has outstanding opportunities for solitude or a primitive and unconfined type of recreation; (3) has at least ten thousand acres of land or is of sufficient size and character as to make practicable its preservation and use in an unimpaired condition; and (4) may also contain ecological, geological, or other features of scientific, educational, scenic, or historical value.[19]

Though recreation and scenery are obviously part of what makes wilderness worth preserving, this definition also suggests how a wilderness aesthetic has achieved meaningful stature. To speak of "the earth and its community of life," to favor the "forces of nature" over those of man, is to admit the value of nature's processes. In this definition the processes themselves become part of the rationale for protecting a piece of landscape from other, non-natural, processes. And the processes of nature are what this definition sets out to protect. Throughout, the emphasis is on the land itself, not the ostensible benefits to mankind of preserving that land; the adjective "untrammeled" modifies "the earth and its community," not the human spirit, which presumably is equally unfettered when it encounters wilderness. The result of implementing this definition would be a place with rich recreational, scenic, and spiritual rewards, but the primary impulse is to preserve the dynamic system of untouched nature. "The aim," the report goes on to say, "is to perpetuate a blend of natural plant and animal life in which man's influence is not apparent."[20] By emphasizing the "plant and animal life" to be protected, rather than a scenic but static wild landscape, the commission chooses to see nature as something in flux, something dynamic.

Of the total acreage in the Forest Preserve at the time the Temporary Study Commission issued its reports, 43 percent was recommended for wilderness classification and another 5 percent for primitive, which would be added to the wilderness category as soon as possible. The remaining 52 percent would be classified wild forest. In these areas, considered "less fragile, in ecological terms, than those selected for wilderness or primitive," the Conservation Department would be permitted to proceed with recreational developments more or less as it had in the past. (Obviously, some of the rationale for distinguishing between wilderness and wild-forest status derived from purely practical issues such as size and administrative manageability, not exclusively from ecological or any other kind of fragility.) The commission emphasized that developments like leantos, fire towers, and "other administrative structures" were not necessarily encouraged in wild-forest areas and that their use had to be "compatibl[e] with a wild forest environment." The importance of the wild-forest areas lay in the political need to leave substantial acreage in the hands of the more development-minded elements within the Conservation Department (and thus available to nonwilderness forms of recreation like snowmobiling) and in the way in which what was allowed in those areas emphasized the required purity of the wilderness and primitive areas.[21]

In 1972, when the Adirondack Park Agency issued its State Land Master Plan to govern the administration of the Forest Preserve, the wilderness aesthetic was again stressed:

> Virtually every Adirondack ecosystem is represented in these wilderness areas—from the alpine, sub-alpine and boreal (spruce-fir) communities of the higher mountains through various mixtures of hardwoods of the middle elevations to the lowland lakes and ponds and a variety of wetland environments—truly an unparalleled spectrum of wilderness resources for this and future generations of New Yorkers.[22]

It is hard to miss the stress put here on ecological communities and systems, and the connection between them and the rationale for preserving wilderness.

In its discussion of the plant and animal communities of the wilderness areas, the Temporary Study Commission especially showed how it viewed nature as a working, comprehensive system. For one thing, it insisted that exotic species of flora and fauna were not to be introduced in wilderness areas. By establishing as the standard the natural community as it existed before European contact, the commission advanced an idea of natural harmony similar to that of George Perkins Marsh. But whereas

Marsh feared interference in this harmony on utilitarian grounds, the commission preferred the original biota for the simple fact of its originality. The very existence and presumed successful interaction of original plants and animals made them the desiderata.

Maintaining animal populations in their original numbers and species would preclude managing the forest to keep up a deer herd simply to meet the requirements of hunters. "The goal of all wildlife management in the Adirondack Park should be to foster a wild Adirondack environment and all the flora and fauna historically associated with that environment."[23] This passage appeared on the same page as a picture of a white-tailed deer with the caption, "Whitetail deer are the most important big game animal in the Adirondacks." But the hidden message of the text was that the state should not promote deer populations on the Forest Preserve. The white-tailed deer did not exist in large numbers in the original Adirondacks; the presence of a large herd in modern times was the direct result of human interference and implied an altered environment. By favoring an original wildlife population over one more useful for hunters, the commission was subtly advancing a wilderness aesthetic, in which all indigenous species, not just game animals, were accorded a protected niche in the Adirondack environment. "Emphasis on game animals is important," wrote the commission, admitting the role of hunting in the local economy, "but it should be balanced with the needs of other species."[24]

Among the species that the commission hoped to see encouraged were predators, several of which had been extirpated from the area. When the commission wrote, "The natural and beneficial role of the predator has become widely recognized," it confirmed what naturalists and wildlife specialists had known for years, but it treated in other than purely scientific terms the existence of the native predators it listed: "We must be wise enough to give such creatures the kind of protection they need and grateful that we have the knowledge to do so." The Canadian zoologist and wildlife specialist Dr. C. H. D. Clarke, hired as consultant by the commission, urged the reintroduction of wolves. He took special care to point out that wolves would be of no practical use and would not even exercise much control on the deer population, but "their simple presence adds wilderness atmosphere that is a positive value. . . . If wolves were reestablished in the Adirondacks, it would be an enlightened act, much to the credit of the people involved."[25] The presence in the Adirondacks of species that previous generations had done all they could to kill off had become an aesthetic necessity, as well as a measure of the judgment and morality of mankind. The absence of extirpated species was regrettable partly because the environment was to that degree less beautiful or useful, but even more because it indicated the extent to which it failed to satisfy the standard of wilderness.

As a symbol of the relationship between the indigenous wildlife and wilderness, the commission chose the moose. Moose had inhabited the Adirondacks until the middle of the nineteenth century but had vanished by about the time of the Civil War. Modern research has suggested that the primary culprit in the disappearance of this animal may not have been hunting, as was long thought, but the white-tailed deer. As lumbering and fires opened up thousands of acres of the Adirondacks to new growth, the habitat became much more favorable for deer, which do not prosper in a mature, closed-canopy forest, and the deer population increased dramatically. Unfortunately, deer commonly carry a roundworm or nematode to which they have a natural resistance but which is usually fatal to moose inhabiting the same range.[26]

Thus the explosion in the deer population accounted for the demise of the Adirondack moose. And thus the white-tailed deer was an omnipresent reminder of man's interference in the Adirondack environment, while the moose symbolized the wilderness which was and might be again. The Temporary Study Commission hoped that the moose could be successfully reintroduced in the parts of the Forest Preserve where decades of preservation had reduced the deer population to levels approximating those before the advent of lumbering. As Dr. Clarke put it, emphasizing the aesthetic value, "It would be nice to have a few moose to round out the picture."[27]

No single recommendation of this commission better illustrates its commitment to wilderness, even though the very act of reintroducing an extirpated species involves human interference in the environment. But in this case, the interference is calculated to restore the landscape, not to use it. The Temporary Study Commission was declaring that it preferred restoring wilderness purity to mollifying the deer hunters. It also was manifesting its abandonment of the primacy of the deer-hunting tradition, which had been so important in establishing the region's image in the nineteenth century and which depended on a view of nature requiring human mastery over a wild animal; the new aesthetic minimized such displays, encouraging a more passive appreciation. The white-tailed deer, moreover, in addition to being patent evidence of how human activity had altered the Adirondack environment, was a touchy economic issue. Many local merchants and innkeepers, who catered to autumn deer hunters, wanted the state to produce more deer, not fewer. They overtly favored managing the Forest Preserve to improve the deer habitat and were unconcerned about the niceties of Article XIV.[28] When the Temporary Study Commission indicated its preference for the indigenous moose, it manifested a radical dedication to wilderness as such. Dr. Clarke wrote, "Wildlife is, more than anything else, the hallmark of quality." And quality in the Adirondacks, as both Clarke and the Temporary Study Commission defined it, was the degree to which the Forest Preserve approached the purity of the original wilderness.[29]

As I write this last chapter, there are moose in the Adirondacks. Several have been seen at widely separated spots; a friend of mine saw one swimming across Long Lake in September of 1983. According to the wildlife specialist of the Adirondack Park Agency, these moose are thought to have wandered in from Ontario or northern New England. More important, they are thought to have a good chance of surviving—if they settle down in the older and thus wilder parts of the Forest Preserve, where they are less likely to encounter either a large deer herd or hunters.[30] The return of moose to the Adirondacks is an event of great significance—aesthetically, historically, symbolically. It demonstrates the persistence or rebirth of wilderness in the Adirondacks. It makes the Adirondack environment that much more appealing. It marks a turning point in the history of the Adirondacks, the point where natural processes have reasserted their possession of the landscape to the extent that an ancient resident is able to return to its ancient home. To the wilderness lover, it also suggests that natural processes may be more reliable than human plans: despite much talk about the reintroduction of extirpated species, nothing substantive has been done. Yet the moose has come back; its return suggests that, given a chance, natural processes can restore the old mix of dynamism and balance.

▲▲▲▲▲▲▲

A recent controversy concerning wilderness illustrates the current situation. Just east of the West Canada Lakes Wilderness Area and north of the town of Speculator in the central Adirondacks is a piece of land known as Perkins Clearing. For years, title to the roughly 19,000 acres of this parcel was divided between the state and International Paper Company in a complicated checkerboard pattern of dozens of small lots. One of the recommendations of the Temporary Study Commission was that the state should move to consolidate its holdings by exchanging some of its lands for an equal or larger acreage owned by International Paper. The Adirondack Park Agency also supported such an exchange and promoted it in the State Land Master Plan of 1972. Any exchange of Forest Preserve land requires a constitutional amendment, and such authorization for Perkins Clearing was duly passed by New York voters in 1979. As a result the state gained 10,344 acres immediately adjacent to its West Canada Lakes Wilderness Area in exchange for 7,133 acres located away from the wilderness area and closer to roads. Thus the state acquired a large parcel of contiguous lands, while International Paper consolidated its holdings and ended up with acreage that it could log more efficiently.

A problem arose, however, when the state moved to classify its new property (combining this with land already in the public domain but not currently part of the West Canada Lakes Wilderness, the state had some 17,000 acres to classify), as it was charged to do under the State Land Master Plan. Since the Perkins Clearing parcel was contiguous to the West Canada Lakes Wilderness Area, environmentalists—including the Adirondack Mountain Club, the Association for the Protection of the Adirondacks, the Atlantic Chapter of the Sierra Club, and the Adirondack Council—wanted it designated wilderness and immediately declared part of the existing wilderness area. In addition to the intrinsic wilderness value of the parcel in question, these groups feared that a less protective classification would threaten the West Canada Lakes Wilderness by opening up its core to motorized use and too many hunters. They argued, moreover, that such a designation had been the original intent of the Temporary Study Commission and the State Land Master Plan; any deviation from strict wilderness classification would be in violation of what voters had expected when they approved the exchange.

Local residents and an assortment of sportsmen's organizations, on the other hand, wanted at least some of the land classified as wild forest; this would have permitted greater road access and float-plane landings on Whitney Lake near the center of the parcel. They argued that complete wilderness classification would prohibit hunters and fishermen from using the more isolated parts of Perkins Clearing, that it would take money out of the local economy, and that it was but one of the latest efforts by an elite minority to "lock up" land for hikers and birdwatchers. In the face of this opposition, the Adirondack Park Agency began to retreat from its original advocacy of strict, inclusive wilderness status, advancing the case for some sort of mix of wilderness and wild-forest classification. This move found little favor with local residents, and it enraged conservationists who accused the Agency of "reneg[ing] on a commitment to the voters of the state."[31]

On January 20, 1984, the Park Agency issued its position on Perkins Clearing; in an effort to reach compromise among the various factions, it recommended classifying about 15,000 acres as wilderness and prohibiting float-plane landings, but placing about 1,900 acres in the wild-forest category. As the *Hamilton County News*, a local newspaper that consistently opposed wilderness classification, commented, "The Adirondack Park Agency has apparently managed to offend both environmentalists and sportsmen." The attempted compromise was short-lived, however, for a technical error was discovered in the maps accompanying the final report. The agency was forced to withdraw its decision, hold new hearings, and invite written and oral testimony from anyone interested. In its next effort at compromise, issued on April 16, 1984, the agency leaned slightly further away from the wilderness position. It voted to move 304 more acres from wilderness to wild-forest classification and to allow seasonal float-plane use of Whitney Lake. Again, virtually no one was happy. The Hamilton County Board of Supervisors, representing local anti-wilderness sentiment, unanimously voted to sue the Park Agency over its decision, which, the supervisors declared, demonstrated "the continued failure of the park agency to understand or respect the people of the Adirondacks." Environmentalists were equally offended: the Adirondack Mountain Club suggested that New Yorkers write to Governor Mario Cuomo and ask that he override the agency's decision. The more radical Adirondack Council entered its own lawsuit against the agency. Declaring that the action "condradicts all that wilderness stands for, all that modern wilderness management principles advocate, all that we as a society have espoused as wilderness policy," the council sued "to compel the state to reaffirm true wilderness status for the West Canada Lakes Wilderness." If the agency were not confronted on the issue, contended the council's Director, George Davis, "none of our magnificent Adirondack wilderness areas would be safe from the roar of the internal combustion engine."[32]

This controversy shows that the wilderness lobby is alive and active; its position has been well represented in magazines and newsletters. At the same time, the persistence of a substantial number of people to whom wilderness is irrelevant or who find it antagonistic to their needs reminds us that our society remains ambivalent about wilderness. Today, no less than at any time during the last century and a half, New Yorkers have not made up their collective mind about what to do with wilderness or the Adirondacks.

# Notes

## Introduction

1. George D. Davis, *Man and the Adirondack Environment: A Primer* (Blue Mountain Lake, N.Y.: Adirondack Museum, 1977); Michael G. DiNunzio, *Adirondack Wildguide: A Natural History of the Adirondack Park* (Elizabethtown, N.Y.: Adirondack Conservancy Committee and Adirondack Council, 1984).
2. The expression "environmental attitude" comes from Yi-Fu Tuan, *Topophilia: A Study of Environmental Perception, Attitudes, and Values* (Englewood Cliffs, N.J.: Prentice-Hall, 1974). Tuan's definition of "attitude" is on p. 4. In organizing my thinking on this subject, I found especially useful his chapters "Culture, Experience, and Environmental Attitudes," "Environment, Perception, and World Views," and "Topophilia and Environment."
3. Clyde Kluckhohn and Henry A. Murray, "The Determinants of Personality," in *Personality in Nature, Society, and Culture*, ed. Kluckhohn and Murray (New York: Alfred A. Knopf, 1948), p. 45.
4. The meaning of "Adirondack" is obscure; see my Introduction to Russell M. L. Carson, *Peaks and People of the Adirondacks* (Glens Falls, N.Y.: Adirondack Mountain Club, 1973), pp. xxxiv–xxxviii.
5. Aldo Leopold, *A Sand County Almanac, with Essays on Conservation from Round River* (San Francisco: Sierra Club, 1970), pp. 237–95. J. Baird Callicott explores the aesthetic implications of Leopold's ethic in "The Land Aesthetic," *Environmental Review* 7 (Winter 1983): 345–58. My definition of a wilderness aesthetic obviously omits much of what attracts people to the wilderness today—chiefly the challenge of survival away from the amenities and protections of civilization. This omission is a calculated one: as I hope to show, the aesthetic I am talking about here, at least in the case of the Adirondacks, is the critical element in modern statutory preservation.
6. Frank Graham, Jr., *The Adirondack Park: A Political History* (New York: Alfred A. Knopf, 1978); Norman J. VanValkenburgh, *The Adirondack Forest Preserve: A Chronology* (Blue Mountain Lake, N.Y.: Adirondack Museum, 1979); Roger C. Thompson, "The Doctrine

of Wilderness: A Study of the Policy and Politics of the Adirondack Preserve-Park," Ph.D. diss., State University College of Forestry, Syracuse University, 1962.
7. Roderick Nash, *Wilderness and the American Mind* (3rd ed.; New Haven, Conn.: Yale University Press, 1982), p. 1.
8. Public Law 88-577, Sept. 3, 1964, U.S.C. 16, § 1131. On the political and legislative steps leading up to the passage of the Wilderness Act see Nash, *Wilderness and the American Mind*, pp. 220–25.
9. But Tuan (*Topophilia*, pp. 102–12) argues that, because of certain changes in culture and attitudes toward nature, the only real "wilderness" is in the city.
10. Henry David Thoreau, *The Maine Woods* (Princeton, N.J.: Princeton University Press, 1972), p. 219.

## Chapter I First Impressions

1. Among the most useful secondary works on American attitudes toward nature are the following: Roderick Nash, *Wilderness and the American Mind* (3rd ed.; New Haven, Conn.: Yale University Press, 1982); Hans Huth, *Nature and the American: Three Centuries of Changing Attitudes* (Berkeley: University of California Press, 1957); Peter N. Carroll, *Puritanism and the Wilderness: The Intellectual Significance of the New England Frontier, 1629–1700* (New York: Columbia University Press, 1969); Leo Marx, *The Machine in the Garden: Technology and the Pastoral Ideal in America* (London: Oxford University Press, 1964); Arthur A. Ekirch, Jr., *Man and Nature in America* (New York: Columbia University Press, 1963); Alan Heimart, "Puritanism, the Wilderness and the Frontier," *New England Quarterly* 26 (Sept. 1953): 361–82; Perry Miller, *Errand into the Wilderness* (Cambridge, Mass.: Belknap Press, Harvard University Press, 1956), esp. pp. 204–16; Samuel P. Hays, *Conservation and the Gospel of Efficiency: The Progressive Conservation Movement, 1890–1920* (Cambridge, Mass.: Harvard University Press, 1959); Annette Kolodney, *The Lay of the Land: Metaphor as Experience in American Life and Letters* (Chapel Hill: University Press of North Carolina, 1975); Carolyn Merchant, *The Death of Nature: Women, Ecology, and the Scientific Revolution* (New York: Harper and Row, 1980); Lee Clark Mitchell, *Witnesses to a Vanishing America: The Nineteenth Century* (Princeton, N.J.: Princeton University Press, 1981); Barbara Novak, *Nature and Culture: American Landscape and Painting, 1825–1875* (New York: Oxford University Press, 1980); Cecelia Tichi, *New World, New Earth: Environmental Reform in American Literature from the Puritans to Whitman* (New Haven, Conn.: Yale University Press, 1979).
2. James DeKay, the zoologist of the Natural History Survey, was told that in 1815 a party of Canadian Indians ascended the Oswegatchie

River and "in a few weeks" collected three hundred beaver pelts. This can reasonably be taken as evidence of prior Indian use of the area (James E. DeKay, *Zoology of New York; Or, the New York Fauna* [2 vols.], Part I of *Natural History of New York* [Albany, N.Y.: Carroll and Cook, 1842], Vol. I, p. 73). But Indian activity in the Adirondack wilderness was slight, as is shown by the archaeological record and by the difficulty with which Thomas Pownall queried Indians about the region. Undoubtedly, Indians traveled through the area, and they must have had some settlements there, at least in the summer, but the scarcity of game caused by the climate and elevation, compared with other parts of New York, would have made the Adirondacks relatively uninviting. The maps of Indian sites in New York in William A. Ritchie, *The Archaeology of New York State* (rev. ed.; New York: Doubleday, 1965), pp. 4–5, 10–11, and 40–41, indicate relatively little Indian activity in the Adirondacks compared with that in the rest of the state.
3. Nash, *Wilderness and the American Mind*, pp. 8–22.
4. Richard Slotkin, *Regeneration Through Violence: The Mythology of the American Frontier, 1600–1860* (Middletown, Conn.: Wesleyan University Press, 1973), pp. 122 ff., offers one the latest discussions of this fear; see also Nash, *Wilderness and the American Mind*, pp. 29–30.
5. See Samuel H. Monk, *The Sublime: A Study of Critical Theories in XVIII-Century England* (New York: Modern Language Association of America, 1935), pp. 164–232. The changing attitude toward a particular feature of nature, mountains, is brilliantly discussed in Marjorie Hope Nicolson, *Mountain Gloom and Mountain Glory: The Development of the Aesthetics of the Infinite* (New York: W. W. Norton, 1963).
6. Alexis de Tocqueville, *Democracy in America*, ed. Phillips Bradley (2 vols.; New York: Random House, 1945), Vol. II, p. 78, cited in Nash, *Wilderness and the American Mind*, p. 23; Thomas Jefferson, *Notes on the State of Virginia*, ed. William Peden (Chapel Hill: University Press of North Carolina for the Institute of Early American History and Culture at Williamsburg, 1955), p. 19.
7. Edmund Burke, *A Philosophical Enquiry into the Origins of Our Ideas of the Sublime and the Beautiful*, ed. James T. Boulton (New York: Columbia University Press, 1958), p. 124; William Gilpin, *Remarks on Forest Scenery and Other Woodland Views* (2 vols.; London: R. Blamire, 1791). See Monk, *The Sublime*, and Nicolson, *Mountain Gloom*, for the English acceptance of the idea of the sublime. On the American acceptance, see Nash, *Wilderness and the American Mind*, pp. 44–66, and Huth, *Nature and the American*, pp. 30–53.
8. Burke, *Philosophical Enquiry*, p. 57.
9. Gilpin, *Remarks*, Vol. I, p. 127.

10. In a narrative of his travels, Cartier described the view from Mont Royal and thus provided what became, in the English translation published by John Florio in 1580, the first mention in English of the Adirondacks: "On the Northe side of it there are manye hilles to be seene, running Weaste and Easte, and as *manye more on the South*" (my emphasis) (Jacques Cartier, *A Short and Brief Narration of the Two Navigations and Discoveries to the Northwest Partes Called Newe Fraunce* [London: H. Bynneman, 1580], p. 54). William Chapman White, in *Adirondack Country* (New York: Alfred A. Knopf, 1954), p. 3, gives 1536 for the date of Cartier's ascent of Mont Royal. Samuel Eliot Morison, in *The European Discovery of America: The Northern Voyages* (New York: Oxford University Press, 1971), pp. 414–15, has 1535. See also William K. Verner, "Introduction," *Adirondack Bibliography Supplement, 1956–1965*, ed. Dorothy Plum (Blue Mountain Lake, N.Y.: Adirondack Museum, 1973), p. ix. Champlain's visit to the Adirondacks included his taking part in a battle between his Algonquin allies and a band of Iroquois whom they encountered near the present site of Crown Point (Samuel de Champlain, *Voyages of Samuel de Champlain, 1604–1618*, ed. W. L. Grant [New York: C. Scribner's Sons, 1907], pp. 163–66). For evidence of the Dutch belief in unicorns, see E. B. O'Callaghan, ed., *Documentary History of New York* (4 vols.; Albany, N.Y.: Weed, Parsons, 1850–1851), Vol. IV, p. 119; for the typical English map of the mid-eighteenth century, see the map drawn by Lewis Evans for Peter Kalm in 1750, printed as endpapers in Lawrence Henry Gipson, *Lewis Evans* (Philadelphia: Historical Society of Pennsylvania, 1939).
11. Evans' *General Map* and *Analysis* (originally published Philadelphia: B. Franklin and D. Hall, 1755) are reprinted in Gipson, *Lewis Evans*. See *Analysis*, p. 11.
12. William Johnson to Goldsboro Banyar, April 6, 1770, in Sir William Johnson, *The Papers of Sir William Johnson* (13 vols.; Albany: University of the State of New York, 1921–1962), Vol. XII, pp. 814–15; Archibald Campbell, "A Field Book of the Survey of . . . Part of the North Bounds of the Lands Purchased for the Benefit of Joseph Totten and Stephen Crossfield and Their Associates, 1772," in *Annual Report of the State Engineer and Surveyor of New York, 1903* (Assembly Document No. 65, 1904; Albany, N.Y.: J. B. Lyon, Jan. 15, 1904), pp. 431–32.
13. Thomas Pownall, *Topographical Description of the Dominions of the United States of America*, ed. Lois Mulkearn (Pittsburgh: University of Pittsburgh Press, 1949), pp. 50–51. This essay by Pownall, an expansion of a 1776 effort, was not published during his lifetime, being made available for the first time in Mulkearn's edition. Evans, *Analysis*, p. 9, in the margin next to the passage cited in note 11 above, had "Cooughsaghrage"; on the *General Map*, in large letters across the entire Adirondack region, running southwest to northeast, Evans

printed "COUXSAXRAGE," and in a note on the map he said that in Indian words like this one the letter X was to be pronounced like a Greek chi. The modern spelling is "Couchsachraga."
14. James Macauley, *The Natural, Statistical and Civil History of the State of New-York* (3 vols.; New York: Gould and Banks, 1829), Vol. II, pp. 12, 7; Joseph Henry, "Topographical Sketch of the State of New York," *Transactions of the Albany Institute* 1 (1830): 87–112, reprinted in *Scientific Writings of Joseph Henry* (3 vols.; Washington, D.C.: Smithsonian Institution, 1886), Vol. I, pp. 8–36. Henry gives the height of Whiteface as 2,686 feet (p. 20 of *Scientific Writings*). See also Thomas F. Gordon, *Gazetteer of the State of New York* (Philadelphia: the author, 1836), p. 448.
15. Macauley, *Natural, Statistical and Civil History*, Vol. II, p. 94.
16. Ibid., p. 105; Thomas Jefferson to Martha Jefferson Randolph, May 31, 1791, in *The Works of Thomas Jefferson*, ed. Paul Liecester Ford (12 vols.; New York: G. P. Putnam's Sons, 1904), Vol. VI, p. 264.
17. Timothy Dwight, *Travels in New-England and New-York* (4 vols.; New Haven, Conn.: S. Converse, 1822), Vol. III, pp. 244–51.
18. Ibid., p. 252. For later development on the lakes, see Frank Graham, Jr., *The Adirondack Park: A Political History* (New York: Alfred A. Knopf, 1978), and Harvey H. Kaiser, *Great Camps of the Adirondacks* (Boston: David R. Godine, 1982).
19. The best examples of this scholarly enterprise are probably Henry Nash Smith, *Virgin Land: The American West as Symbol and Myth* (New York: Harvard University Press, 1950), esp. pp. 123–83, and Marx, *The Machine in the Garden*, esp. pp. 73–144. For a more recent example, by a cultural geographer, see John R. Stilgoe, *The Common Landscape of America, 1580–1845* (New Haven, Conn.: Yale University Press, 1982), pp. 135–208.
20. Smith, *Virgin Land*, pp. 123 ff.; Marx, *The Machine in the Garden*, passim.
21. Timothy Dwight, a conservative Federalist, would probably not have received kindly the idea that he agreed with Thomas Jefferson on anything; the fact that these two men expressed similar views on aesthetics and the middle landscape indicates the pervasiveness of certain cultural attitudes.
22. Norman J. VanValkenburgh, *The Adirondack Forest Preserve* (Blue Mountain Lake, N.Y.: Adirondack Museum, 1979), pp. 3–18.
23. Alfred Lee Donaldson, *A History of the Adirondacks* (2 vols.; New York: Century, 1921), Vol. I, p. 213, Vol. II, pp. 31–32; Arthur H. Masten, *The Story of Adirondac* (privately printed, New York, 1923), p. 32; Ted Aber and Stella King, *The History of Hamilton County* (Lake Pleasant, N.Y.: Great Wilderness Books, 1965), p. 750. New York Forestry Commission, *Report* (Assembly Document No. 36, 1885; Albany, N.Y.: Weed, Parsons, 1885).

24. New York State Canal Board, "Report Relating to the Survey of the Several Branches of the Hudson River" (Senate Document No. 61, 1840; Albany, N.Y.: N. pub., 1840).

## Chapter II Progress or Nature

1. John A. Dix, "Report of the Secretary of State in Relation to a Geological Survey of the State," in *Documents of the Assembly of the State of New York, 1836* (Assembly Document No. 9; Albany, N.Y.: N. pub., 1836). The best account of the background, establishment, and work of the New York Natural History Survey is Michele Alexis La Clerque Aldrich, "New York Natural History Survey," Ph.D. diss., University of Texas at Austin, 1974. I am indebted to this thoroughly researched study for much of my discussion of the creation and aims of the Survey.
2. Cecil J. Schneer, "Ebenezer Emmons and the Foundation of American Geology," *Isis* 60 (Winter 1969): 450; Andrew Denny Rodgers III, *John Torrey: A Story of North American Botany* (New York: Hafner, 1965); John Mason Clarke, *James Hall of Albany: Geologist and Paleontologist* (Albany, N.Y.: N. pub., 1923); Samuel Reznick, "The Emergence of a Scientific Community in New York State a Century Ago," *New York History* 43 (July 1962): 215; William H. Goetzmann, *Exploration and Empire: The Explorer and Scientist in the Winning of the American West* (New York: W. W. Norton, 1966), p. 355. The New York Natural History Survey was "classic" in its comprehensiveness, its aim to embrace all of nature. In dividing its labors among a number of autonomous scientists, it differed in organization from most of the other surveys, which usually had one chief scientist with a host of assistants.
3. Dirk J. Struik, *Yankee Science in the Making* (New York: Collier, 1962), pp. 237–60; Goetzmann, *Exploration*, pp. 355–56; Ebenezer Emmons, *Geology of New-York*, Part II: *Comprising the Second Geological District* (Albany, N.Y.: Carroll and Cook, 1842), p. 1.
4. The only useful biographical sources on Emmons are the articles by George P. Merrill in the *Dictionary of American Biography*, Vol. VI (New York: Scribner, 1931), p. 149, and by Cecil J. Schneer in the *Dictionary of Scientific Biography*, Vol. IV (New York: Scribner, 1971), pp. 363–65. See also Ebenezer Emmons, *American Geology* (Albany, N.Y.: Sprague, 1855). There is no collection of Emmons' correspondence or papers. A few letters from Emmons to other scientists exist, but they contain no insights into his work in the Adirondacks. On Emmons' later career, see Markes Johnson, "The Second Geological Career of Ebenezer Emmons: Success and Failure in the Southern States, 1850–1860," in *The Geological Sciences in the Antebellum South*, ed. James Corgan (University: University of Alabama Press, 1982), pp. 142–70.

5. Edmund Burke, *A Philosophical Enquiry into the Origin of Our Ideas of the Sublime and Beautiful*, ed. James T. Boulton (New York: Columbia University Press, 1958). Emmons, *Geology of New-York*, p. 267; William C. Redfield, "Some Account of Two Visits to the Mountains in Essex County, New York, in the Years 1836 and 1837; with a Sketch of the Northern Sources of the Hudson," *American Journal of Science and Arts* 33 (July–Dec. 1837): 316. William Redfield was not officially connected with the Natural History Survey but had been invited by Emmons to participate in field explorations; see my Introduction to Russell M. L. Carson, *Peaks and People of the Adirondacks* (Glens Falls, N.Y.: Adirondack Mountain Club, 1973), pp. lxi–lxiv.
6. Ebenezer Emmons, "Fifth Annual Report of the Survey of the Second Geological District," in *Documents of the Assembly of the State of New York, 1841* (Assembly Document No. 150, 1841; Albany, N.Y.: N. pub., 1841), Vol. V, p. 115; Ebenezer Emmons, "Third Annual Report of the Survey of the Second Geological District," in *Documents of the Assembly of the State of New York, 1839* (Assembly Document No. 275, 1839; Albany, N.Y.: N. pub., 1839), Vol. V, p. 226.
7. Emmons, *Geology of New-York*, pp. 36–37; the animal that Emmons and others referred to as "panther" or "mountain lion" is properly called "puma."
8. Ebenezer Emmons, "Report of E. Emmons, Geologist of the 2d Geological District of the State of New York," in *Documents of the Assembly of the State of New York, 1838* (Assembly Document No. 200, 1838; Albany, N.Y.: N. pub., 1838), Vol. IV, pp. 247–48.
9. Emmons, *Geology of New-York*, p. 218; Ebenezer Emmons, "First Annual Report of the Second Geological District of the State of New York," in *Documents of the Assembly of the State of New York, 1837* (Assembly Document No. 161, 1837; Albany, N.Y.: N. pub., 1837), Vol. II, p. 103. On the resistance of American scientists to Lyell's doctrine of uniformitarianism (the position that only those geological forces currently operative had shaped the earth), see George H. Daniels, *Science in American Society* (New York: Alfred A. Knopf, 1971), pp. 206–22. By the time he wrote *American Geology* (p. 2), Emmons had changed his mind and rejected catastrophism (the position that accepted the historical reality of the biblical flood and other ancient past phenomena).
10. James E. DeKay, *Zoology of New York; Or, the New York Fauna* (2 vols.; Albany, N.Y.: Carroll and Cook, 1842–1844), Vol. I, pp. 28, 32, 43.
11. John Torrey, *A Flora of the State of New York*, (2 vols., Albany, N.Y.: Carroll and Cook, 1843), Vol. II, pp. 95, 231; see also Torrey to Benjamin Silliman, Aug. 23, 1837, John Torrey Papers, Library of the New York Botanical Gardens, Brooklyn, N.Y. Torrey does not supply either scientific or common names of the alpine plants he found on Marcy.

12. On the Marcy climb, see Carson, *Peaks and People*, pp. 53–55 and my Introduction, pp. xliii–li; Torrey to Silliman, Aug. 23, 1837, Torrey Papers; Redfield, "Some Account," pp. 301–23; James Hall's letter to *Albany Daily Advertiser*, Aug. 15, 1837.
13. Lewis C. Beck, "Report on the Mineralogical and Chemical Department of the Survey," in *Documents of the Assembly of the State of New York, 1841*, Vol. II (Assembly Document No. 150, 1841; Albany, N.Y.: N. pub., 1841. Emmons, *Geology of New-York*, p. 3; Emmons, "Report of E. Emmons," p. 185; Emmons, "Third Annual Report," p. 224.
14. Emmons, *Geology of New-York*, p. 165; Dix, "Report of the Secretary of State." On the American inclination to associate mineral wealth with mountainous or otherwise apparently useless land, see John R. Stilgoe, "Fair Fields and Blasted Rock: American Land Classification Systems and Landscape Aesthetics," *American Studies* 32 (Spring 1981): 26.
15. Emmons, *Geology of New-York*, , pp. 418–21, 224, 28–29; David Henderson to Archibald McIntyre, Sept. 8, 1833, quoted in Arthur H. Masten, *The Story of Adirondac* (privately printed, New York, 1923), p. 62.
16. Emmons, *Geology of New-York*, pp. 250, 245, 261, 263; Emmons, "First Annual Report," pp. 130–31, 224–25.
17. Masten, *Story of Adirondac*, pp. 129–43; Harold K. Hochschild, *The MacIntyre Mine: From Failure to Fortune* (Blue Mountain Lake, N.Y.: Adirondack Museum, 1962), p. 11.
18. In addition to Henry Nash Smith, *Virgin Land: The American West as Symbol and Myth* (Cambridge, Mass.: Harvard University Press, 1950), pp. 123–44, and Leo Marx, *The Machine in the Garden: Technology and the Pastoral Ideal in America* (New York and London: Oxford University Press, 1964), pp. 73–144, see also Morton White and Lucia White, *The Intellectual versus the City: From Thomas Jefferson to Frank Lloyd Wright* (New York: Mentor Books, 1977), pp. 6–35. Roderick Nash, *Wilderness and the American Mind* (3rd ed.; New Haven, Conn.: Yale University Press, 1982), pp. 38–43.
19. Emmons, "Third Annual Report," pp. 224–25.
20. Thomas F. Gordon, *Gazetteer of the State of New York* (Philadelphia: the author, 1836), p. 476; Emmons, *Geology of New-York*, p. 415; New York State Canal Board, "Report Relating to the Survey of the Several Branches of the Hudson River," (Senate Document No. 61, 1840; Albany, N.Y.: N. pub., 1840), p. 21; William C. H. Waddell, *Northern New York* (New York: G. P. Putnam, 1855), p. 14 (italics in original).
21. Lardner Vanuxem, *Geology of New York, Part III: Comprising the Survey of the Third Geological District* (Albany, N.Y.: Carroll and Cook, 1842), p. 256; Emmons, "Third Annual Report," p. 226; New York State Canal Board, "Report," p. 21; Emmons, *Agriculture of*

*New York* (5 vols.; Albany, N.Y.: Carroll and Cook, 1846–1854), Vol. I, p. 5.
22. New York State Canal Board, "Report," pp. 7, 14 (italics in original); Emmons, "Third Annual Report," p. 227.
23. Emmons, *Geology of New-York*, pp. 415, 203; Emmons, "Third Annual Report," pp. 227–29; "Memorial of George A. Simmons and Six Other Gentlemen . . . Stating the Results of a Survey of a Railroad and Steamboat Route from Lake Champlain to the County of Oneida," in *Documents of the Senate of the State of New York* (Senate Document No. 73, 1846; Albany, N.Y.: N. pub., 1846), Vol. III, pp. 10–20; Waddell, *Northern New York*, p. 15. See also *New York Times*, July 7, 1855; this corespondent was Henry Raymond, publisher and editor of the *Times*.
24. Emmons, "Fifth Annual Report," p. 125; New York State Canal Board, "Report," p. 8.
25. Frank Graham, Jr., *The Adirondack Park: A Political History* (New York: Alfred A. Knopf, 1978), pp. 31–32, 94, 132.
26. Emmons, "First Annual Report," p. 105; Ebenezer Emmons, "Fourth Annual Report of the Survey of the Second Geological District," in *Documents of the Assembly of the State of New York, 1840* (Assembly Document No. 50, 1840; Albany, N.Y.: N. pub., 1840), Vol. II, p. 296. On the emergence of conservationist sentiment in the Jacksonian era, see Lee Clark Mitchell, *Witnesses to a Vanishing America: The Ninetenth Century* (Princeton, N.J.: Princeton University Press, 1981), pp. 28–29.
27. Emmons, *Geology of New-York*, p. 416; Emmons, "Fifth Annual Report," p. 120.
28. Vanuxem, *Geology*, p. 256.
29. Emmons, "Third Annual Report," p. 226.

## Chapter III
### Romantic Sportsmen and Travelers

1. Joel T. Headley, *The Adirondack; Or, Life in the Woods* (New York: Baker and Scribner, 1849), p. i. On the subsequent editions and expansions of Headley, see my Introduction to the 1982 reprint (Harrison, N.Y.: Harbor Hill Books, 1982), pp. 10–14. On romantic travel literature, see Roderick Nash, *Wilderness and the American Mind* (3rd ed.; New Haven, Conn.: Yale University Press, 1982), pp. 60–66; Hans Huth, *Nature and the American: Three Centuries of Changing Attitudes* (Berkeley: University of California Press, 1957), pp. 71–86.
2. Nash, *Wilderness and the American Mind*, pp. 67–83; Huth, *Nature and the American*, pp. 71–128.
3. See E. R. Wallace, *Descriptive Guide to the Adirondacks*, appended to H. Perry Smith, *The Modern Babes in the Woods; Or, Summerings in the Adirondacks* (Hartford, Conn.: Columbian, 1872), p. 432.

On the Adirondack guideboat and its role in opening up the wilderness, see Kenneth Durant and Helen Durant, *The Adirondack Guide-Boat* (Camden, Maine: International Marine and Adirondack Museum, 1980).
4. Ralph Waldo Emerson, "The Adirondacs: A Journal Dedicated to My Fellow Travellers in August, 1858," *May-Day and Other Poems* (Boston: Ticknor and Fields, 1867), pp. 41–62. Subsequent verse quotations from Emerson are from this poem. On this camping trip, see also William James Stillman, *The Autobiography of a Journalist* (2 vols.; Cambridge, Mass.: Houghton, Mifflin, 1901), Vol. I, pp. 239–81. William F. Martin began building his hotel on Lower Saranac in 1849; it soon became one of the best known hostelries in the Adirondacks (Alfred Lee Donaldson, *A History of the Adirondacks* [2 vols.; New York: Century, 1921], Vol. I, pp. 292–304). On the allocation of guides in Emerson's party, see Stillman, *Autobiography*, Vol. I, pp. 246, 250. This camping trip, a famous episode in Adirondack history, is best described in Stillman, *Autobiography*, Vol.I, pp. 239–81; see also Donaldson, *History of the Adirondacks*, Vol. I, pp. 172–89, and Paul F. Jamieson, "Emerson in the Adirondacks," *New York History* 39 (July 1958): 215–37. Curiously, Emerson's stay in the Adirondack wilderness has been paid little attention by his biographers. For example, Gay Wilson Allen, *Waldo Emerson* (New York: Viking, 1981), briefly discusses Emerson's use of blank verse in the poem he wrote about the trip and incorrectly asserts that the party stayed in Stillman's "hunting lodge" (pp. 635–37). In fact, they camped in a temporary shelter constructed of saplings and spruce bark. Stillman memorialized the trip with a large painting, which now hangs in the Concord, Massachusetts, Free Public Library. Stillman also took photographs; these, among the earliest photographs of the central Adirondacks, are now in the collection of the Adirondack Museum.
5. Jamieson, "Emerson," pp. 222–23.
6. See E. R. Wallace, *Descriptive Guide to the Adirondacks: Revised and Enlarged* (Syracuse, N.Y.: Watson Gill, 1895), pp. 476–77.
7. Alfred B. Street, *Woods and Waters; Or, the Saranacs and Racket* (New York: M. Doolady, 1860), p. 190; T. Addison Richards, "A Forest Story," *Harper's New Monthly Magazine* 19 (June–Nov. 1859): 318; Charles Dudley Warner, "The Adirondacks Verified: A-Hunting of the Deer," *The Atlantic Monthly* 41 (April 1878): 524.
8. For typical descriptions of jacklighting, see Thomas Bangs Thorpe, "A Visit to 'John Brown's Tract,'" *Harper's New Monthly Magazine*, 19 (June–Nov. 1859): 175; S. H. Hammond, *Wild Northern Scenes; Or, Sporting Adventures with the Rifle and the Rod* (New York: Derby and Jackson, 1857), pp. 92–93; Headley, *The Adirondack*, pp. 184–89; or Street, *Woods and Waters*, pp. 82–93.
9. For a particularly maudlin example of the anthropomorphic attitude, see Warner, "The Adirondacks Verified," pp. 525–29, where this

otherwise rather cynical observer of the Gilded Age describes how a doe sacrifices herself to save her fawn from hounds and hunters.
10. Headley, *The Adirondack*, pp. 140–41.
11. Henry L. Ziegenfuss, "Piseco and T Lake Falls," *Forest and Stream* 18 (Feb. 16, 1882), 44–45.
12. Thorpe, "A Visit," pp. 170–71; F. S. Stallknecht and Charles E. Whitehead, "Sporting Tour in August, 1858," *Frank Leslie's Illustrated Weekly Newspaper* 6 (Nov. 1858): 378.
13. Warder H. Cadbury, "Biographical Sketch," in *A. F. Tait: Artist in the Adirondacks* (Blue Mountain Lake, N.Y.: Adirondack Museum, 1974), pp. 9–10.
14. Edmund Burke, *Philosophical Enquiry into the Origin of Our Ideas of the Sublime and Beautiful*, ed. James T. Boulton (New York: Columbia University Press, 1958). For analyses of Burke, see Boulton's Introduction, pp. xv–cxxvii; Samuel H. Monk, *The Sublime: A Study of Critical Theories in XVIII-Century England* (New York: Modern Language Association, 1935); Huth, *Nature and the American*, pp. 11–12; Barbara Novak, *Nature and Culture: American Landscape and Painting, 1825–1875* (New York: Oxford University Press, 1980), pp. 34–44; Earl A. Powell, "Luminism and the American Sublime," in *American Light: The Luminist Movement, 1850–1875*, ed. John Wilmerding (Washington, D.C.: National Gallery of Art, 1980), pp. 69–94.
15. Thorpe, "A Visit," p. 170; John Todd, *Long Lake* (Pittsfield, Mass.: E. P. Little, 1845), pp. 22–23.
16. Headley, *The Adirondack*, pp. 60–61, 67, 71–72; Charles Fenno Hoffman, *Wild Scenes in the Forest and Prairie* (New York: W. H. Colyer, 1843), p. 36; Jervis McEntee, "Diary of 1851 Summer Spent in Adirondacks, 1851," MS 67-19, Adirondack Museum, n.p.; Burke, *Philosophical Enquiry*, p. 124.
17. Headley, *The Adirondack*, pp. 174, 145.
18. Ibid., pp. 181–82.
19. Todd, *Long Lake*, pp. 92, 29; Henry J. Raymond, "A Week in the Wilderness," *New York Times*, June 26, 1855.
20. S. H. Hammond, *Hills, Lakes, and Forest Streams; Or, A Tramp in the Woods* (New York: J. C. Derby, 1854), p. 175; Henry Nash Smith, *Virgin Land: The American West as Symbol and Myth* (Cambridge, Mass.: Harvard University Press, 1950); Leo Marx, *The Machine in the Garden: Technology and the Pastoral Ideal in America* (London: Oxford University Press, 1964); John R. Stilgoe, "Fair Fields and Blasted Rock: American Land Classification Systems and Landscape Aesthetics," *American Studies* 32 (Spring 1981): 21–22, and Cecelia Tichi, *New World, New Earth: Environmental Reform in American Literature from the Puritans Through Whitman* (New Haven, Conn.: Yale University Press, 1979).
21. William Gilpin, *Observations on the Western Parts of England,*

*Relative Chiefly to Picturesque Beauty* (London: T. Cadell and W. Davies, 1798), p. 328 (italics in original).

22. Thomas Cole, personal journal, quoted in Louis Legrand Noble, *The Life and Works of Thomas Cole*, ed. Elliot S. Vesell (Cambridge, Mass.: Belknap Press, Harvard University Press, 1964), p. 177; Street, *Woods and Waters*, p. 31. For illustrative examples of the common use of this motif, see the works by Sanford Gifford, Frederick Church, Thomas Cole, Asher B. Durand, George Caleb Bingham, Thomas Doughty, Homer Dodge Martin, and Jasper Francis Cropsey in *The Natural Paradise: Painting in America, 1800–1950*, ed. Kynaston McShine (New York: Museum of Modern Art, 1976), pp. 21, 38, 49, 58, 61, 62, 71, 91, 92, 96.

23. Cole, in Noble, *Life and Works of Thomas Cole*, p. 179; Headley, *The Adirondack*, p. 146; McEntee, "Diary"; Richards, "Forest Story," p. 466; Noble, *Life and Works*, p. 280.

24. Hammond, *Hills, Lakes*, pp. 143–44; Street, *Woods and Waters*, pp. 238–39, 43, 285–86. For a somewhat different discussion of the romantic response to process in nature, see James McIntosh, *Thoreau as Romantic Naturalist* (Ithaca, N.Y.: Cornell University Press, 1974), pp. 55–58.

25. Street, *Woods and Waters*, p. 302; Todd, *Long Lake*, p. 64.

26. Todd, *Long Lake*, pp. 65–68; Stillman, *Autobiography*, Vol. I, p. 214; Richard Slotkin, *Regeneration Through Violence: The Mythology of the American Frontier, 1600–1860* (Middletown, Conn.: Wesleyan University Press, 1973), pp. 94–145; Peter Carroll, *Puritanism and the Wilderness: The Intellectual Significance of the New England Frontier, 1629–1700* (New York: Columbia University Press, 1969), pp. 11, 74–75, 111–14; Nash, *Wilderness and the American Mind*, pp. 33–38.

27. Headley, *The Adirondack*, p. 44, where the pronouns are second person. For the sake of readability I have changed them to first person.

28. For comments on Emerson's response to the idea of technological progress and for a brief discussion of Emerson's visit to the Adirondacks, see Joseph Jones, "Thought's New-Found Path and the Wilderness: 'The Adirondacs,'" in *Emerson: Prospect and Retrospect*, ed. Joel Porte (Harvard English Studies, vol. 10; Cambridge, Mass.: Harvard University Press, 1982), pp. 105–19.

29. Emerson's visit to Yosemite in 1871 and his encounter there with John Muir are well known, but since Emerson refused Muir's invitation to join him on a camping trip and stayed in a comfortable inn, we can hardly call that journey a genuine wilderness experience (Allen, *Waldo Emerson*, pp. 650–51; see also Stephen Fox, *John Muir and His Legacy: The American Conservation Movement* [Boston: Little, Brown, 1981], pp. 4–6).

30. Ralph Waldo Emerson, *The Complete Works of Ralph Waldo Emerson* (Centenary Edition, Boston: Houghton, Mifflin, 1903–1904), Vol.

I, p. 10. Nash (*Wilderness and the American Mind*, p. 86) quotes this very sentence as evidence of Emerson's positive response to wilderness.
31. William James Stillman, *The Old Rome and the New and Other Studies* (London: Grant Richards, 1897), p. 293.
32. Street, *Woods and Waters*, pp. 95–96.
33. Street, *Woods and Waters*, p. 12.
34. S. H. Hammond and L. W. Mansfield, *Country Margins and Rambles of a Journalist* (New York: J. C. Derby, 1855), pp. 317–19; Street, *Woods and Waters*, pp. 99–101, 106–17; William James Stillman, "Sketchings," *The Crayon* 2 (July–Dec. 1855): 280–81, 296, 328–29; Richards, "Forest Story," p. 319.
35. Hammond, *Wild Northern Scenes*, pp. 33–34, 82–84.

## Chapter IV The Gilded Age

1. The best source on Murray's life is Warder H. Cadbury's Introduction to the 1970 reprint of Murray's *Adventures in the Wilderness* (Syracuse, N.Y.: Syracuse University Press and Adirondack Museum), pp. *40–52*; the pagination in this volume can be confusing, the Murray text is duplicated by photo offset with original page numbers, and Cadbury's introduction is paginated with italicized Arabic numerals. See also Alfred Lee Donaldson, *A History of the Adirondacks* (2 vols.; New York: Century, 1921), Vol. I, pp. 190–201; Roderick Nash, *Wilderness and the American Mind* (3rd ed.; New Haven, Conn.: Yale University Press, 1982), p. 116; Frank Graham, Jr., *The Adirondack Park: A Political History* (New York: Alfred A. Knopf, 1978), pp. 23–30. Murray's name appears in the hotel's register, a typescript of which is at the Adirondack Museum (Cadbury, "Introduction," p. *32*).
2. William H. H. Murray, *Adventures in the Wilderness; Or, Camp-Life in the Adirondacks* (Boston: Fields, Osgood, 1869), pp. 9–14; Cadbury, "Introduction," p. *40*; Donaldson, *History of the Adirondacks*, Vol. I, pp. 243–72; Graham, *Adirondack Park*, pp. 45–52.
3. For a similar discussion of stylistic differences, see Cadbury, "Introduction," pp. *62–63*.
4. *Forest and Stream* 38 (Jan. 28, 1892): 74; Kate Field, "Among the Adirondacks: Murray's Fools—A Plain Talk About This Wilderness," *New-York Daily Tribune*, Aug. 12, 1869; Wachusett [pseud.], "With the Multitudes in the Wilderness," *Boston Daily Advertiser*, July 17, 19, 22, 23, 24, 26, 30, 1869 (the passage quoted is from the July 17 issue). On the basis of entries in hotel registers, William K. Verner has tentatively identified Wachusett as George B. Wood (see Cadbury, "Introduction," p. *40*). See also Edward B. Osborne, *Letters from the Woods; Random Rhymes; Annual Addresses* (Poughkeepsie, N.Y.: N. pub., 1893), p. 38.
5. Thomas Bangs Thorpe, "The Abuses of the Backwoods," *Appleton's*

*Journal* 2 (Dec. 1869): 564. For a modern expression of the patronizing response to novices in the woods, see Joseph Bruchac, "High Peaks and Herd Paths," *Adirondack Life* 7 (Summer 1976): 12–13, 47–49, 56–57.
6. Charles Dudley Warner, "The Adirondacks Verified: Camping Out," *The Atlantic Monthly* 41 (Jan.–June 1878), pp. 755–60; *Forest and Stream* 20 (May 3, 1883): 263 and 30 (July 12, 1888): 489.
7. See Thomas L. Altherr, "The American Hunter-Naturalist and the Development of the Code of Sportsmanship," *Journal of Sport History* 5 (Spring 1978): 7–22.
8. For a pre-Murray example of this frequent lament, see Alfred B. Street, *Woods and Waters. Or, the Saranacs and Racket* (New York: M. Doolady, 1860), p. xix, where Street declares that shooting deer is becoming more difficult because of an increase in the number of sportsmen.
9. The *Forest and Stream* deer editorials are far too numerous to list; for a typical sample, see 24 (1885): 2, 21, 41, 81, 101, 162, 181, 221, 266, 305, 365, 405, 445, and 485. For editorials on logging, see, for example, 20 (1883): 22, 142, 481, and 484–85.
10. *Forest and Stream*, 15 (Sept. 16, 1880): 125 and 18 (April 13, 1883): 206. Nessmuk's Adirondack writings have been collected and reprinted in *The Adirondack Letters of George Washington Sears*, ed. Dan Brenan (Blue Mtn. Lake, N.Y.: Adirondack Museum, 1962).
11. Ibid. 20 (April 12, 1883): 209–10 and 30 (July 19, 1888): 51.
12. *New-York Daily Tribune*, Aug. 12, 1869; Cadbury, "Introduction," pp. 46–48; Osborne, *Letters*, p. 44; W. H. H. Murray, "The Adirondacks: Murray on Murray's Fools, His Reply to His Calumniators," *New-York Daily Tribune*, Oct. 23, 1869 (this letter was reprinted in the *Boston Journal*, Oct. 30, 1869, as "The Adirondacks: Mr. Murray's Reply to His Calumniators," and in the Adirondack Museum reprint of *Adventures in the Wilderness*, at the end of the book after the text, but with continued italicized pagination from Cadbury's introduction, pp. 77–95).
13. "Murray's Reply," pp. 93–94, in ibid.
14. In 1875, a letter to *Forest and Stream* reported that Murray was hunting near Cranberry Lake and unjustly accused him of hounding deer out of season; a few weeks later a friend of Murray's wrote to insist that Murray had never killed a deer before hounds in his life (*Forest and Stream* 5 [Sept. 2, 1875]: 57 and 5 [Nov. 25, 1875]: 251). On the "democratic dilemma," see also Cadbury, "Introduction," pp. 71–75.
15. Nash, *Wilderness and the American Mind*, p. 116; Hans Huth, *Nature and the American: Three Centuries of Changing Attitudes* (Berkeley: University of California Press, 1957), p. 110; Graham, *Adirondack Park*, pp. 23–30.
16. Colvin's annual reports on his surveying were submitted to the state legislature between 1873 and 1897 and are cited below. One statement of Colvin's that might indicate a preservationist position is the

following, found in his *Report on the Topographical Survey for the Year 1873* (Senate document No. 98, 1874; Albany, N.Y.: Weed, Parsons, 1874), hereafter cited as *Second Topo*: writing of the high peak region, he suggests it "should be forever preserved in its natural wilderness condition as a forest park or timber reserve" (p. 166). The important qualifier here, of course, is "timber reserve." It is likely that, in visualizing the preservation of "wilderness," Colvin did not foresee an absolute prohibition on logging.

17. *Who's Who in New York* (New York: L. R. Hamersby, 1904), pp. 138–39; "The Adirondack Survey," *New-York Daily Tribune*, March 5, 1883, cited in Marvin Wolf Kranz, "Pioneering in Conservation: A History of the Conservation Movement in New York State, 1865–1903," Ph.D. diss., Syracuse University 1961, p. 46; Verplanck Colvin, *Report on the Adirondack State Land Survey to the Year 1884 with a Description of the Location of the Boundaries of the Great Land Patents* (Assembly Document No. 126, 1884; Albany, N.Y.: Weed, Parsons, 1884), p. 26; Colvin, *Second Topo*, pp. 161–62.
18. Verplanck Colvin, *Seventh Annual Report on the Progress of the Topographical Survey of the Adirondack Region of New York, to the Year 1879, Containing the Condensed Reports for the Years 1874–75–76–77 and '78* (Assembly Document No. 87, 1879; Albany, N.Y.: Weed, Parsons, 1880), p. 67; hereafter cited as *Seventh Topo*.
19. Colvin, *Seventh Topo*, p. 66.
20. Ibid., p. 89; *Forest and Stream* 19 (Aug. 1882): 22.
21. Colvin, *Second Topo*, p. 55; Colvin, *Seventh Topo*, pp. 23–24.
22. Colvin, *Seventh Topo*, p. 301.
23. Colvin, *Seventh Topo*, pp. 361, 83–101.
24. George Perkins Marsh, *Man and Nature; Or, Physical Geography as Modified by Human Action* (New York: Charles Scribner, 1864); David Lowenthal, *George Perkins Marsh: Versatile Vermonter* (New York: Columbia University Press, 1958), pp. 267–68; Verplanck Colvin, *Ascent and Barometrical Measurement of Mount Seward* (Albany, N.Y.: Argus, 1872). Fears about the deterioration of the Adirondack watershed also surfaced in the first and only report of the New York State Park Commission (of which Colvin was the secretary), created by the legislature in 1872 (Commissioners of State Parks, *First Annual Report of the Commissioners of State Parks* [Senate Document 102, 1873; Albany, N.Y.: Weed, Parsons, 1874]). The connection between Marsh's warnings about watershed and fears about lumbering in the Adirondacks is discussed in the next chapter. The only known reference by Colvin to Marsh appears in a letter from Colvin to the *New York Tribune*, March 17, 1902, where Colvin refers to Marsh's work by its 1864 title, *Man and Nature*. This letter was pointed out to me by William K. Verner, who found it cited in an unpublished manuscript on Colvin by Joseph Jillisky.
25. James Russell Lowell, "Marsh's Man and Nature," *North American*

Review 99 (1864): 320; Marsh, *Man and Nature*, pp. 15–17 and passim; Roger B. Stein, *John Ruskin and Aesthetic Thought in America, 1840–1900* (Cambridge, Mass.: Harvard University Press, 1967), pp. 164–65.
26. Verplanck Colvin, "The Discovery of the Source of the Hudson," in Russell M. L. Carson, *Peaks and People of the Adirondacks* (Garden City, N.Y.: Doubleday, Page, 1927; rpt. Glens Falls, N.Y.: Adirondack Mountain Club, 1973), pp. 138–44. This account was not published during Colvin's lifetime. It was owned by Mills Blake, Colvin's assistant, and lent to Carson for inclusion in *Peaks and People*.
27. Marsh, *Man and Nature*, p. 464.
28. Colvin, *Seventh Topo*, pp. 193, 146.
29. Marsh, *Man and Nature*, p. 30.
30. Verplanck Colvin, *Annual Report of the Superintendent of the Adirondack Survey* (Assembly Document No. 1883; 177, Albany, N.Y.: N. pub., 1883), p. 22; hereafter cited as *Eleventh Topo*.
31. As Marsh wrote in *Man and Nature*, "The fact that, of all organic beings, man alone is to be regarded as essentially a destructive power . . . tends to prove that, though living in physical nature, he is not of her, that he is of more exalted parentage, and belongs to a higher order of existences than those born of her womb and submissive to her dictates" (pp. 36–37); see Lowenthal, *George Perkins Marsh*, pp. 270–76. Kranz, in "Pioneering in Conservation," p. 47, writes that Colvin in the middle of his career "called for absolute preservation," and Frank Bergon in his headnotes for *The Wilderness Reader* (New York: Mentor, 1980), p. 188, writes that "Colvin appealed to all interests to protect the wilderness for posterity." These are incorrect assessments of Colvin's views. Throughout his career Colvin advocated various schemes that were utterly inconsistent with wilderness preservation.
32. Colvin, *Second Topo*, p. 45; Colvin, *Seventh Topo*, pp. 49–50; Colvin, *Eleventh Topo*, p. 27; Verplanck Colvin, *Report on the Progress of the State Land Survey of the State of New York* (Senate Document No. 48, 1891; Albany, N.Y.: James B. Lyon, 1891), pp. 47–48 and p. 27, where Colvin reacted positively to a large lumbering operation he encountered in southern St. Lawrence County.
33. Verplanck Colvin, *Report on a Topographical Survey of the Adirondack Wilderness of New York* (Government Document [no No.]; Albany, N.Y.: Argus, 1873), pp. 41, 30; Colvin, *Second Topo*, pp. 288, 105. Colvin repeatedly pushed this scheme in his reports and other writings, most notably in a speech he delivered to the New York Board of Trade and Transportation on Washington's Birthday, 1885; to emphasize his point concerning the future value of Adirondack drinking water to New York City, Colvin brought to this banquet a huge cake of Adirondack ice and thus contributed ice and water for a toast (the teetotaling Colvin would never have toasted with wine).

This speech was published as a pamphlet, *The Adirondacks: Speech Delivered at the Annual Banquet of the New York Board of Trade and Transportation, Washington's Birthday, 1885* (New York: George F. Nesbit, 1885). See also Colvin, *Eleventh Topo*, p. 8.
34. *Forest and Stream* 17 (Dec. 15, 1881): 386 and 15 (Nov. 25, 1880): 325.
35. Colvin, *Seventh Topo*, pp. 7–8.
36. Ibid., p. 8.
37. In Verplanck Colvin, *Report on the Progress of the State Land Survey* (Senate Document No. 32, 1893; Albany, N.Y.: N. pub., 1893), pp. 37–38, hereafter cited as *Eighth Land*.
38. Verplanck Colvin, *Report of the Superintendent of the State Land Survey of the State of New York* (Senate Document No. 42, 1896; Albany: Wynkoop Hallenbeck Crawford, 1896), pp. 90–91.
39. One result of the Marshall brothers' reading in the Colvin reports was their successful effort to climb all the high peaks over 4,000 feet above sea level; this helped set off the modern boom in recreational climbing in the Adirondacks. Robert Marshall's little book about the forty-six peaks that the then-current topographic maps indicated as satisfying their altitude criterion was his first published response to wilderness: *The High Peaks of the Adirondacks* (Albany, N.Y.: Adirondack Mountain Club, 1922). On Marshall, see Nash, *Wilderness and the American Mind*, pp. 200–208; Stephen Fox, *John Muir and His Legacy: The American Conservation Movement* (Boston: Little, Brown, 1981), pp. 206–12. In a letter to me (June 30, 1979), George Marshall wrote of the impact of Colvin on himself and his brother: "There was a definite influence. We greatly admired him. . . . We read the Colvin Reports, especially the accounts of his extraordinary trips in the mountains and into the Adirondack wilderness. We were also interested in his hypsometry and mappings and drawings, and they excited us too. . . . Colvin, because of what he represented in his Adirondack exploration and enthusiasms, could not have helped stimulating the enthusiasms of two young Adirondackers."

## Chapter V Wilderness Preserved

1. Ebenezer Emmons, "First Annual Report of the Second Geological District of the State of New York." in *Documents of the Assembly of the State of New York, 1837* (Assembly Document No. 161, 1837; Albany, N.Y.: N. pub., 1837), Vol. II, p. 105; Ebenezer Emmons, "Fourth Annual Report of the Survey of the Second Geological District," in *Documents of the Assembly of the State of New York, 1840* (Assembly Document No. 50, 1840; Albany, N.Y.: N. pub., 1840), p. 926; W. W. Ely, "A Trip to the Wilderness," *Moore's Rural New Yorker* 11 (1860): 289; *New York Times*, Aug. 9, 1864.
2. Alfred Lee Donaldson, *A History of the Adirondacks* (2 vols.; New York: Century, 1921), Vol. II, pp. 150–59; Harold K. Hochschild,

*Lumberjacks and Rivermen in the Central Adirondacks, 1850–1950* (Blue Mountain Lake, N.Y.: Adirondack Museum, 1962); William F. Fox, *A History of the Lumber Industry in the State of New York* (U.S. Department of Agriculture, Bureau of Forestry Bulletin No. 34; Washington, D.C.: Government Printing Office, 1902).

3. George Perkins Marsh, *Man and Nature; Or, Physical Geography as Modified by Human Action* (New York: Charles Scribner, 1864; rpt. ed. David Lowenthal, Cambridge, Mass.: Belknap Press, Harvard University Press, 1965). All subsequent references to Marsh are to the Lowenthal reprint of the 1864 edition of *Man and Nature*. The important role played by Marsh in influencing opinion on Adirondack matters is suggested in Marvin Wolf Kranz, "Pioneering in Conservation: A History of the Conservation Movement in New York State, 1865–1903," Ph.D. diss., Syracuse University, 1961, p. 41; in William K. Verner, "Wilderness and the Adirondacks: An Historical View," *The Living Wilderness* 33 (Winter 1969): 34; and in Frank Graham, Jr., *The Adirondack Park: A Political History* (New York: Alfred A. Knopf, 1978), pp. 67, 75. My discussion of conservation in the Adirondacks depends heavily on Kranz for facts and chronology.

4. Marsh, *Man and Nature*, pp. 3, 42–43, 119, 186. The 1864 edition of *Man and Nature* specifically addressed Adirondack issues, as did subsequent editions. Marsh noted the extensive forests in the Adirondack region and acknowledged (thinking, apparently, of the Park Commission) that conservation proposals were being considered. He commented approvingly on the fact that other than utilitarian motives seemed to be behind them, but he went on to insist that the main reason for protection of forests in the Adirondacks was to save the watershed. He concluded his discussion with the importance of maintaining the water level in the Hudson (pp. 203–5). See also George Perkins Marsh, *The Earth as Modified by Human Action* (New York: Scribner and Armstrong, 1874), pp. 327–29. Marsh's views on the Adirondacks are also discussed (with a somewhat different emphasis) in Craig W. Allin, *The Politics of Wilderness Preservation* (Westport, Conn.: Greenwood, 1982), pp. 26–27, 30–31.

5. *Laws of New York, 1872*, chap. 848; New York State Commissioners of State Parks, *First Annual Report* (Senate Document No. 102, 1873; Albany, N.Y.: Weed, Parsons, 1874), pp. 13–19. The New York effort to legislate watershed control by public ownership and protection thus antedated by several years the first similar attempt on the federal level. In 1876, legislation was introduced in Congress to insure that "all public timber lands adjacent to the sources of affluents of all the rivers be withdrawn from public sale and entry." Like the Adirondack Park proposal, this effort failed to win sufficient friends. The Forest Reserve Act of 1891, however, officially recognized watershed protection as an important and legitimate reason for protecting federally

owned forested land (Harold K. Steen, *The U.S. Forest Service: A History* [Seattle: University of Washington Press, 1976], p. 123). On Hough and the Adirondacks, see Arthur A. Ekirch, Jr., "Franklin B. Hough: First Citizen of the Adirondacks," *Environmental Review* 7 (Fall 1983): 271–74.

6. *Forest and Stream* 1 (Sept. 11, 1873): 73; *New York Times*, July 6, 1873, and Feb. 28, 1874.
7. Alonzo B. Cornell, *Public Papers of Alonzo B. Cornell, Governor of the State of New York, 1882* (Albany, N.Y.: E. H. Bender's Sons, 1883), annual message to legislature, Jan. 3, 1882; *Forest and Stream* 19 (Jan. 25, 1883): 502 and 21 (Dec. 13, 1883): 381; see also *Forest and Stream* 20 (Feb. 8, 1883): 22 and 34 (Jan. 23, 1890): 1.
8. *Laws of New York, 1883*, chap. 13; Kranz, "Pioneering in Conservation," p. 147.
9. The Sargent Commission Report is officially titled Forestry Commission, *Report* (Assembly Document No. 36, 1885; Albany, N.Y.: Weed, Parsons, 1885); *Laws of New York, 1885*, chap. 283.
10. S. B. Sutton, *Charles Sprague Sargent and the Arnold Arboretum* (Cambridge, Mass.: Harvard University Press, 1970), pp. 97–104; Graham, *Adirondack Park*, p. 105; Norman J. VanValkenburgh, *The Adirondack Forest Preserve* (Blue Mountain Lake, N.Y.: Adirondack Museum, 1979), pp. 32–34.
11. *Garden and Forest* 3 (March 12, 1890): 121. The reference to a sanitarium derives from the establishment in the Saranac Lake area of several sanitaria devoted to the treatment of tuberculosis; see Donaldson, *History of the Adirondacks*, Vol. I, pp. 273–88; Graham, *Adirondack Park*, pp. 51–52.
12. *Harper's Weekly* 29 (Jan. 24, 1885), 56, 58; see also *Harper's Weekly* 28 (Dec. 6, 1884), 795, 802–3, where Rix's engravings of "Destruction of Forests in the Adirondacks" appear, one on the front cover.
13. For example, see William James Stillman, "Sketchings," *The Crayon* 2 (July–Dec. 1855), 280–81, 296, 328–29. A. Judd Northrup, *Camps and Tramps in the Adirondacks* (Syracuse, N.Y.: Davis, Bardeen, 1880), p. 222; Charles Dudley Warner, "The Adirondacks Verified: A Fight with a Trout," *The Atlantic Monthly* 41 (Jan.–June 1878): 343; L. E. Chittenden, *Personal Reminiscences, 1840–1890* (New York: Richmond, Croscup, 1893), p. 167; *Forest and Stream* 1 (Nov. 27, 1873): 244; *Forest and Stream* 2 (Feb. 19, 1874): 21; *Forest and Stream* 4 (May 13, 1875): 212; *Forest and Stream* 15 (Sept. 16, 1880): 125; *Forest and Stream* 18 (April 13, 1883): 206.
14. On the rise of scientific forestry in America, see Samuel P. Hays, *Conservation and the Gospel of Efficiency: The Progressive Conservation Movement, 1890–1920* (New York: Atheneum, 1969), pp. 27–48.
15. Commissioners of State Parks, *First Annual Report*, pp. 5, 20.

16. New York State Senate, "Report of the Special Committee on State Lands in the Adirondack Region," (Senate Document No. 23, 1884; Albany, N.Y.: N. pub., 1884).
17. *Harper's Weekly* 28 (Dec. 6, 1884): 805; ibid. 29 (Feb. 7, 1885): 82–85; ibid. 29 (May 30, 1885): 338; *Forest and Stream* 24 (Jan. 29, 1885): 2; *Forest and Stream* 23 (Jan. 22, 1885): 502; *Forest and Stream* 24 (May 21, 1885): 325; *New York Times*, May 30, 1885. The *Times* was more sanguine about Basselin's appointment, suggesting that a lumberman could make a valuable contribution to the Forestry Commission's work, but later (Feb. 26, 1890) it pointed to Basselin's presence as one source of the commission's incompetence.
18. *New York Times*, Sept. 16, 18, 23, 25, Oct. 4, 6, 1889; New York State Forestry Commission, *First Annual Report* (Assembly Document No. 103, 1886; Albany, N.Y.: N. pub., 1886), p. 13.
19. Hays, *Conservation*, passim, esp. pp. 1–4, 261–76.
20. See *New York Times*, Feb. 26, 1890; see also Assembly Committee on Public Lands and Forestry, *Reports of the Majority and Minority . . . Relative to the Administration of the Laws in Relation to the Forest Preserve by the Forest Commission* (Assembly Document No. 81, 1891, Albany, N.Y.: Weed, Parsons, 1891), where the need for reorganization of the Forestry Commission was urged. See also *Garden and Forest* 2 (July 19, 1889): 345 and 4 (June 10, 1891): 265.
21. *Laws of New York*, 1892, chap. 707. Since 1892 the state has acquired much of the then private land, but the park boundary has grown to include some six million acres of the Adirondack region, and the state owns only about two-fifths of the total. Roderick Nash, in *Wilderness and the American Mind* (3rd ed.; New Haven, Conn.: Yale University Press, 1982), p. 108, asserts that the Adirondack Park legislation was evidence that "the recreational rationale for wilderness preservation had finally achieved equal legal recognition with more practical concerns." I believe that this exaggerates the case.
22. New York State Forestry Commission, *Annual Report . . . for the Year Ending December 31, 1891* (Assembly Document No. 34, 1892; Albany, N.Y.: James B. Lyon, 1892), pp. 26, 96.
23. Commissioners of State Parks, *First Annual Report*, pp. 20–21; *Forest and Stream* 28 (May 5, 1887): 325; see also *Forest and Stream* 21 (Jan. 3, 1884): 450–51 and 38 (Jan. 28, 1892): 76; and *Garden and Forest* 2 (Oct. 16, 1889): 493 and 3 (June 11, 1890): 282. See also *New York Tribune*, Feb. 20, 1893; *New York Times*, Sept. 16, 1889, Oct. 1, 1889, Feb. 8, 1890, May 27, June 10, 1891.
24. *Laws of New York*, 1892, chap. 707.
25. "Communication of the Adirondack Park Association . . . ," in *An Act Creating a State Forest Park in the Adirondack Region* (Senate Document No. 39, 1891; Albany, N.Y.: Weed, Parsons, 1891); *New York Times*, March 19, April 5, 1893; *Garden and Forest* 6 (April 19, 1893): 171.

26. Article VII, Section 7, of New York State Constitution, approved November 1894, going into effect January 1, 1895 (italics added).
27. New York Board of Trade and Transportation to Governor Roswell Flower, quoted in Kranz, "Pioneering in Conservation," p. 378. Kranz apparently found the letter quoted in Edwin Small, "The Adirondack Region" (M.A. thesis, Yale University, 1934), p. 123, which I have not seen.
28. Kranz, "Pioneering in Conservation," pp. 391–93; *New York Times*, April 11, March 2, 1894.
29. Kranz, "Pioneering in Conservation," pp. 394–95.
30. Ibid., pp. 396–98; *New York Tribune*, Aug. 27, 1894; New York State Constitutional Convention, *Revised Record of the Constitutional Convention of the State of New York: May 8, 1894–September 29, 1894*, 5 vols. (Albany, N.Y.: August 1900), Vol. IV, pp. 124–39.
31. Constitutional Convention, *Revised Record*, p. 152.
32. Ibid., p. 148; *New York Times*, Aug. 28, 1894; *New York Tribune*, Sept. 15, 1894; *Garden and Forest* 7 (Sept. 12, 1894): 361.
33. Martin L. Fausold, *Gifford Pinchot: Bull Moose Progressive* (Syracuse, N.Y.: Syracuse University Press, 1961), p. 8; Harold T. Pinkett, *Gifford Pinchot: Private and Public Forester* (Urbana: University of Illinois Press, 1970), pp. 32–34; Gifford Pinchot, *Breaking New Ground* (Seattle: University of Washington Press, 1972), p. 74.
34. Pinkett, *Gifford Pinchot*, p. 33; Pinchot, *Breaking New Ground*, pp. 182–84; Pinchot to Thomas H. Wagstaff, Dec. 10, 1896, quoted in Pinkett, *Gifford Pinchot*, p. 34.
35. *New York Times* and *New York Tribune*, Sept. 11, 1894; *Forest and Stream* 43 (Oct. 20, 1894): 231. *Forest and Stream* was not alone in believing that the forever wild strictures would eventually be lifted. State foresters, soon after Article VII, Section 7 was adopted, began preparing management plans for the Forest Preserve in order to be ready when "the present constitutional restrictions are removed" (Fox, *History of the Lumber Industry*, p. 46). The fact that the forever-wild provision was seen as temporary by most of the people involved in its original passage has been consistently ignored by historians; see Nash, *Wilderness and the American Mind*, pp. 120–21; Michael Frome, *Battle for the Wilderness* (New York: Praeger, 1974), pp. 113, 191; Jane Eblen Keller, *Adirondack Wilderness: A Story of Man and Nature* (Syracuse, N.Y.: Syracuse University Press, 1980), pp. 173, 175, 183.

CHAPTER VI WILDERNESS AND THE CONSERVATION BUREAUCRACY

1. Marvin Wolf Kranz, "Pioneering in Conservation: A History of the Conservation Movement in New York State, 1865–1903," Ph.D. diss., Syracuse University, 1961, pp. 420–22.
2. Frank Graham, Jr., *The Adirondack Park: A Political History* (New

York: Alfred A. Knopf, 1978); Norman VanValkenburgh, *The Adirondack Forest Preserve* (Blue Mountain Lake, N.Y.: Adirondack Museum, 1979); Roger C. Thompson, "The Doctrine of Wilderness: A Study of the Adirondack Preserve-Park," Ph.D. diss., State University College of Forestry, Syracuse University, 1962. For evidence of how the changes within the New York conservation bureaucracy paralleled similar developments in the National Park Service, see Alfred Runte, *National Parks: The American Experience* (Lincoln: University of Nebraska Press, 1979), pp. 106–38.

3. Fisheries, Game and Forests Commission, *Second Annual Report* (Albany, N.Y.: State Printer, 1897), p. 132.
4. Fisheries, Game and Forests Commission, *Third Annual Report* (Albany, N.Y.: State Printer, 1898), pp. 327–44; Alfred Lee Donaldson, *A History of the Adirondacks* (2 vols.; New York: Century, 1921), Vol. II, pp. 228–30.
5. William F. Fox, *The Adirondack Black Spruce* (Albany, N.Y.: J. B. Lyon, 1895); William F. Fox, *A History of the Lumber Industry in the State of New York* (first published in *Sixth Annual Report* of Forest, Fish and Game Commission [Albany, N.Y.: State Printer, 1901]; then Washington, D.C.: U.S. Government Printing Office, 1902; and finally Harrison, N.Y.: Harbor Hill Books, 1976); Forest, Fish and Game Commission, *Annual Reports for 1907–1908–1909* (Albany, N.Y.: State Printer, 1910), pp. 73–77.
6. Fisheries, Game and Forests Commission, *Third Annual Report*, pp. 327–32.
7. Ibid., p. 333. Throughout the rest of this study I use the expression "forever wild" as a noun, meaning the constitutional restriction and its consequences; this conforms to the popular usage of the term by local conservationists.
8. Fisheries, Game and Forests Commission, *Third Annual Report*, p. 334.
9. Ibid., p. 337. See Samuel P. Hays, *Conservation and the Gospel of Efficiency: The Progressive Conservation Movement, 1890–1920* (New York: Atheneum, 1969), passim.
10. John Todd, *Long Lake* (Pittsfield, Mass.: E. P. Little, 1845), p. 92.
11. Fisheries, Game and Forests Commission, *Fourth Annual Report* (Albany, N.Y.: State Printer, 1899), p. 358. An interesting and often described feature of Fernow's tenure with the College of Forestry was his supervision of an experimental forest plot near Axton on the Raquette River. Largely because the land was in nearly useless condition when it was handed over to him and also because Fernow managed to offend most of his superiors, the entire undertaking was a failure; see Graham, *Adirondack Park*, pp. 150–55.
12. Fisheries, Game and Forests Commission, *Fourth Annual Report*, p. 366. National Forest policies at this time acknowledged the importance of recreation (though timber management and watershed pro-

tection, of course, were the chief concern). The vision of both Fox and Fernow of a judicious mix of timber harvest, recreation, and watershed conservation was precisely what Pinchot was aiming for in the federally owned forests; see Harold K. Steen, *The U.S. Forest Service: A History* (Seattle: University of Washington Press, 1976), p. 113–17.
13. Forest, Fish and Game Commission, *Sixth Annual Report*, pp. 15, 17–19. Although the name of this agency changed, the numbering of reports continued with the sequence begun in 1895 (Steen, *U.S. Forest Service*, pp. 47–68).
14. Forest, Fish and Game Commission, *Seventh Annual Report* (Albany, N.Y.: State Printer, 1902), p. 30.
15. New York State Conservation Commission, *Fourth Annual Report* (2 vols.; Albany, N.Y.: State Printer, 1915), Vol. I, p. 43.
16. Graham, *Adirondack Park*, pp. 197–207. VanValkenburgh, *Adirondack Forest Preserve*, 105–07; New York State Conservation Commission, *Third Annual Report* (2 vols.; Albany, N.Y.: State Printer, 1914), Vol. II, pp. 66–67.
17. Conservation Commission, *Third Annual Report*, Vol. II, pp. 57, 60.
18. Conservation Commission, *Fourth Annual Report*, Vol. II, pp. 76–89.
19. David M. Ellis et al., *A History of New York State* (Ithaca, N.Y.: Cornell University Press and New York State Historical Association, 1967), pp. 376–92. A look at any of the official reports cited above will confirm the bureaucracy's predilection for timber management.
20. A. Judd Northrup, *Camps and Tramps in the Adirondacks* (Syracuse, N.Y.: Davis, Bardeen, 1880); A. Judd Northrup, "Fishes and Fishing in the Adirondacks: From the Sportsman's Point of View," in Forest, Fish and Game Commission, *Eighth and Ninth Annual Reports* (Albany, N.Y.: State Printer, 1904), pp. 275–94.
21. Northrup, "Fishes and Fishing," pp. 282, 290.
22. Ibid., p. 287.
23. Forest, Fish and Game Commission, *Fourteenth Annual Report* (Albany, N.Y.: State Printer, 1909), p. 44. For a contemporary example of the complaint that wilderness "locks up" resources, see *Hamilton County News*, Sept. 7, 1983, for local concern over the possible wilderness classification of the Perkins Clearing area. This affair is briefly discussed in Chapter VIII.
24. Forest, Fish and Game Commission, *Fifteenth Annual Report* (Albany, N.Y.: State Printer, 1910), p. 63.
25. Ibid., p. 190. The idea that wilderness is the place for the pursuit of manly values has also appealed to strict preservationists, an Adirondack example of whom would be Robert Marshall. See Stephen Fox, *John Muir and His Legacy: The American Conservation Movement* (Boston: Little, Brown, 1981), pp. 206–12; Roderick Nash, *Wilderness and the American Mind* (3rd ed.; New Haven, Conn.: Yale University Press, 1982), pp. 200–208.
26. New York State Conservation Commission, *Ninth Annual Report*

(Albany, N.Y.: State Printer, 1920), pp. 105, 120. The 1915 *Report* also showed a new interest in the recreational and aesthetic potential of the Forest Preserve.
27. Conservation Commission, *Ninth Annual Report*, pp. 113–14.
28. Ibid., pp. 94–100. On the view from Haystack see Robert Marshall, *The High Peaks of the Adirondacks* (Albany, N.Y.: Adirondack Mountain Club, 1922), p. 13.
29. Conservation Commission, *Ninth Annual Report*, pp. 104–8.
30. Ibid., p. 109.
31. Ibid., pp. 4–8. On early twentieth-century anti-modernism, see Nash, *Wilderness and the American Mind*, pp. 141–60; Peter Schmitt, *Back to Nature: The Arcadian Myth in Urban America* (New York: Oxford University Press, 1969). For a more recent and somewhat iconoclastic treatment of this subject, see Jackson Lears, *No Place of Grace: Antimodernism and the Transformation of American Culture, 1880–1920* (New York: Pantheon, 1981).
32. Conservation Commission, *Ninth Annual Report*, pp. 116–17.
33. Ibid., p. 117. Graham, *Adirondack Park*, pp. 144–45.
34. New York State Conservation Commission, *Eighth Annual Report* (Albany, N.Y.: State Printer, 1919), pp. 100–101; New York State Conservation Commission, *Twelfth Annual Report* (Albany, N.Y.: State Printer, 1923), pp. 134–35.
35. Steen, *U.S. Forest Service*, 119–20; Runte, *National Parks*, 103–4.
36. New York State Conservation Commission, *Twenty-First Annual Report* (Albany, N.Y.: State Printer, 1932), p. 22.
37. New York State Conservation Commission, *Twenty-Fourth Annual Report* (Albany, N.Y.: State Printer, 1935), pp. 23–24; VanValkenburgh, *Adirondack Forest Preserve*, p. 168.
38. Graham, *Adirondack Park*, pp. 184–87; VanValkenburgh, *Adirondack Forest Preserve*, pp. 149–54.
39. New York State Conservation Commission, *Thirtieth Annual Report* (Albany, N.Y.: State Printer, 1941), p. 125.
40. On the road controversy, see Graham, *Adirondack Park*, pp. 190–96, VanValkenburgh, *Adirondack Forest Preserve*, pp. 172–73. *American Forests* ran an article by Osborne defending the construction of the truck roads with a reply from Robert Marshall (42 [Jan. 1936]: 3–6); this was also published by that journal as a separate pamphlet of seven pages.

## Chapter VII A Wilderness Aesthetic

1. Frank Graham, Jr., *The Adirondack Park: A Political History* (New York: Alfred A. Knopf, 1978), pp. 159–71, 184–207. Despite a lack of adequate documentation, Graham provides the best summary of the politics of wilderness in the Adirondacks in the twentieth century. See also Norman J. VanValkenburgh, *The Adirondack Forest*

*Preserve* (Blue Mountain Lake, N.Y.: Adirondack Museum, 1979), passim. The types of threats to wilderness have been varied; the conservation bureaucracy has advocated everything from roads to bobsled runs, while private interests have pushed interstate highways, timber harvest, and a host of other projects calculated to bring in money to the local towns and villages. Most of these projects have been defeated either in the courts or by the electorate when amendments to forever wild have been voted on.

2. For example, see the discussions in Roderick Nash, *Wilderness and the American Mind* (3rd ed.; New Haven, Conn.: Yale University Press, 1982), pp. 161–237, and Stephen Fox, *John Muir and His Legacy: The American Conservation Movement* (Boston: Little, Brown, 1981), passim.

3. "Save the Wilderness," *Nature Magazine* 20 (Nov. 1932): 203. This is an unsigned editorial arguing against a proposed amendment to the New York constitution that would have removed the constitutional protection of the Forest Preserve and delegated authority over it to the legislature; the amendment failed.

4. VanValkenburgh, *Adirondack Forest Preserve*, p. 317. The amendment would have permitted the state to lease, sell, or exchange Forest Preserve lands.

5. VanValkenburgh, *Adirondack Forest Preserve*, pp. 115–19; *Adirondack Park*, Graham, pp. 170–71, 79–87. The worst offender in the tradition of misreading the rationale for defending the constitutional prohibition on logging is Jane Eblen Keller, *Adirondack Wilderness: A Story of Man and Nature* (Syracuse, N.Y.: Syracuse University Press, 1980), especially pp. 171. Among other things, Keller insists that the 1885 law establishing the Forest Preserve specifically prohibited lumbering on state lands; it did nothing of the sort.

6. Fox, *John Muir*, pp. 3–99; Nash, *Wilderness and the American Mind*, pp. 122–40.

7. Paul Jamieson, ed., *The Adirondack Reader* (2nd ed.; Glens Falls, N.Y.: Adirondack Mountain Club, 1982). Jamieson, a professor emeritus of English at St. Lawrence University, is one of the most industrious and intelligent students of Adirondack literature. His twice-issued *Adirondack Reader* is an invaluable resource; see Neal S. Burdick's review of the second edition in *Environmental Review* 7 (Fall 1983): 291–92.

8. For example, see Stephen Birmingham, "The Beautiful, Bedeviled Adirondacks," *Holiday* 36 (Aug. 1964): 42–47, 89–94; Ralph Knight, "New York Wilderness," *Saturday Evening Post* 233 (Aug. 27, 1960): 52–53, 56.

9. Robert Marshall's most important statement on the need for preserving wilderness was his article, "The Problem of the Wilderness," *Scientific Monthly* 30 (Feb. 1930): 141–48. See also Nash, *Wilderness and the American Mind*, pp. 141–60, 200–271. Fox outlines well the

various impulses behind the modern wilderness preservation movement (*John Muir*, pp. 103–47, 218–49). A standard work on antimodernism and the resulting interest in wilderness recreation is Peter Schmitt, *Back to Nature: The Arcadian Myth in Urban America* (New York: Oxford University Press, 1969), pp. 167–76.
10. All the biographical information on Abbott comes from the introduction by Vincent Engels in Henry Abbott, *The Birch Bark Books of Henry Abbott* (Harrison, N.Y.: Harbor Hill Books, 1980), pp. v–xiii.
11. Abbott, *Birch Bark Books*, pp. 81, 105, 6; Abbott's retreat from the conventional hostility can be traced on pp. 6, 40–41, 115, 242. The subject of changing attitudes toward predators is discussed in Susan L. Flader, *Thinking like a Mountain: Aldo Leopold and the Evolution of an Ecological Attitude Toward Deer, Wolves, and Forests* (Columbia: University of Missouri Press, 1974).
12. Abbott, *Birch Bark Books*, pp. 103, 207–9, 213.
13. Ibid., pp. 216–18.
14. Ibid., pp. 10, 41.
15. Ibid., pp. 241, 194, 204.
16. Ibid., p. 246.
17. Ibid., p. 254.
18. Ibid., p. 248.
19. Ibid., p. 52.
20. A landmark in the practical application of ecological knowledge was James W. Toumey, *Foundations of Silviculture upon an Ecological Basis* (New York: J. Wiley, 1928).
21. Abbott, *Birch Bark Books*, p. 91; see p. 173 for a similar example. The Cold River Country Abbott was here describing is the site of Mount Seward, the logging of which so offended Colvin; hence we must assume that Abbott was incorrect in postulating the absolute virginity of the region. The fact that it appeared so, however, suggests the relativity of the term *wilderness*.
22. Henry David Thoreau, "Walking," in *Excursions*, Vol. IX of *The Writings of Henry David Thoreau* (Boston: Houghton, Mifflin, 1893), pp. 278–79: "Hope and the future for me are not in lawns and cultivated fields, not in towns and cities, but in the impervious and quaking swamps. . . . I derive more of my subsistence from the swamps which surround my native town than from the cultivated gardens in the village. . . . Yes, though you may think me perverse, if it were proposed to me to dwell in the neighborhood of the most beautiful garden that ever human art contrived, or else of a Dismal Swamp, I should certainly decide for the swamp." The notion that Western culture is antipathetic to nature has been recently and forcefully advanced in Frederick Turner, *Beyond Geography: The Western Spirit Against the Wilderness* (New York: Viking, 1980). Turner begins his discussion of the Western mind with the nomads of ancient Mesopotamia and finds thereafter a mentality that is consistently anti-nature, anti-sex, anti-women.

23. Abbott, *Birch Bark Books*, pp. 173, 240.
24. A. B. Recknagel, *The Forests of New York* (New York: MacMillan, 1923), pp. 69–74.
25. Graham, *Adirondack Park*, pp. 173–76, 200–207. To be sure, Abbott was not necessarily the most significant synthesizer of these traditions. I would argue that the great achievement of John Muir is his ability to marry the transcendentalism of Emerson with the scientific inclination he acquired as a student at Madison. For example, throughout his best-known book, *The Mountains of California* (Berkeley: Ten Speed Press, 1977), especially in the famous account of the view from Mount Ritter (pp. 68–70), Muir shows that conventional romantic aesthetics are inadequate for appreciating the grandeur of nature. By acknowledging the role of glaciers in shaping the landscape, Muir is able to move into a new grasp of time, one emphasizing process and mutability, and thus achieves a sense of transcendence unavailable to the romantic.
26. Rachel Carson, *The Edge of the Sea* (Boston: Houghton, Mifflin, 1955), p. 250.

CHAPTER VIII THE INSTITUTIONALIZATION OF A WILDERNESS AESTHETIC

1. The acreage figure comes from the report for 1953 of the Joint Legislative Committee on Natural Resources (Albany, N.Y.: N. pub., 1953), p. 44. The reports of this committee, bound separately for each year, can be found in certain New York State libraries (e.g., State Library in Albany, New York Public Library, Adirondack Museum in Blue Mountain Lake). My citations will supply the year and page number with the abbreviation JLCNR: thus the citation for this reference would be JLCNR (1953), p. 44. See also Frank Graham, Jr., *The Adirondack Park: A Political History* (New York: Alfred A. Knopf, 1978), pp. 208–9.
2. Graham, *Adirondack Park*, pp. 196, 210–11; Norman J. VanValkenburgh, *The Adirondack Forest Preserve* (Blue Mountain Lake, N.Y.: Adirondack Museum, 1979), pp. 196–208.
3. *New York State Conservationist* 6 (Oct.–Nov. 1951): 1. The putative author of these questions was *Conservationist* Editor Pieter W. Fosburgh; Graham, *Adirondack Park*, p. 210.
4. *New York State Conservationist*, 6 (Dec.–Jan. 1951–52): 1.
5. For evidence of the Conservation Department's continuing preoccupation with developed forms of recreation, see its *Forty-Third Annual Report* (Albany: State Printer, 1954), pp. 44–46.
6. *New York State Conservationist*, 6 (Dec.–Jan. 1951–52): 4.
7. Ibid., pp. 5–7. For an excellent, though biased, summary of the frustrations felt by the conservation bureaucracy in its efforts to open up the Forest Preserve to more developed forms of recreation as well as

conservative exploitation of natural resources, see Roger C. Thompson, "Politics in the Wilderness: New York's Adirondack Forest Preserve," *Forest History* 6 (Winter 1963): 14–23. A professional forester, Thompson shows little sympathy for absolute wilderness preservation.

8. The April–May and June–July 1952 issues of the *New York State Conservationist* were full of letters defending wilderness in the Forest Preserve. Most did not investigate the complexities of the controversy, arguing simply for maintenance of the status quo. One, however, from Oakleigh Thorne II of the Yale Conservation Program, did cite positive reasons for preserving wilderness; Thorne argued that "the Preserve is of great scientific value as wilderness area where natural phenomena govern its appearance, undisturbed by man; that is, as an ecological norm where natural succession can take place without man's modification of it. Since the preserve is made up of many different types of field and forest in many stages of development, it is important to leave it undisturbed, so as to trace the natural changes that take place within it over a period of time" (6 [June–July 1952]: 28). The idea of wilderness as a natural laboratory for scientific study had been advanced by Aldo Leopold in his *Sand County Almanac, with Essays on Conservation from Round River* (New York: Sierra Club and Ballantine, 1970), pp. 272–76. See also JLCNR (1953), pp. 35–37; Graham, *Adirondack Park*, pp. 200–207.

9. JLCNR (1954), pp. 65–69.

10. Ibid., p. 87 (italics in original). Paul Schaefer immediately responded to Foss's worries about the constitutionality of state-constructed and state-owned facilities on the Forest Preserve. According to Schaefer, repeated opinions rendered by the courts and state attorneys general made Foss's concern superfluous (*New York State Conservationist* 6 [Feb.–March 1952]: 3–4).

11. JLCNR (1954), p. 89. The articles in the *New York State Conservationist* had also broached the possibility of zoning (6 [Dec.–Jan. 1951–1952]: 6); hence the use of the word "first" is figurative. Foss's proposal reflected the current position of the Conservation Department. As early as 1934, Robert Marshall had made a similar proposal (untitled column, *High Spots* 11 [Jan. 1934]: 14). Foss's declaration that the bureaucracy intended to adopt a hands-off treatment of the wilderness areas was by no means unanimously accepted throughout the Conservation Department. In the late 1960s, William Petty, the forest ranger in charge of Cold River Country on the western edge of the high peaks—one of the wildest and most remote pieces of the Forest Preserve—was permitting extensive developments that intruded on the area's wilderness character. These included horse trails, stables, unnecessary bridges, and administrative vehicular use of what were supposed to be foot paths.

12. JLCNR (1960), pp. 83–140.

13. *New York Times,* July 30, 1967; Graham, *Adirondack Park,* pp. 219–29.
14. On the establishment and political controversy surrounding the Adirondack Park Agency, see Graham, *Adirondack Park,* pp. 230–74. On the agency's efforts to introduce and enforce regional zoning, see Richard A. Liroff and G. Gordon Davis, *Protecting Open Space: Land Use Controls in the Adirondack Park* (Cambridge, Mass.: Ballinger, 1981).
15. Leopold, *Sand County Almanac,* pp. 237–64. In this commitment to preserving ecosystems, New York was lagging far behind the National Park Service, which made a similar commitment with the Everglades National Park in the 1930s; see Alfred Runte, *National Parks: The American Experience* (Lincoln: University of Nebraska Press, 1979), pp. 106–37, and Graham, *Adirondack Park,* pp. 242–43.
16. The Temporary Study Commission issued two documents; these were distributed to legislators and others concerned with the future of the Adirondacks and were quickly published by the Adirondack Museum. The first was *The Future of the Adirondack Park* (Blue Mountain Lake, N.Y.: Adirondack Museum, 1971), hereafter referred to as *Future;* the second was *The Future of the Adirondacks,* Vol II: *The Technical Reports* (Blue Mountain Lake, N.Y.: Adirondack Museum, 1971), hereafter referred to as *Technical Reports. Future* was a brief, comprehensive statement of the commission's recommendations, with a summary of its research and background information. The *Technical Reports* were lengthy monographs on seven distinct issues: *Private and Public Lands,* Vols. A and B; *Wildlife; Forests, Minerals, Water and Air; Transportation and the Economy; Recreation; Local Government;* and *Financial Implementation.* The citations for this reference are *Technical Reports: Private and Public Lands;* Vol. B, p. 23, and *Future,* p. 44.
17. Temporary Study Commission, *Technical Reports: Private and Public Lands,* Vol. B, pp. 23–24, 29.
18. Ibid., p. 25. When the Adirondack Park Agency issued its *Adirondack Park State Land Master Plan* (N. pub., 1972), based on and designed to implement the study commission's recommendations, it made a significant addition to the goals for wilderness: besides the *"perpetuation* of natural plant and animal communities," the agency instructed the wilderness managers to "achieve" such communities (p. 9).
19. Temporary Study Commission, *Technical Reports: Private and Public Lands,* Vol. B, p. 25; Temporary Study Commission, *Future,* p. 45. A draft report, "Unit Planning for Wilderness Management" (typescript, Dec. 31, 1982), sent to me by its author, Norman VanValkenburgh, director of the Conservation Department's Division of Lands and Forests, points out the many ambiguities and problems in this definition. Among other things, qualifying or vague words like "gen-

erally," "appears," "primarily," "substantially," and "character" beg the question of a concrete definition of wilderness.
20. Temporary Study Commission, *Future*, p. 45.
21. Temporary Study Commission, *Technical Reports: Private and Public Lands*, Vol. B, p. 27; Temporary Study Commission, *Future*, p. 44.
22. Adirondack Park Agency, *State Land Master Plan*, p. 11.
23. Temporary Study Commission, *Future*, p. 53.
24. C. W. Severinghaus and C. P. Brown, "History of the White-Tailed Deer in New York," *New York Fish and Game Journal* 3 (July 1956): 136; Temporary Study Commission, *Technical Reports: Wildlife*, p. 6; Temporary Study Commission, *Future*, p. 54. On the evolving attitude toward wildlife management in the National Parks, see Roland H. Wauer and William R. Supernaugh, "Wildlife Management in the National Parks," *National Parks* 57 (July–Aug. 1983): 12–16.
25. Temporary Study Commission, *Future*, pp. 55–56; Temporary Study Commission, *Technical Reports: Wildlife*, p. 29.
26. Temporary Study Commission, *Technical Reports: Wildlife*, p. 30; Philip G. Terrie, "R.I.P. the Adirondack Moose," *Adirondack Life* 4 (Fall 1973): 40–45.
27. Temporary Study Commission, *Technical Reports: Wildlife*, p. 30.
28. The connection between the size of the deer herd and wilderness is well understood by most people who live in the Adirondacks. They know that the longer a parcel of land has been in the Forest Preserve, the fewer the deer likely to be found there. I know of several Adirondack residents who every winter cut branches off cedar trees on state land to feed deer. The discussion of wildlife in the *New York State Conservationist* 6 (Dec.–Jan. 1951–52): 5 played on local hostility to forever wild by emphasizing how timber harvest or management would promote a larger deer population.
29. Temporary Study Commission, *Future*, p. 56.
30. Dennis Aprill, "The Moose Came Back," *Adirondack Life* 14 (March–April 1983): 14–17, 40–42.
31. *Hamilton County News*, Sept. 7, Dec. 21, 1983; *New York Times*, Dec. 11, 1983. Adirondack Council, "Action Alert" (undated newsletter); Neil F. Woodworth, "Perkins Clearing: A Forest Preserve Controversy," *Adirondac* 47 (Oct.–Nov. 1983): 6–10. For evidence of continuing hostility to wilderness within the conservation bureaucracy, see the letter to *Adirondac* from State Forest Ranger John F. Seifts (48 [Jan. 1984]: 41) opposing wilderness classification for Perkins Clearing.
32. James C. Dawson, "Perkins Clearing Compromise," *Adirondac* 48 (Feb.–March 1984): 34–35; James C. Dawson, "Perkins Clearing: The Second Time Around," *Adirondac* 48 (June 1984): 38–39; *Hamilton County News*, Feb. 1, 1984, April 25, 1984 and June 13, 1984; Adirondack Council, "Special Mid-Year Appeal" (newsletter, dated only 1984). For the establishment and purpose of the Council, see Mason Smith, "Adirondack Council," *Adirondack Life* 12 (Jan.–Feb. 1981): 25–27, 52–55.

# A Note on Sources

The historian working on an Adirondack subject begins with the *Adirondack Bibliography* (Gabriels, N.Y.: Adirondack Mountain Club, 1958) and the *Adirondack Bibliography Supplement, 1956–1965* (Blue Mountain Lake, N.Y.: Adirondack Museum, 1973), both compiled by Dorothy A. Plum. These valuable volumes contain over ten thousand entries arranged by subject—e.g., recreation, conservation, natural history—and date. It is regrettable that the series is not being updated.

Among the basic chronicles of the region, Alfred Lee Donaldson's comprehensive *A History of the Adirondacks*, 2 vols. (New York: Century, 1921), is marred by factual errors, idiosyncratic organization, and a lack of analysis. The best modern history is Frank Graham, Jr., *The Adirondack Park: A Political History* (New York: Alfred A. Knopf, 1978). Graham, a popular historian, is especially thorough in describing the establishment of the Adirondack Park Agency and its problems in effecting land-use planning and curbs on the development of private land in the park. Norman J. VanValkenburgh, *The Adirondack Forest Preserve: A Chronology* (Ann Arbor, Mich.: University Microfilms International; Blue Mountain Lake, N.Y.: Adirondack Museum, 1979), presents a year-by-year account of legislative, judicial, and constitutional activity relative to the Forest Preserve. (It was first compiled as an in-house memorandum by the Director of Lands and Forests of the New York State Department of Environmental Conservation.) William Chapman White's *Adirondack Country* (New York: Alfred A. Knopf, 1954), provides a beautifully written introduction to local history, culture, and the environment.

Two Ph.D. dissertations are also important to Adirondack research. Marvin Wolf Kranz, "Pioneering in Conservation: A History of the Conservation Movement in New York State, 1865–1903" (Syracuse University, 1961), attempts to survey all conservation activity in New York during the latter part of the nineteenth century. Roger C. Thompson, "The Doctrine of Wilderness: A Study of the Policy and Politics of the Adirondack Preserve-Park" (State University College of Forestry, Syracuse University, 1962), discusses the judicial and legislative history of the Forest Preserve up to the 1950s; while the research is impeccable, the professional forester's bias against statutory protection of wilderness is often evident.

The books most useful to my understanding of the environmental aesthetics of the first Adirondack visitors are Marjorie Hope Nicolson, *Mountain Gloom and Mountain Glory: The Development of The Aesthetics of the Infinite* (New York: W. W. Norton, 1963), and Roderick Nash, *Wilderness and the American Mind*, 3rd ed. (New Haven, Conn.: Yale University Press, 1982). The former is a brilliant discussion of changes in English attitudes about the landscape. The latter is the starting point for all historians dealing with the American wilderness; although I differ with Nash on several points, I believe that his is the seminal work on American wilderness values. Yi-Fu Tuan, *Topophilia: A Study of Environmental Perception, Attitudes, and Values* (Englewood Cliffs, N.J.: Prentice-Hall, 1974), provides a good general introduction to environmental aesthetics as a function of culture. I have also relied on two American Studies classics: Henry Nash Smith, *Virgin Land: The American West as Symbol and Myth* (Cambridge, Mass.: Harvard University Press, 1950), and Leo Marx, *The Machine in the Garden: Technology and the Pastoral Ideal in America* (London: Oxford University Press, 1964).

The primary sources for study of the New York Natural History Survey are the annual and final reports of the Survey itself, particularly those written by Ebenezer Emmons. His annual reports may be found in the published *Documents of the Assembly of the State of New York* (Albany, N.Y.: N. pub., 1837–1841), as follows: "First Annual Report of the Second Geological District of the State of New York" (Assembly Document No. 161, 1837), Vol. II; "Report of E. Emmons, Geologist of the 2d Geological District of the State of New York" (Assembly Document No. 200, 1838), Vol. IV; "Third Annual Report of the Survey of the Second Geological District," (Assembly Document No. 275, 1839), Vol.V; "Fourth Annual Report of the Survey of the Second Geological District," (Assembly No. 50, 1840), Vol. II; "Fifth Annual Report of the Survey of the Second Geological District," (Assembly Document No. 150, 1841), Vol V.. Emmons' final report was *Geology of New-York, Part II: Comprising the Second Geological District* (Albany, N.Y.: Carroll and Cook, 1842). Two other important final reports are James E. DeKay, *Zoology of New York; Or, The New York Fauna*, 2 vols. (Albany, N.Y.: Carroll and Cook, 1842–1844), and John Torrey, *A Flora of the State of New York*, 2 vols. (Albany, N.Y.: Carroll and Cook, 1843). Emmons' annual reports and all the final reports are illustrated with engravings, some in color. A useful secondary source is Michele Alexis La Clerque Aldrich, "New York Natural History Survey" (Ph.D. Dissertation, University of Texas, 1974).

Among the rich primary sources from the age of the romantic traveler, Joel T. Headley's *The Adirondack; Or, Life in the Woods* (New York: Baker and Scribner, 1849) is one of the best. Other typical examples of romantic travel and sporting narratives include S. H. Hammond, *Hills, Lakes and Forest Streams; Or a Tramp in the Woods* (New York: J. C. Derby, 1854), and *Wild Northern Scenes; Or, Sporting Adventures with the Rifle and Rod* (New York: Derby and Jackson, 1857); Charles Fenno

## A Note on Sources

Hoffman, *Wild Scenes in the Forest and Prairie* (New York: W. H. Colyer, 1843); A. B. Street, *Woods and Waters: Or, the Saranacs and Racket* (New York: M. Doolady, 1860); John Todd, *Long Lake* (Pittsfield, Mass.: E. P. Little, 1845). For secondary works in addition to Nash, *Wilderness and the American Mind*, see Hans Huth, *Nature and the American: Three Centuries of Changing Attitudes* (Berkeley: University of California Press, 1957); Edward H. Foster, *The Civilized Wilderness: Backgrounds to American Romantic Literature, 1817–1860* (New York: Free Press, 1975); and Barbara Novak, *Nature and Culture: American Landscape and Painting, 1825–1875* (New York: Oxford University Press, 1980).

The significance of W. H. H. Murray to the Adirondacks is discussed in Warder H. Cadbury's Introduction to the 1970 Adirondack Museum reprint of Murray's *Adventures in the Wilderness; Or, Camp-Life in the Adirondacks* (Syracuse, N.Y.: Syracuse University Press and Adirondack Museum). This essay cites all the important reactions to Murray and Murray's Fools and reprints Murray's own response to his critics. For representative sporting narratives and editorials on Adirondack issues, see *Forest and Stream*; most issues, from the magazine's establishment in 1871 through the end of the century, contain articles on the Adirondacks.

Verplanck Colvin's reports were submitted to the state legislature between 1873, the first year of the Adirondack Survey, and 1900, when his job was terminated; the last three reports were not published. From 1873 to 1883, Colvin's work was primarily involved with topography and mapping; beginning in 1884, he was further charged with locating and identifying the boundaries of all parcels of state land, and the project became known as the State Land Survey. Although all the reports are informative, probably the most interesting is *Seventh Annual Report on the Progress of the Topographical Survey of the Adirondack Region of New York, to the Year 1879, Containing the Condensed Reports for the Years 1874–75–76–77 and '78* (Assembly Document No. 87, 1879; Albany, N.Y.: Weed, Parsons, 1880). This lengthy book (536 pages) contains stirring accounts of exploration in the high peaks, as well as Colvin's essay "The Winter Fauna of Mount Marcy."

On the legislative and judicial steps leading to the creation of the Adirondack Forest Preserve, see Kranz, "Pioneering in Conservation"; VanValkenburgh, *Adirondack Forest Preserve*; and Donaldson, *History of the Adirondacks*. The central primary document is what has come to be known as the Sargent (New York Forestry) Commission Report, titled simply "Report" in *Documents of the Assembly of the State of New York, 1885* (Assembly Document No. 36, 1885; Albany, N.Y.: Weed, Parsons, 1885). Also essential is the record of the 1894 constitutional convention: *Revised Record of the Constitutional Convention of the State of New York: May 8, 1894–September 29, 1894*, 5 vols. (Albany, N.Y.: Argus, 1900). Important periodicals paying attention to Adirondack affairs were *Forest and Stream, Garden and Forest, Harper's Weekly*, and the New York *Times* and *Tribune*. George Perkins Marsh, *Man and Nature; Or, Physical Geography as Modified by Human Action* (New York: Charles Scribner, 1864), is the basic text on the beginnings of conservation in America. For more about Marsh himself, see David Lowenthal's biography, *George Perkins Marsh: Versatile Vermonter* (New York: Columbia University Press, 1958). A useful history of conservation activity throughout the country in this era is Samuel P. Hays, *Conservation and the Gospel of Efficiency: The Progressive Conservation Movement, 1890–1920* (1959; reprint, New York: Atheneum, 1969).

The New York State conservation bureaucracy has issued copious reports throughout its existence, whatever the name of its chief agency: Forestry Commission (1885–1894), Fisheries, Game and Forests Commission (1895–1899), Forest, Fish and Game Commission (1900–1910), Conservation Commission (1911–1926), Conservation Department (1927–1969), Department of Environmental Conservation (since 1970). From 1897 to 1901 there was also Forest Preserve Board. The annual and occasional reports of these agencies illuminate changing institutional values with respect to forests, wildlife, and the idea of wilderness. Two important works on federal conservation bureaucracies are Harold K. Steen, *The U.S. Forest Service: A History* (Seattle: University of Washington Press, 1976) and Alfred Runte, *National Parks: The American Experience* (Lincoln: University of Nebraska Press, 1979). These are best read in conjunction with Robert Shankland, *Steve Mather of the National Parks* (New York: Alfred A. Knopf, 1951), and Harold T. Pinkett, *Gifford Pinchot: Private and Public Forester* (Urbana: University of Illinois Press, 1970).

The political, legislative, and judicial background of the cultural shifts manifested in the writings of Henry Abbott are discussed in Graham, *Adirondack Park*; Thompson, "Doctrine of Wilderness"; and VanValkenburgh, *Adirondack Forest Preserve*. The general subject of the cultural context of twentieth-century American environmental attitudes and aesthetics has been neglected. Perhaps because environmentalists working on twentieth-century topics have stressed politics and policy, we know less than we should about the expression of environmental values in contemporary culture; in marked contrast, numerous culturally based studies provide rich resources for the nineteenth century. Among the efforts to redress this neglect of the twentieth century, the following studies are noteworthy: Susan Flader, *Thinking Like a Mountain: Aldo Leopold and the Evolution of an Ecological Attitude Toward Deer, Wolves, and Forests* (Columbia: University of Missouri Press, 1974), and Donald Worster, *Nature's Economy: The Roots of Ecology* (San Francisco: Sierra Club, 1977).

The annual reports of the Joint Legislative Committee on Natural Resources—known through much of the 1950s and early 1960s as the Pomeroy Committee, after Assemblyman (later State Senator) Robert Watson Pomeroy, its chair—provide the best view of the position of the conservation bureaucracy throughout that period. Unlike the *Conservationist*, the official organ of New York's Conservation Department, the documents assembled by the Pomeroy Committee reveal division and debate within the department. Additional primary sources for my last chapter are the reports of the Temporary Study Commission (*The Future of the Adirondack Park* [Blue Mountain Lake, N.Y.: Adirondack Museum, 1971]; *The Future of the Adirondacks*, Vol. II: *The Technical Reports* [Blue Mountain Lake, N.Y.: Adirondack Museum, 1971]), and of the Adirondack Park Agency, especially the *Adirondack Park State Land Master Plan* (no publication information, 1972). One can follow the more recent fortunes of and threats to New York wilderness in the local and state press, and in the publications and newsletters of conservation organizations: the Adirondack Mountain Club, the Association for the Protection of the Adirondacks, and the Adirondack Council.

# Index

Abbott, Henry: appreciation of, of wilderness, 142–43; *Birch Bark Books* of, 141–42, 147, 148; career of, 140–41; importance of, 148–49; inconsistencies of, 142; and logging, 143–44; and process, 141, 144–45, 147; reaction of, to being lost, 142–43
Adams, Campbell W., 104
Adirondack Council, 163–64
Adirondack Forest Preserve, 7; and blowdown, 150–51; creation of, 92, 96–97, 99–100; prohibition on logging in, 98, 99, 104–9, 112, 121–23, 153. *See also* Article VII, Section 7; Recreation
Adirondack Mountain Club, 4, 163–64
Adirondack Mountains National Park Proposal, 155
*Adirondack; Or, Life in the Woods, The* (Headley), 44
Adirondack Park, 8, 125, 155; creation of, 102–3; logging in, 102–8, 125
Adirondack Park Agency, 155–56, 162; and Perkins Clearing, 163–65. *See also* Private Land Use and Development Plan; State Land Master Plan
Adirondack Park Association, 103
*Adirondack Reader* (Jamieson), 139

Adirondack region: defined, 5; early image of, 7–8, 19–22, 36–37
*Adventures in the Wilderness; Or, Camp-Life in the Adirondacks* (Murray), 68–71, 131
Aesthetics. *See* Beautiful, the; Burke, Edmund; Sublime, the; Wilderness aesthetic
Agassiz, Louis, 46, 62
Agriculture, 23, 25. *See also* Middle landscape ideal
Agriculture, U.S. Department of, 122
American Forestry Association, 105
Ampersand Lake, 89
Anti-modernism, 131, 140
Apperson, John S., 136, 148
Article XIV: adoption of, 151; attack on, from Conservation Department, 151–52; interpreted, 156–57
Article VII, Section 7, 92; adoption of, 104–8; amendments to, 137, 191; hostility toward, of conservation bureaucracy, 109–12, 121–24, 126–28, 187; use of, to protect wilderness, 136; and utilitarianism, 137; violations of, by conservation bureaucracy, 129. *See also* Watershed; Wilderness

203

Association for the Protection of the Adirondacks, 4, 134, 163
Ausable Chasm, 30
Ausable River, 22, 30
Automobiles, 131–32
Avalanche Lake, 130
Avalanche Pass, 130

Basselin, Theodore, 100
Beautiful, the: defined, 17–18; and New York Natural History Survey, 29–32; and romantic writers, 52–53
Beaver River, 84
Benedict, Farrand, 39
Blowdown, 150–51
Blue Line, 102
Blue Mountain, 86
Bobsled case, 133–34
Bog River, 57, 64, 66, 83
Burke, Edmund: and *Philosophical Enquiry*, 17–19; influence of, on New York Natural History Survey, 30–32; influence of, on romantics, 51–53, 55; landscape classifications of, 18, 19, 23, 30, 57, 126

Campbell, Archibald, 20–21
Canal Board, New York, 37, 38, 39
Canals, 38–40, 87, 106. *See also* Erie Canal
Carson, Rachel, 148–49
Cartier, Jacques, 19, 170
Champlain, Samuel de, 19
Civilian Conservation Corps, 134
Clarke, C. H. D., 160–62
Colden, Lake, 130
Colden, Mount, 30, 130
Cold River, 126, 134, 145–46, 194
Cole, Thomas, 55–56
Colvin, Verplanck: and conservation, 86–88, 182; conservatism of, 87–90; early career of, 78; field work of, 78–81; inconsistency of, 77, 86–87, 89–90; influence of G. P. Marsh on, 81–85, 181; and logging, 86–87, 180–81; and Park Commission, 95; plan of, for aqueduct, 87, 182; romanticism and, 77; wilderness aesthetic of, 77, 79, 80, 81–86, 90

Conservation: early signs of, 40; and romantics, 66–67. *See also* Watershed
Conservation bureaucracy. *See* Conservation Commission; Conservation Department; Environmental Conservation, New York State Department of; Fisheries, Game and Forest Commission; Forest, Fish and Game Commission
Conservation Commission: commitment of, to recreation, 128–30, 132–33; creation of, 122; hostility of, to Article VII, Section 7, 123–24, 126–28; 1914 report of, 124; 1919 report of, 128; position of, on hydroelectric dams, 123–24; utilitarianism of, 124
Conservation Department: attack of, on forever wild, 150–52, 154; commitment of, to recreation, 133–35, 154, 157, 159; creation of, 133
*Conservationist*, 151, 153
Cornell, Alonzo B., 96
Constitutional Conventions: of 1894, 104–8; of 1915, 138; of 1938, 150
Couchsachraga, 20, 170–71
Cranberry Lake, 75
Cuomo, Mario, 164

Dams, logging. *See* Logging
Dams, storage and hydroelectric, 109, 123–24
Davis, George, 164
DeKay, James, 33

## Index

Dix, John Adams, 27, 34
Duck Hole, 126, 134
Duryea, Perry, 153
Dwight, Timothy, 23, 24

Elitism, 72–76; Colvin's objection to, 88
Ely, W. W., 92
Emerson, Ralph Waldo, 45, 46–47, 59–65, 131; and John Muir, 178; and *Nature*, 60
Emmons, Ebenezer, 7, 29, 127; ambivalence toward wilderness of, 29, 31–32, 42–43; and Burkean vocabulary, 30; and canals, 38–40; and conservation, 40–41, 92; early years of, 29; and middle landscape ideal, 36–38; pantheism of, 31; reputation of, 27; utilitarianism of, 31–32, 34–35, 36
Environmental attitude, 6
Environmental Conservation, New York State Department of, 5
Erie Canal, 95, 111
Evans, Lewis, 20, 21

Fernow, Bernhard, 105, 121, 188; hostility of, toward Article VII, Section 7, 121–22
Field, Kate, 75, 76
"Fifty Years of Conservation," 133
Firetruck roads, 134
Fisher (mammal), 33
Fisheries, Game and Forest Commission: creation of, 109; 1897 report of, 110; 1898 report of, 121
Fishing, 49–50, 125–26
Follensby Pond, 46–47, 60, 62, 65
*Forest and Stream*: and conservation, 95–96, 100, 101, 103, 107; and elitism, 72, 74
Forest, Fish and Game Commission: creation of, 122; 1903 report of, 125
Forest Preserve. *See* Adirondack Forest Preserve
Forestry, scientific, 95, 97, 99, 100, 103, 106, 121
Forestry, U.S. Division of, 122
Forestry Commission: competence of, 100–101, 104, 106, 137; corruption of, 101; creation of, 5, 96–97, 100
Forest Service, U.S., 132, 153
Forever wild. *See* Adirondack Forest Preserve; Article XIV; Article VII, Section 7; Wilderness
Forked Lake, 52–53, 144
Fosburgh, Pieter W., 151, 193
Foss, William M., 153–54
Fox, William F.: early career of, 110–11; hostility of, toward wilderness, 111, 121; opinions of, on forestry, 111–12, 121–23; utilitarianism of, 111
Friends of the Forest Preserve, 153
Fulton Chain, 88

*Garden and Forest*, 97–98, 101, 102, 103, 105, 106
George, Lake, 22–23
Gilpin, William, 18, 19, 55
Glens Falls, 74
Gothics, Mount, 79
Graham, Frank, Jr., 110, 136, 138
Gray, Asa, 27

Hall, James, 27
Hamilton County, 22, 30, 34, 36, 49, 122; Board of Supervisors, 164
*Hamilton County News*, 164
Hammond, Samuel H., 54, 57, 64, 66–67
Hanging Spear Falls, 130
*Harper's Weekly*, 98, 100
Hays, Samuel, 101, 108
Haystack, Mount, 129

Headley, Joel T., 70; and *Adirondack*, 44; and hunting, 49; and middle landscape ideal, 54; as romantic writer, 44, 45, 52, 59, 64, 126
Henderson, David, 35
High Peaks, 5, 52–53, 129–30
Hitchcock, Edward, 29
Hoffman, Charles Fenno, 52
Hough, B. Franklin, 95
Hudson River, 22, 35, 39, 95, 96, 106
Hunting, 125–26, 160–62; with hounds, 47–48; with jacklights, 48; regulation of, 73–74; romantic travelers and, 47–49

Indian Lake, 30
Indian Pass, 32, 52–53, 55–56, 130
Indians, 16, 21, 168–69
Interior, U.S. Department of, 155
International Paper Company, 163

Jamieson, Paul, 139
Jefferson, Thomas, 17, 22
John Brown's Tract, 51
Johnson, Sir William, 20, 21
Joint Legislative Committee on Natural Resources (Pomeroy Committee), 153–55, 156, 200–201

Keene Valley, 25
Kluckhohn, Clyde, 6

Lake Placid, 133
Landscape painting, 18, 45, 55
Leopold, Aldo, 8, 156
Littlefield, F. W., 152
Logging: abuses of, 88, 93, 98, 111; in Adirondack Park, 102–8, 125; dams constructed for, 74, 87; early signs of, 66; and forest fires, 93, 161; on Mount Seward, 89–90; in Murray era, 73, 74; public perception of, 98–99, 100–101, 108; threat to watershed of, 94, 99; threat to wilderness of, 144. *See also* Forestry, scientific
Long Lake (lake), 5, 22, 39, 51, 53, 87, 143, 162
Long Lake (town), 25, 58, 71
Lowell, James Russell, 46, 82

Macauley, James, 22
McClure, David, 104–6, 108, 136
McEntee, Jervis, 52, 55–56
McIntyre, Mount, 5, 130
McIntyre iron mine, 35–36, 39, 40
*Man and Nature* (Marsh), 81–82, 84–85, 93–95
Marcy, Mount, 29, 52–53, 80–81, 83, 129–30; alpine plants on, 5, 33; first ascent of, 33
Marsh, George Perkins: and Adirondacks, 184; and conservation, 81, 93–95, 105, 121, 160; and environmental aesthetics, 81–85, 139, 159; and *Man and Nature*, 81–82, 84–85, 93–95; utilitarianism of, 86, 182
Marshall, George, 91, 183
Marshall, Robert, 90–91, 136, 140, 183
Martin's Hotel, 46
Marx, Leo, 24
Mather, Fred, 79–80
Middle landscape ideal, 23–25, 36–38, 54; and scenery, 54–55
Mining, 34; of hypersthene, 34–35; of iron, 25, 26, 34–36
Mitchell, Lee Clark, 41
Moose, 56, 57, 161–62
Muir, John, 90, 138, 178, 193
Murray, Henry A., 6
Murray, William H. H.: and *Adventures in the Wilderness*, 68–71, 131; career of, 68–69; and hunting, 180; response of, to elitism, 75–76

# Index

"Murray's Fools," 70–73, 88

Nash, Roderick, 10, 16, 140
National Park Service, 132
*Nature* (Emerson), 60
*Nature Magazine*, 137
Nessmuk. *See* Sears, George Washington
Newcomb, 25, 35
New York Board of Trade and Transportation, 104, 108, 136, 137
*New York Daily Tribune*, 101, 106, 107
New York Natural History Survey, 10, 32, 34, 39–40, 76; establishment of, 27–28. *See also* Emmons, Ebenezer
New York State College of Forestry (Cornell), 121, 188
*New York Times*, 92–93, 96, 100–101, 103, 105, 106, 107
Nippletop, Mount, 31
Noble, Louis, 56
Northrup, A. Judd, 125–26

Old Forge, 40
Olympics (Winter, 1932), 133–34
Opalescent River, 130
Osborne, Lithgow, 134
Oswegatchie River, 22, 84, 168
Owl's Head, 53, 55

Panther Gorge, 81, 130
Park Commission (of 1872), 95, 99, 103
Perkins Clearing, 163–65
Petty, William, 194
*Philosophical Enquiry into the Origins of Our Ideas of the Sublime and the Beautiful* (Burke), 17–19
Pinchot, Gifford, 106–7, 109, 121, 122
Pine Brook, 144
Piseco Trout Club, 49

Pomeroy Committee. *See* Joint Legislative Committee on Natural Resources
Pownall, Thomas, 21
Preservation, 101, 136–38, 153
Private Land Use and Development Plan, 155–56
Process, in nature, 56–58, 84–85, 139, 141, 145–47, 152, 158. *See also* Abbott, Henry; Wilderness aesthetic

Railroads, 40, 70, 93
Raquette Falls, 124
Raquette Lake, 22, 42, 54, 75, 122
Raquette Lake House, 69
Raquette River, 22, 39, 46, 63, 66, 88; proposal of dam for, 124
Recknagle, A. B., 147–48
Recreation: as threat to wilderness, 133–35, 157; use of Forest Preserve for, 103, 105, 125–35, 144. *See also* Fishing; Hunting
Redfield, William C., 30
Richards, T. A., 56
Rix, Julian, 98, 129
Rockefeller, Lawrence, 155
Rockefeller, Nelson, 155, 156
Romanticism, 16–17, 42, 44, 59, 126, 148; of Conservation Commission, 131; environmental aesthetics of, 8; popular, 45
Romantic travelers, 44–45; camping habits of, 46–50; discomfort in the wilderness of, 50–51; fears of being lost of, 58–59; pantheism of, 65; and scenery, 51–58
Roosevelt, Theodore, 127–28
Round Pond, 40, 87

St. Regis River, 22
Sanford Lake, 35
Saranac Lake (town), 25, 40, 70
Saranac Lakes, 46, 57, 65, 91

Saranac River, 22, 55; proposal of dam for, 124
Sargent, Charles Sprague, 96, 97, 98
Sargent Commission, 96–97
Scenery, aesthetics of, 17; and conservation bureaucracy, 129–30; early responses to, 22–23; and New York Natural History Survey, 30–32; and romantic travelers, 51–58
Schaefer, Paul, 136, 148, 153
Schroon Lake, 55
Schroon Mountain, 55
Sears, George Washington (pseud. "Nessmuk"), 74, 87–88
Seward, Mount, 89–90, 130
Sierra Club, 163
Skiff, J. Victor, 153
Smith, Bige, 140, 144
Smith, Henry Nash, 24
South Pond, 142
Special Advisory Committee on the State Forest Preserve, 153
Speculator, 162
State Land Master Plan, 156, 159–63
Stillman, William James, 46, 58, 64, 66, 176
Street, Alfred B., 57, 58, 64, 65, 70, 126
Sublime, the, 23; defined, 18–19; and New York Natural History Survey, 30, 32; and romantic writers, 52
Swamps, 5–6, 20, 37, 57, 124

Tait, Arthur Fitzwilliam, 50–51
Teal, Edwin Way, 153
Tear of the Clouds, Lake, 5, 83
Temporary Study Commission on the Future of the Adirondacks, 155–63
Thompson, James, 17
Thompson, Roger, 110

Thoreau, Henry David, 12, 147, 192
Thorne, Oakleigh, II, 194
Thorpe, Thomas Bangs, 51, 70, 72, 76
Tocqueville, Alexis de, 17
Todd, John, 51, 54, 58, 121
Torrey, John, 27, 33
Transatlantic cable, 59, 61–63
Tupper Lake, 57

Vanuxem, Lardner, 42–43
VanValkenburgh, Norman, 110

"Wachusett" (pseud.), 71
Warner, Charles Dudley, 48, 72, 76
Watershed, 81, 124, 132; deterioration of, 94; protection of, as rationale for conservation, 13, 95–96, 101, 104–6, 111
West Canada Lakes Wilderness Area, 162–64
Whipple, James S., 126–28
Whiteface Mountain, 5, 21
White-tailed deer, 49–50, 152, 160–62, 196; hunting of, 73, 110
Whitney Lake, 163–64
Wilderness: ambivalence toward, 16, 28, 32, 45; appreciation of, 9, 16, 28, 41–42, 60–61, 64–67, 82–86, 137–43; definition of, 10–12, 157–58; as escape, 41–43, 65–67, 131; hostility toward, 9, 12, 16, 57–58, 109, 121, 127–28, 152; lobby for, 9, 136–38, 140, 153, 163–64; as obstacle to civilization, 16, 20, 28, 33–34, 37–38; preservation of, as such, 12, 136–37, 144; and utilitarianism, 21, 28, 31–32, 42, 76, 102
Wilderness Act (federal, 1964), 10–11, 157
Wilderness aesthetic: in Adiron-

dacks, 138–40, 148, 156–62; and Burkean aesthetic, 19, 30–32, 55; defined, 8–9, 146–47, 167. *See also* Abbott, Henry; Colvin, Verplanck
Wilderness Society, 90

Wilson, Woodrow, 132
Wolf, 33, 56, 160
Wolverine, 33

Zoning of Forest Preserve, 152–55, 157–59, 194

LIBRARY OF DAVIDSON COLLEGE

Books on
must be pres

# *Give God the Glory!*

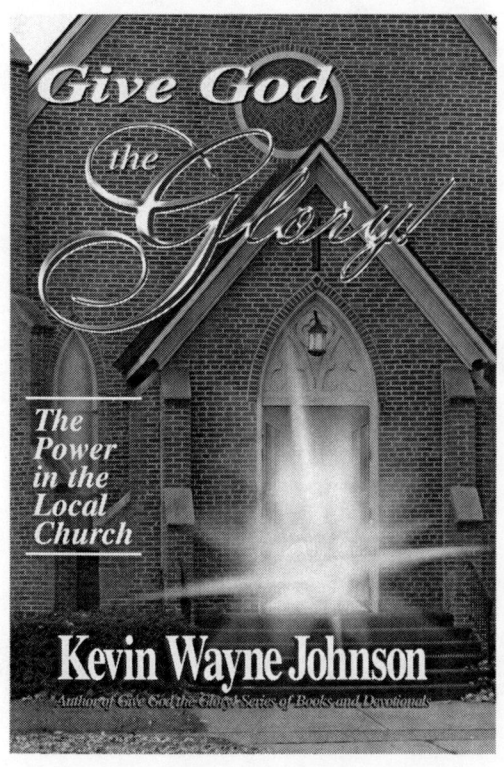

## *The Power in the Local Church*

# *Give God the Glory!*

# The Power in the Local Church

## Kevin Wayne Johnson

www.writingforthelord.com &
www.writingforthelord.org

*Give God the Glory!* series of books and devotionals
*The Power in the Local Church*
Retail Price: $19.95
©2010 by Kevin Wayne Johnson

Written by Kevin Wayne Johnson
Cover Concept by Kevin Wayne Johnson
Cover Design by The Mazzocchi Group Graphic Design
Zendra Mazzocchi-Manley, Three Rivers, MI USA
1 (877) 842-6916

Edited and Designed by Hallagen Ink
Tanya Brockett, MBA, Crozet, VA USA
1 (434) 409-7058

Distributed throughout the United States of America, Canada, and internationally by:
   (1)  STL Distribution of North America
       522 Princeton Drive
       Johnson City, TN 37601 USA
       1 (800) 289-2772
       1 (888) 785-2432 Stock Check
       www.stl-distribution.com
   (2)  Black Christian Book Distributors, LLC
       8528 Davis Boulevard, Suite 134
       N. Richlands, TX 76180 USA
       1 (214) 764-4029
       www.BlackCBC.com
   (3)  Amazon.com, Barnes & Noble Booksellers, and 11 other strategic distribution partners throughout the United States of America, United Kingdom, and Canada.

**All Rights Reserved.** No part of this book may be reproduced by any mechanical, photographic, or electronic process, or in the form of any audio recording. No part of this book may be stored in a retrieval system, transmitted, or otherwise copied for public or private use without prior written permission of the publisher, other than for "fair use" as brief quotations embodied in articles and reviews.

Unless otherwise noted, all Scripture references are taken from the King James Version of *The Holy Bible*, The New Open Bible Study Edition, Thomas Nelson, Incorporated, 1990. Other versions include the New International Version (NIV), Amplified Version (Amplified), New Living Translation (NLT), New Century Version (NCV), the New King James Version (NKJV), The Message, and New International Reader's Version (NIRV). Some of the names used in Parts I, II, and III, are fictitious characters.

ISBN: 978-0-9705902-5-1

Library of Congress Control Number: 2009943628

Printed in the United States of America

---

**Attention colleges; universities; non-profits; hospitals; prisons; independent bookstores; regional, national, and international suppliers; corporations; civic organizations; churches/church bookstores; libraries; and publishers:**

Quantity discounts are available for bulk purchases of this book for educational training purposes, fund-raising, or gift giving. Special books, booklets, articles, or book excerpts can also be created to fit your specific needs, as requested.

For special quotes, information, or for answers to your questions, contact us at: www.writingforthelord.org or www.writingforthelord.com (Web sites); http://GiveGodtheGlory.wordpress.com (our blog); Kevin@writingforthelord.com (e-mail); (443) 535-0475 (phone); (410) 340-8633 (cell)

# *Endorsements*

***Give God the Glory!*** *The Power in the Local Church* (Book #7 in the series) has received testimonials from many local, regional, national, and international readers and book reviewers.

"A revelation is unveiled after flipping through the first ten pages of this book. Awesomely written, filled with wisdom, power, and instruction. I highly recommend this book!"

—**Resa Mitchell**,
Resa Mitchell Report Gospel Magazine

"Kevin Wayne Johnson has delivered a much needed and important look at this compelling issue. Bravo, Kevin!"

—**Marilyn White**, Publisher
*Precious Times Magazine*

"Kevin Wayne Johnson delivers another powerful glimpse into his best-selling book series: ***Give God the Glory!*** A thorough look into the power that resides inside of the local church is clearly written and revealed in this book. A must read for all who sincerely desire to Give God the Glory while understanding the role of the local church in that regard."

—**Willie Jolley**, CSP, Best Selling Author
and host of the Willie Jolley Radio Show

"Where two or three are gathered there is power! *The Power in the Local Church* will teach you about the purpose of church and our roles as Christians… Not only will this book inspire us, but it will allow our souls to grow."

—**Linda Pate**, Proprietor, Precious Memories Reading and Collectibles Bookstore

"This book really made me wonder how many parents, grandmothers, Sunday school teachers, pastors, and evangelists today are indefatigably sowing richly in the lives of our young people so they will not only grow up in the power and wisdom of God, but also write books like Give God the Glory! The Power in the Local Church to help others in their life-walk with God."

—**C. Paschal Eze**, preacher, author of eleven books including *Prosperity Power Kit* and *Rebranding Race*

"Just when I think that you have surpassed excellence in your former work, once again I am awed by the soundness, the relevance, the depth of research, and the impeccable ability demonstrated to masterfully weave the spiritual and the practical together... My love and appreciation for the Church has deepened as a result of reading this great literary work. Thank you, Kevin, for your obedience and for sharing your gift with the world."

—**Paulette C. Holloway**, LICSW, LCSW-C
Director, Bethany Christian Services of Maryland

"Once again, Kevin Wayne Johnson has penned an outstanding book! It clearly explains what the Church is, its role in the Kingdom of God, and the power it has been given to operate on earth. The wisdom revealed in this book should be mandatory teaching for every person at the time or before they join a local church. It provides understanding of God's Love, purposes, and desires for the Church, thereby allowing for us to operate on a much higher level."

—**Stephanie L. Jones**, Survivor, Speaker, Author & Sexual Abuse Victim Advocate

# Other Books by Kevin Wayne Johnson

*Winner of seventeen literary/media awards since 2001; also available in Russian, Burmese, Falam, and Ngawn languages*

## As Principal Author:

**Give God the Glory!** *Know God and Do the Will of God Concerning Your Life*, 2001
Fifth printing
[Also available in print-on-demand, Amazon.com Kindle, and e-book formats]

**Give God the Glory!** *Called to be Light in the Workplace*, 2003
Second printing

**Give God the Glory!** *Let Your Light So Shine* (a devotional), 2004
Fourth printing
[Also available in print-on-demand, Amazon.com Kindle, and e-book formats]

**Give God the Glory!** *The Godly Family Life*, 2005
Second printing
[Also available in print-on-demand, Amazon.com Kindle, and e-book formats]

***Give God the Glory!*** Your *Role in* Your *Family*
(a devotional), 2006
Second printing
[Also available in print-on-demand, Amazon.com
Kindle, and e-book formats]

***Give God the Glory!*** *Know God and Do the Will of God Concerning Your Life (STUDY GUIDE)*, 2008
[Also available in print-on-demand, Amazon.com
Kindle, and e-book formats]

| | |
|---|---|
|  | Best Spiritual / Inspirational Book and Trailblazer Award 2010 |
|  | *International Best Books Award Finalist—Religion: Christianity* <br> *USA Book News & JPX Media 2010* |
| 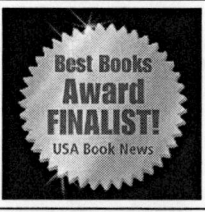 | National Best Books Award Finalist—Religion: Christianity <br> USA Book News & JPX Media 2009 |
| 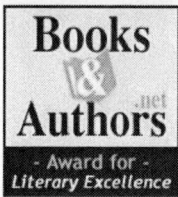 | *Award for Literary Excellence 2008* |

# Other Books with Kevin Wayne Johnson as Contributing Author:

**The Book of Miracles:** *Up Close and Personal*, projected 2011 release date

**Blended Families**, *An Anthology*, 2006
[Christian Small Publishers Association 2008 Non-Fiction Book of the Year]

**The Secret**: *How* His *Word Impacts* Our *Lives*, 2007

*If any man speak, let him speak as the oracles of God; if any man minister, let him do it as of the ability which God giveth:* **that God in all things may be glorified** *through Jesus Christ, to whom be praise and dominion for ever and ever. A-men.*

—1 Peter 4:11 KJV

*Whoever speaks, [let him do it as one who utters] oracles of God; whoever renders service, [let him do it] as with the strength which God furnishes abundantly, so* **that in all things God may be glorified** *through Jesus Christ (the Messiah). To Him be the glory and dominion forever and ever (through endless ages). Amen (so be it).*

—1 Peter 4:11 Amplified

Foundational Scripture (emphasis added) for
*Writing for the Lord* Ministries, LLC

## *In Loving Memory*

As I did with the initial book in this series (2001), I dedicate this book—*The Power in the Local Church*—to the loving memory of my maternal grandmother, *Granny*. She was a God-fearing woman who professed that I would grow up to be a preacher when I was about eight years old as she touched me on my clean-shaven head one day in her home. It is a memory of her that I will never forget. I also vividly remember observing *Granny* on her knees praying to God consistently and persistently, giving me an excellent example to follow.

*Thank you Granny for your Godly example and loving memories!*
*I love you.*

# Contents

Personal Reflections and Acknowledgements .............. xv

Author's Note .......................................................... xix

## Part I
*What is the church?* ....................................................... 1

| Chapter 1. | The Church Defined ................................ 9 |
| Chapter 2. | The Proclamation of the Church ............ 23 |
| Chapter 3. | The Declaration of the Church .............. 41 |

Section Notes ............................................................. 51

## Part II
*What is my role in the local church?* ............................. 53

| Chapter 4. | Service to Others .................................... 59 |
| Chapter 5. | Enjoy God's Blessings ............................ 67 |
| Chapter 6. | Your Role, Your Church ......................... 83 |

Section Notes ............................................................. 104

## Part III
*How do I glorify God by fulfilling my role in the local church?* ............................................................. 107

| Chapter 7. | Good Works .......................................... 111 |
| Chapter 8. | Togetherness ......................................... 121 |
| Chapter 9. | Stay in your Lane .................................. 129 |

Final Thoughts .......................................................... 139

The Establishment of the Local Church
   —A Pictorial View ................................................ 141

A Prayer for the Local Church
by Kevin Wayne Johnson ........................................ 146

*Section Notes* ............................................................ 148

A Reader's Guide:
–A Conversation with Kevin Wayne Johnson
Facilitated by Linda Pate ...................................... 149

–Reading Group Questions and
Topics for Discussion ........................................... 165

Selected Bibliography and Recommended Reading ... 167

Index .......................................................................... 171

# *Personal Reflections and Acknowledgements*

I am sincerely thankful for the awesome and privileged opportunity to share my gift at a time in history when the world needs to understand *the power in the local church*. First and foremost, I acknowledge my Heavenly Father, through Jesus Christ, as my source of life, faith, strength, encouragement, wisdom, understanding, endurance, confidence, boldness, and biblical knowledge. Without Him, this book series would not be possible nor would they reach the thousands and thousands of readers, in many countries around the world that have chosen to support this ministry. When I think about His goodness, and all He's done for me, my soul cries out *Hallelujah,* thank God for saving me!

I thank my late mom, Adele, and my dad, Ernest, his wife, Joyce, my wife, Gail, and my three sons, Kevin, Chris, and Cameron, for their family support, fun, and good times that we share daily. Your steadfast love keeps me going and going. Life is fulfilling because I am surrounded by a loving and caring family.

I want to thank several outstanding publishing industry professionals for their years of support with book design, marketing, creativity, strategic thought, promotion, and advice.

In no particular order, they are: Zendra Manley (The Mazzocchi Group, Three Rivers, Michigan), Pam Perry (Ministry Marketing Solutions, Southfield, Michigan), Larry Carpenter (former President of Standard Publishing and former General Manager of Faithworks, Cincinnati, Ohio), Marsha Sumner (Radio Host—Heaven 1580AM, Lanham, Maryland), Lawrence Wayne (Director, Memphis Black Writer's Conference, Memphis, Tennessee), and Marlene Bagnull (Director, Colorado and Greater Philadelphia Christian Writer's Conference, Langhorne, Pennsylvania).

For negotiating rights to this book series in Russian, Burmese, Falam, and Ngawn, I thank Cindy Riggins (Owner, Riggins International Rights Services, Incorporated, Clarksville, Tennessee).

I also thank Dr. Eugene Williams (mentor, author, and educator), Ella Curry (Chief Executive Officer, EDC Creations Media, Suitland, Maryland), Tanya Brockett (Owner, Hallagen Ink, Crozet, Virginia), Darren Henry (Vice President, Publisher Services, STL-Distribution of North America, Johnson City, Tennessee), Evelyn and Joseph Curtiss (Christian African-American Book Sellers Association, Los Angeles, California), Tony and Yvonne Rose (Chief Executive Officer and Vice President, Amber Communications Group, Incorporated, Phoenix, Arizona), Winston Chaney (Radio Host—WYCB-AM 1340, Lanham, Maryland), Marilyn White (Publisher and Editor in Chief, Precious Times magazine, Newport Beach, California), Les Stobbe (literary agent, Troy, North Carolina), Thea (Black Christian Book Promo, North Richlands, Texas), Kwame Alexander (Founder and Director, Capitol Book Fest, Largo, Maryland; Harrisburg, Pennsylvania; and Charleston, South Carolina), Emmanuel Amevor (Owner, Centerprise BookShop, London England), and the numerous bookstore owners/managers that have hosted outstanding book signing events.

They include: Paul Glenn (Potomac Adventist Health and Bookstore, Silver Spring, Maryland), Leo Gordy (Borders Books & Music, Largo, Maryland), Adrian Killebrew (Tennessee Regular Baptist Bookstore, Memphis, Tennessee), Pastor L. and Sister Pat Williams (Crossroads of Life Christian Bookstore, Hillside, New Jersey), and Linda Pate (Precious Memories Reading and Collectibles, Richmond, Virginia), just to name a few.

I also thank all of the wonderful bishops and pastors across this country, and abroad, for graciously opening your doors and allowing me to introduce this book series to your respective congregations and circles of influence. Since 2001, over fifty of you have welcomed me into your family and I am eternally grateful for your warm hearts.

Thank you to the multiple radio and television personalities, and hosts, for the vast opportunities to spread the gospel of Jesus Christ on the air—live and on tape.

I thank the following authors for their advice, counsel, fellowship, and mentoring: The late Andria Hall, Minister Mary Edwards, Bishop Donald Downing, Yolanda Powell, Allison Gappa Bottke,

Kimberly Brooks, Stephanie Jones, Elder Nicole Simpson, and Kim Jackson.

Thank you, Zendra Manley, for another beautiful cover design that captures the essence of this book. Great job!

Special thanks go to Pastors Pat and Jack Webster, Shiloh Pentecostal Church, *The Christian Love Center*, Somerville, New Jersey, as well as Pastor Robbie Davis and Bishop Robert Davis, Sr., Celebration Church in Columbia, Maryland.

Thank you, Steve Gilliland, for allowing God to use you as the spark that has since caught me on fire to *write for the Lord*. Our relationship dates back to the year 2000 when we first met in midtown Manhattan, New York City. Look at what God has done!

I send an especially grateful acknowledgement to all of my readers and supporters worldwide—thank you, thank you, thank you. Your loyalty and confidence in this book series encourages me to continue my personal ministry work in the Body of Christ. I thank you for your continued word-of-mouth support, for subscribing to our *Give God the Glory!* e-newsletter and blog as the *Writing for the Lord* Ministries family continues to grow and prosper. To you, and everyone involved in this ministry project, I say THANK YOU!

Enjoy God's blessings…

*Kevin Wayne Johnson*
www.writingforthelord.com
www.christianbookseries.com

## Author's Note

I love the church and what is represents. To me, the church is a place of comfort where, joy, peace, tranquility, rest, and contentment permeate the atmosphere. Over the years, the church has consistently and repeatedly provided an untarnished sense of pure power that is almost inconceivable.

*Power* is referenced throughout the Scriptures 242 times! Its first reference is transcribed in Genesis 31:6 (KJV), *"And ye know that with all my **power** I have served your father,"* and concludes in Revelation 20:6 (KJV), *"Blessed and holy is he that hath part in the first resurrection: on such the second death hath no **power**, but they shall be priests of God and of Christ, and shall reign with him a thousand years."* In the former verse, power refers to *ability*. In the latter verse, there is comfort in knowing that the second death, reserved for the unjust, has no power in the life of the believer.

*Church* is referenced throughout the Scriptures 80 times! The Greek word for church is *ekklesia*, meaning *called out ones*. Its first reference can be found in Matthew 16:18 (The Message):

> *Jesus came back, God bless you, Simon, son of Jonah! You didn't get that answer out of books or from teachers. My Father in heaven, God himself, let you in on this secret of who I*

*really am. And now I'm going to tell you who you are, really are. You are Peter, a rock. This is the rock on which I will put together my church, a church so expansive with energy that not even the gates of hell will be able to keep it out.*

The last mention in the Scriptures is located at Revelation 3:14 (NLT), *"Write this letter to the angel of the church in Laodicea. This is the message from the one who is the Amen—the faithful and true witness, the beginning of God's new creation:"* In both instances, the church represents a gathering place of believers who worship, celebrate, and praise the Lord corporately.

Although I have served as an active member and ministry leader in three denominations—African Methodist Episcopal Zion, Pentecostal, and Church of God—since my salvation experience in 1993, the common theme throughout each of these dynamic local churches is that Jesus is Lord! There is power in that name.

I still cherish the memories of my local church as a child. During those formative years, a solid foundation was laid based upon the center verse in the Bible: It is better to trust in the LORD than to put confidence in man (Psalm 118:8 KJV). My parents understood, and valued, the statutes, commandments, and judgments of our Almighty God. These principles were instilled in them through their parents, also at an early age in life.

Both of my grandmothers, Grandma (paternal) and Granny (maternal), were God-fearing women who demonstrated righteousness before God in every aspect of their respective lives. Grandma regularly attended

Sunday morning worship services at Fifth Street Baptist Church, while Granny regularly attended Saturday morning worship services at Ephesus Seventh Day Adventist Church in our hometown of Richmond, Virginia.

Though each observed the Sabbath on different days of the week, I was undeniably convinced that they loved and trusted the Lord with all of their heart (Proverbs 3:6). Their mannerism, discipline, prayer life, service to others, diligence, and lifestyle was on display for all to witness.

I remember our loving interactions as if it were yesterday. In fact, I still recall Granny's prophesy that I would preach the gospel in due season. I was eight years old at the time. It was during the summer of 1968. The power of the gospel in their lives resonates perpetually because of their active involvement in the local church.

While observing their Godly lives week after week and year after year, I spent my impressionable childhood years at Ebenezer Baptist Church, Richmond, Virginia, actively engaged in Sunday school, cub scouts, music, and youth leadership programs. The experience from active engagement was powerful. I remember my scout master, Deacon Ross, and my music teacher, Sister Flowers. They are still active ministry leaders at Ebenezer and I enjoy seeing them as often as I can.

I experienced water baptism at the age of nine. Although I did not quite understand the significance at the time, there was power in this ordinance. I could not explain what I felt but it was real and meaningful. Between the ages of ten and twelve, I recall leading

Sunday morning worship services, along with other youth in the church, from the pulpit, reading Scripture and reciting the Lord's Prayer. There was power in these leadership positions during our annual youth day programs.

My dad served twenty years in the United States Marine Corps. As he approached the end of his career, his love for his family compelled him to decline a promotion to the rank of captain in order to avoid another tour of duty overseas.

During his illustrious career as an enlisted soldier and commissioned officer, Dad served admirably in Okinawa, Japan and Vietnam (twice). His decision not to leave us again was a sincere demonstration of love. In exchange for an overseas tour, Dad retained his rank as first lieutenant and our family relocated from Richmond to Virginia Beach in 1973. Dad would serve his final three years of military service at the Naval Air Station, Norfolk, Virginia. We would not return to Richmond until 1976.

During our time in the Norfolk and Virginia Beach area, and during my pivotal middle and high school years, we did not attend church services regularly. I lost my connection with God, but not my need for Him. Once my dad retired from military service in 1976, we returned home to Richmond and once again actively attended church at Ebenezer. While I temporarily strayed away from the power in the local church for a brief period of time, God's Word kept me from falling. *"Train up a child in the way he should go: and when he is old, he will not depart from it"* (Proverbs 22:6 KJV).

As a result of the solid foundation that my grandmothers' laid for my parents to build upon, who in turn passed their Godly love on to their children, I am able to write this next book in the award-winning **Give God the Glory!** series. This book series has reached a global audience in multiple languages. It is my prayer that you will experience *The Power in the Local Church* and pass this revelation along to the next generation as well as those within your sphere of influence. Notice the multiple references to how people across the globe are revealing the power in the local church. Their acts of service, togetherness, good works, and God's blessings are the true manifestation of the power of God in the hearts of men and women.

Together, let's **Give God the Glory!** as we journey through the power in the local church.

*Kevin Wayne Johnson*

## *The Church by Definition*

…any number of souls, called and united in one vow, in one place, for divine worship, where the pure Word is preached, and the sacraments duly administered, and godly living, after His law, as given by the head of the church, the Lord Jesus Christ.

—Smith's Bible Dictionary

# Revelation of the Church

When Jesus came into the coasts of Caesarea Philippi, he asked his disciples, saying, Whom do men say that I the Son of man am?

And they said, Some say that thou art John the Baptist: some, Elias; and others, Jeremias, or one of the prophets.

He saith unto them, But whom say ye that I am?

And Simon Peter answered and said, Thou art the Christ, the Son of the living God.

And Jesus answered and said unto him, Blessed art thou, Simon Barjona: for flesh and blood hath not revealed it unto thee, but my Father which is in heaven.

And I say also unto thee, That thou art Peter, and upon this rock I will build my church; and the gates of hell shall not prevail against it.

And I will give unto thee the keys of the kingdom of heaven: and whatsoever thou shalt bind on earth shall be bound in heaven: and whatsoever thou shalt loose on earth shall be loosed in heaven.

—Matthew 16:13–19 KJV

# Glory!

*A divine quality. Literally meaning heavy or weighty.*

*It represents the brightness, splendor, and radiance of God's presence as well as His visible revelation of Himself.*

*Our word 'doxology' comes from 'doxa,' the Greek word for Glory.*

# ଓଃ Part I ଛ
## What is the Church?

*And I say also unto thee, That thou art Peter, and upon this rock I will build my church; and the gates of hell shall not prevail against it.*
—Matthew 16:18 KJV

*Now I say to you that you are Peter (which means 'rock'), and upon this rock I will build my church, and all the powers of hell will not conquer it.*
—Matthew 16:18 NLT

## GIVE GOD THE GLORY!

Church means different things to many people. As I recall, my personal experience in the local church began in 1965. Sunday school, music lessons, sing-alongs, reciting Bible verses, Cub Scout activities, and water baptism resonate in my mind vividly. These were some of my earlier remembrances of Ebenezer Baptist Church, my local church as a child.

"Kevin, it's time to go to church. It's 10:30 and we can't be late. Sunday school starts shortly and church services at 11:00," my mom would say. "Are you ready?"

"Yes ma'am. I'm ready," I said without missing a beat.

"What about Eric? Is he ready too? You can't forget your brother," she asked.

"Yes, he said that he's ready to go. He was ready five minutes ago," I stated.

"Are you excited about Sunday school this morning Kevin?" asked mom.

"Yes ma'am, I am. I think that we will continue with last week's lesson about David and his victory over Goliath," I said with a jump. "Brother Bell does a great job in telling the story about David. I enjoy his teaching. I hope that I can teach like that when I grow up." Mom gave me a proud look.

"I'm sure that you will son. Pay close attention in class, learn as much as you can and you will be a great teacher just like Brother Bell." Mom would stare in my eyes and smile when giving positive feedback on these matters. This reinforced her message of hope.

As I smiled at my mom in return, I would look up at her to say, "Thanks mom for taking me and Eric to Sunday school each week. We have lots of fun and learn so much." Getting in the car, I thought about the Sunday school class and the lesson for the day.

"Sure, Kevin. This is what I am supposed to do and I am happy to do it. Just make sure that you do the same when you have children someday."

"Children? Me? Yuck! Now that's a long time from now, isn't it mom? I'm only five years old."

"It is. But it's never too early to start working on good habits that will last a lifetime. The Bible teaches us to *'leave an inheritance to your children's children.'* That's found in the book of Proverbs. It means that we are supposed to make God a priority in our lives, including regular attendance at church and active participation in our local church. It is supposed to be passed down to the children in the family. That means you Kevin. Also, in the book of Proverbs, the Bible teaches us *'to train up a child in the way that he should go, so that when he is old he will not depart from it.'* Always remember this Kevin, it will serve you well."

"Yes ma'am, I will," peaking out of the car window as we rode the seven miles to our local church. We were there in less than ten minutes.

"There's Brother Bell," I shouted, pointing to my Sunday school teacher from the back seat of our car. He was standing on the front steps of the church in clear sight. I knew that Sunday school started in just a few minutes. I couldn't wait.

"Brother Bell, Brother Bell! I'm here! We are right on time. Whew!" I shouted with joy.

"Yes you are Kevin. Nice to see you this morning," said Brother Bell.

"What is today's lesson?" I asked. "I remember the story about David and Goliath from last week."

"Kevin, this week we will discuss how the church empowers its members. There is power in the local church that is specifically intended to encourage, motivate, and inspire us all toward greatness. This power is revealed by God through our collective attendance in a local church. The Bible clearly teaches us that *'Where two or three are gathered together in my name, there I am in the midst of them.'* Kevin, this is found in the book of Matthew, chapter 18. In essence, the church is wherever you are if at least two people are gathered together for the purpose of worshipping God Almighty. Isn't that great?"

"Wow…I've learned a lot and class hasn't started yet. Last week, you taught us about the power of God in the life of young David as he defeated a nine foot giant named Goliath. Thanks Brother Bell, let's go inside to join the others." Kevin ran inside.

"Guess what everybody?" I asked.

"What?" All twelve classmates replied.

"God is in our midst according to the Bible because there are more than two of us gathered to worship Him today. We are empowered to greatness. This power it supposed to be used by us to make this world a much better place for all. When we do so, God gives us the same ability as He gave to David who defeated a mean giant with a single aim from a slingshot. Brother Bell told me so."

"Kevin, now that's the power in the local church," said Brother Bell with a huge smile. He took over and began teaching the week's lesson plan.

"Amen," I said.

# The Growth of the Gospel

## *God is Building His Church— Rapidly*

Across the centuries, Bible-believing Christians have become an ever-larger proportion of the world population. In 1430 A.D., only one person in one hundred was a Bible-believing Christian. Today, one in nine is. This means 600 million out of 6 billion people in the world are Bible-believing Christians. This huge body of believers is growing at a rate of *more than three times* that of the world population!

## Milestone Dates in the Growth of True Christianity

At the dates indicated, a comparison of:
1) The number of Bible-believing Christians, and
2) The total number of people in the world.

| | | |
|---|---|---|
| One per 100 (1%) by | A.D. 1430 | (One to 99 after 1430 years) |
| Two per 100 (2%) by | A.D. 1790 | (One to 49 after 360 years) |
| Three per 100 (3%) by | A.D. 1940 | (One to 32 after 150 years) |
| Four per 100 (4%) by | A.D. 1960 | (One to 24 after 20 years) |
| Five per 100 (5%) by | A.D. 1970 | (One to 19 after 10 years) |
| Six per 100 (6%) by | A.D. 1980 | (One to 16 after 10 years) |
| Seven per 100 (7%) by | A.D. 1983 | (One to 13 after 3 years) |
| Eight per 100 (8%) by | A.D. 1986 | (One to 11 after 3 years) |
| Nine per 100 (9%) by | A.D. 1989 | (One to 10 after 3 years) |
| Ten per 100 (10%) by | A.D. 1993 | (One to 9 after 4 years) |
| Eleven per 100 (11%) by | A.D. 1995 | (One to 8 after 2 years) |

*Source*: Lausanne Statistics Task Force, headed by David Barnett, Ph.D. The intermediate values here were then calculated (exponentially) for these specific milestone dates. Mission Frontiers, Jan–Feb 1996 edition, The Bulletin of the U.S. Center for World Mission, Pasadena, California.

*Give God the Glory!*

# Chapter One

## The Church Defined

*God can do anything, you know—far more than you could ever imagine or guess or request in your wildest dreams! He does it not by pushing us around but by working within us, his Spirit deeply and gently within us. Glory to God in the church! Glory to God in the Messiah, in Jesus! Glory down all the generations! Glory through all millennia! Oh, yes!*

—Ephesians 3:20–21 The Message

# GIVE GOD THE GLORY!

**G**lory to God in the church! This is an intriguing pronouncement that is found in Ephesians 3:20–21 (The Message). Through this entire chapter, God unravels the mystery of the church (verses 1–13) as the Apostle Paul lifts up a prayer for realization concerning the church (verses 14–21).

The ultimate purpose of the church is to bring honor and glory to its head, Jesus Christ. It does this as it fulfills its two purposes related to God's program for the world. The first purpose is evangelism (The Great Commission, Matthew 28:19–20). Evangelism is a two-fold ministry that involves *"baptizing them in the name of the Father, and of the Son, and of the Holy Ghost,"* and *"teaching them to observe all things whatsoever I have commanded you."*

The second is edification—building up one's faith (Ephesians 4:12). Its two goals are *"For the perfecting of the saints"* and *"For the work of the ministry."* The believers who compose the church's membership need to be built up so that they may realize all that God has provided for Christian living and that they may come to spiritual maturity. In a real sense, each member of the church is to be a Christian worker so that the work that God wants to perform through the local church can be accomplished.

Church is defined by its original root word—*ekklesia*. When translated into English, it means *called out ones*. From this, we can derive that there are three scriptural definitions of a church:

*The Church Defined*

1. The entire body of believers (universal) who are saved by or because of their relationship with Jesus Christ (Body of Christ);
2. Those who are assembled together by the bounds of their habitation (a local church); and
3. The bride of Christ.

## What happens at church?

Primarily, Christians attend church to worship God. But worship styles vary from church to church. Sometimes, they even change from week to week. But most churches, unless they are running a special program, have a regular format that is adjusted depending on the people leading it. In some form or another, with varying degrees of style and creativity, expect the following:

**Welcome**—This will give you an insight into what to expect, as well as the workings and passions of the particular congregation.

**Singing/praise**—Led by one or several people, with musical accompaniment by anything from an organ to a band. Songs of praise to God may be sprinkled throughout the worship service or they may be all sung in a block. Some congregations will stand when they sing, others remain seated, and others a combination depending on the song itself. Some congregations encourage clapping or raising hands; others are more traditional.

**Prayer**—You may be invited to kneel, stand, or even to remain in your seat. Do what everyone else does.

**Offering**—Our gifts to God and His cause. Quite often, a bag or plate will be passed among the group for the collection, which will be used to cover the expenses of the local congregation, the premises, or to support a project. Alternatively, an offering box will be placed in a strategic position. It is not compulsory, of course, to give an offering or donation, so if you choose not to or are caught unawares, don't be embarrassed.

**Sermon**—This might begin with a drama or story to get everyone's attention and focus on the topic or theme. The sermon is usually an expansion of somebody's thoughts on a theme, and may include a Bible passage or story, or several. If the Bible or God isn't a central theme in the sermon, you may want to rethink your purpose for attending this church.

**Winding up**—A worship service will usually end with a prayer, called a benediction. There may also be more singing. Some churches will include an invitation for anyone who wishes to publicly respond to an invitation from the presenter to be a follower of Jesus.[1]

## Glossary of Church Speak

A selection of church terms and the context for their use are captured in table 1, which follows.

**TABLE 1.** Church terms to know and understand

| Church Term | Description |
|---|---|
| **Church** | Can refer to a local congregation (First Baptist Church of Centreville), the building where they meet (the church on the corner of Maple and Main), or a denomination (Methodist Church, Adventist Church). |
| **Denomination** | A group of local congregations that shares a name and certain beliefs. |
| **Doxology** | A short song of praise to God, often sung at the beginning of a worship service. |
| **Baptism** | Immersion in water as a public acknowledgement of one's belief that Jesus is Lord and Savior. Baptism is also evidence of repentance for one's sin. |
| **Communion** | A worship service in which Christians celebrate Jesus' death for their sins by eating small pieces of bread (symbolic of His body) and drinking grape juice (symbolic of His blood). |

## A Look into the Sabbath

In the fourth of the Ten Commandments (Exodus 20:8–11), God's Word teaches us:

*Remember the Sabbath day by keeping it holy. Six days you shall labor and do all your work, but the seventh day is a Sabbath to the LORD your God. On it you shall not do any work, neither you, nor your son or daughter, nor your manservant or maidservant, nor your animals, nor the alien within your gates. For in six days the LORD made the heavens and the earth, the sea, and all that is in them, but he rested on the seventh day. Therefore the LORD blessed the Sabbath day and made it holy.*

—NIV

*Remember to observe the Sabbath day by keeping it holy. You have six days each week for your ordinary work, but the seventh day is a Sabbath day of rest dedicated to the LORD your God. On that day no one in your household may do any work. This includes you, your sons and daughters, your male and female servants, your livestock, and any foreigners living among you. For in six days the LORD made the heavens, the earth, the sea, and everything in them; but on the seventh day he rested. That is why the LORD blessed the Sabbath day and set it apart as holy.*

—NLT

A mere superficial reading of this commandment would suggest that you do not work on the Lord's day, keeping it holy instead. But there's more to keeping the day holy than ceasing from everyday employment. Notice, the command tells us only *what not to do*, it does not tell us *what to do* in order to keep the day holy. It's left to us to examine whether our activities on that day in fact "keep it holy," something that over the millennia since Moses' day, we've not been good at. Is it right, then, to worship our Creator on the Sabbath? Is that a "holy" activity? Of course it is. Let's examine 1 Chronicles 16:29:

*Ascribe to the Lord the glory due His name. Bring an offering and come before Him; worship the Lord in the beauty of holiness and in holy array.*

—Amplified and NLT

In fact, you can't do better than that. Since God has been so good to us all week long, we should love to come and worship Him. In worship we express our thanks and gratitude, we adore Him, we give Him all the glory and we praise His name. That's worship. So do you celebrate the Sabbath? Is it any different from the other six days? Or is it more of the same, rushing around and not really finding a rest in God—or a focus on Him? Isaiah says if we endeavor to make a real difference between our days and God's, and decide to honor Him instead of doing as we please on the Sabbath, *"then you will find your joy in the Lord"* (Isaiah 58:14). If we all kept God's day holy, according to His instructions, think what a change there would be in our communities. The elderly in rest homes would be visited more; the sick and dying in hospitals would be encouraged and comforted. If all kept the Sabbath as intended, the disadvantaged in the community would come to know that people care about them. Eventually, all of these groups would anticipate the arrival of the Sabbath day with pleasure. For ourselves, life's pressures would ease, and it would go a long way toward repairing broken relationships in our families. Busy parents might spend more time with their children in both worship and amid nature. [2]

## Ideas for a Sabbath

Why not experiment with a Sabbath this weekend? Here are some suggestions of things to do:
- Visit an aged-care facility. Older people are often very lonely.
- Invite your family to a special lunch, then take something you've prepared to a shut-in.
- Take a walk in a national or state park where there's natural beauty.
- Visit a new church.
- Enjoy fellowship.

*But if we walk in the light, as he is in the light, we have fellowship with one another, and the blood of Jesus, his Son, purifies us from all sin.*
—1 John 1:7 NIV

*Those who had respect for the Lord talked with one another. They cheered each other up. And the Lord heard them. A list of people and what they did was written on a scroll in front of him. It included the names of those who respected the Lord and honored him.*
—Malachi 3:16 NIRV

## Gang Hideout Becomes a Church

For years, the A&M Body Shop in Somerville, Massachusetts, USA, was known as the headquarters for an Irish-American gang that dealt in illegal drugs and gambling. The group committed murder to achieve its goals. A trapdoor provided entry to an underground room that was reputedly used to get rid of bodies. But today the former body shop has been transformed into a church. Collin Green, the pastor of the Somerville Church of God, said that his congregation had no idea of the building's sordid past until shortly before they signed papers to purchase it. Green said his church is open to everyone, including former gang members. Former gangster, John Martorano, who confessed to twenty killings, said *"I think it's great"* that the building is being used for a church. *"I'm all for religion."*[3]

Analyzing Pastor Green's motivation and intent, we have to get past the name on a building, or the need for a physical building to fulfill God's vision in the earth. To this end, God *is* where two or three gather together in the name of Lord:

*For where two or three are gathered together in my name, there am I in the midst of them.*
—Matthew 18:20 KJV

*Take this most seriously: A yes on earth is yes in heaven; a no on earth is no in heaven. What you say to one another is eternal. I mean this. When two of you get together on anything at all on earth and make a prayer of it, my Father in heaven goes into action. And when two or three of you are together because of me, you can be sure that I'll be there.*
—Matthew 18:20 The Message

## Church and Suicide

Analyzing data taken from a survey of nearly 37,000 people that was conducted by Canada's Community Health Survey, psychiatrist Daniel Rasic at the University of Manitoba found that people who attend church are half as likely to commit suicide as non-attendees. Rasic took into consideration that affiliation with a church provides attendees with a built-in support system, and he found that his statistics held even when he ruled out that factor. While the study does not attempt to explain why church attendance reduces the likelihood of suicide, Rasic suggests that it may have to do with the fact that most religions teach against suicide and the life-long religious people are less likely to suffer from mental illness such as depression.[4]

## Church Growth

In the year that ended June 30, 2009, Seventh Day Adventists added more than one million people to their membership. This is the sixth consecutive year that the church has experienced growth in excess of one million. An average of 2,818 people joined the church daily during the most recent period, bringing global membership to just over sixteen million. Church leaders had projected that world membership would be seventeen million by 2009. However, corrected membership reports from several regions caused membership to remain at about sixteen million.[5]

## *Major Historical Events in the Church*

1. The Apostolic Period—30-70 AD: Jesus is crucified, Christian faith begins to spread; The Church is born. Apostle Paul's first through fourth missionary journeys throughout Macedonia and Asia Minor with Barnabus and Silas.
2. The Spread of the Catholic Church—70-132 AD: The Universal church spreads despite persecution and opposition.
3. The Age of the Christian Church—312-590 AD: Constantine names Christianity as the "World Religion," people are persecuted for not being Christian, The Council of Nicea, At Antioch, disciples are referred to as Christians for the first time (Acts 11:26).
4. The Middle Ages—590-1517 AD: The church goes on many "crusades" to the Holy Land to expel the Jews, The Catholic Church becomes a "business."
5. The Protestant Reformation—1517-1648: Martin Luther 95 thesis posted up, Martin Luther opposes the Catholic Church.

## *Review and Discussion*

1. Why does the church exist?
   _____
   _____

2. Why do we need to belong to a local church assembly?
   _____
   _____

3. How do you know if you are in the right church?
   _____
   _____

4. How does God speak through a pastor on behalf of the members?
   _____
   _____

5. Name some of the benefits of belonging to a local church?
   _____
   _____

***GIVE GOD THE GLORY!***

# Chapter Two

## The Proclamation of the Church

*All the believers devoted themselves to the apostles' teaching, and to fellowship, and to sharing in meals (including the Lord's Supper), and to prayer. A deep sense of awe came over them all, and the apostles performed many miraculous signs and wonders. And all the believers met together in one place and shared everything they had. They sold their property and possessions and shared the money with those in need. They worshiped together at the Temple each day, met in homes for the Lord's Supper, and shared their meals with great joy and generosity—all the while praising God and enjoying the goodwill of all the people. And each day the Lord added to their fellowship those who were being saved.*

—Acts 2:42–47 NLT

The practices of the early church established outstanding examples for today's church. The pattern set here, in Acts 2:42–47, is normative throughout this age. They publicly profess, or proclaim, their faith through baptism, and join in fellowship, edification, and service within the assembly of God's people.

**The Fellowship of the Believers**

*They devoted themselves to the apostles' teaching and to the fellowship, to the breaking of bread and to prayer. Everyone was filled with awe, and many wonders and miraculous signs were done by the apostles. All the believers were together and had everything in common. Selling their possessions and goods, they gave to anyone as he had need. Every day they continued to meet together in the temple courts. They broke bread in their homes and ate together with glad and sincere hearts, praising God and enjoying the favor of all the people. And the Lord added to their number daily those who were being saved.*

—Acts 2:42–47 NIV

The above passage records the first meeting of the first local church. From this passage, seven benefits of participation in the local church are immediately apparent:

1. Instruction: *"continued stedfastly in the apostles' doctrine,"*
2. Fellowship: *"and fellowship,"*
3. Observance of the ordinances: *"breaking of bread,"*
4. Corporate prayer: *"prayers,"*
5. Effective outreach: *"fear came upon every soul,"*
6. Common cause: *"had all things common,"* and
7. Mutual assistance: *"parted them to all men, as every man had need."*

In addition to these, four other benefits of participation in the local church are clear. They are:

### Worship

*And on the first day of the week, when we were assembled together to break bread [the Lord's Supper], Paul discoursed with them, intending to leave the next morning; and he kept on with his message until midnight.*

—Acts 20:7 Amplified

### Discipline

*If a fellow believer hurts you, go and tell him—work it out between the two of you. If he listens, you've made a friend. If he won't listen, take one or two others along so that the presence of witnesses will keep things honest, and try again. If he still won't listen, tell the church. If he won't listen to the church, you'll have to start over from scratch, confront him with the need for repentance, and offer again God's forgiving love.*

—Matthew 18:15–17 The Message

### Pastoral oversight

*The elders who are among you I exhort, I who am a fellow elder and a witness of the sufferings of Christ, and also a partaker of the glory that will be revealed: Shepherd the flock of God which is among you, serving as overseers, not by compulsion but willingly, not for dishonest gain but eagerly; nor as being lords over those entrusted to you, but being examples to the flock;*

—1 Peter 5:1–3 NKJV

*And now, a word to you who are elders in the churches. I, too, am an elder and a witness to the sufferings of Christ. And I, too, will share in his glory when he is revealed to the whole world. As a fellow elder, I appeal to you: Care for the flock that God has entrusted to you. Watch over it willingly, not grudgingly—not for what you will get out of it, but because you are eager to serve God. Don't lord it over the people assigned to your care, but lead them by your own good example.*

—1 Peter 5:1–3 NLT

### Obedience to God's command

*Let us not give up meeting together, as some are in the habit of doing, but let us encourage one another—and all the more as you see the Day approaching.*

—Hebrews 10:25 NIV

Participation in the local church is not optional for the child of God. It is imperative and yields eternal benefits!

## Why does God Want Us to Go to Church?

The church functions in a state of "oneness." The Scriptures are a clear revelation of the fact that God (our Heavenly Father) is the source of the church, Jesus (our advocate and Savior) is the head of the church, and the Holy Spirit (our Comforter) is the guide, helper, enabler, or embodiment of power within the church. Thus, the triune God is equal in deity, omnipotence [power], omniscience [knowledge], omnipresence [present at all times], as the Father, Son, and Holy Spirit. Source, in this context, refers to the origin and creator of that from which any act, movement, or effect proceeds. The reason that we attend church is to learn and understand how the triune God operates as one.

<u>**God** is our Source</u>:

a. In Hebrews 11:6, simply stated—*He is.*

   *Without faith no one can please God. Anyone who comes to God must believe that he is real and that he rewards those who truly want to find him.*

   —NCV

> *But without faith it is impossible to please and be satisfactory to Him. For whoever would come near to God must [necessarily] believe that God exists and that He is the rewarder of those who earnestly and diligently seek Him [out].*
>
> —Amplified

b. He is the "I Am" (Exodus 3:6–7; 13–14). He is always in the present.

> *Moreover He said, "I am the God of your father—the God of Abraham, the God of Isaac, and the God of Jacob." And Moses hid his face, for he was afraid to look upon God. And the LORD said: "I have surely seen the oppression of My people who are in Egypt, and have heard their cry because of their taskmasters, for I know their sorrows.*
>
> —3:6–7 NKJV

> *Then Moses said to God, "Suppose I go to the People of Israel and I tell them, 'The God of your fathers sent me to you'; and they ask me, 'What is his name?' What do I tell them?" God said to Moses, "I-AM-WHO-I-AM. Tell the People of Israel, 'I-AM sent me to you.'"*
>
> —3:13–14 The Message

c. He is incomprehensible, yet the church can know Him (1 Corinthians 2:9–16).

> *That is what the Scriptures mean when they say, "No eye has seen, no ear has heard, and no mind has imagined what God has prepared*

*for those who love him." But it was to us that God revealed these things by his Spirit. For his Spirit searches out everything and shows us God's deep secrets. No one can know a person's thoughts except that person's own spirit, and no one can know God's thoughts except God's own Spirit. And we have received God's Spirit (not the world's spirit), so we can know the wonderful things God has freely given us. When we tell you these things, we do not use words that come from human wisdom. Instead, we speak words given to us by the Spirit, using the Spirit's words to explain spiritual truths. But people who aren't spiritual can't receive these truths from God's Spirit. It all sounds foolish to them and they can't understand it, for only those who are spiritual can understand what the Spirit means. Those who are spiritual can evaluate all things, but they themselves cannot be evaluated by others. For, "Who can know the LORD's thoughts? Who knows enough to teach him?" But we understand these things, for we have the mind of Christ.*

—NLT

**Jesus** is the Head of the church:
*I have not stopped thanking God for you. I always remember you in my prayers. I pray to the God of our Lord Jesus Christ. God is the glorious Father. I keep asking him to give you the wisdom and understanding that come from the Holy Spirit. I want you to know God better. I also pray that your mind might see more*

*clearly. Then you will know the hope God has chosen you to receive. You will know that the things God's people will receive are rich and glorious. And you will know his great power. It can't be compared with anything else. It is at work for us who believe. It is like the mighty strength God showed when he raised Christ from the dead. He seated him at his right hand in his heavenly kingdom. There Christ sits far above all who rule and have authority. He also sits far above all powers and kings. He is above every title that can be given in this world and in the world to come. God placed all things under Christ's rule. He appointed him to be ruler over everything for the church. The church is Christ's body. It is filled by Christ. He fills everything in every way.*

—Ephesians 1:16–23 NIRV

a. He is the way, the truth, and the life

*Jesus answered, "I am the way and the truth and the life. No one comes to the Father except through me."*

—John 14:6 NIRV

b. He is divine

*I am the true vine; my Father is the gardener. He cuts off every branch of mine that does not produce fruit. And he trims and cleans every branch that produces fruit so that it will produce even more fruit. You are already clean because of the words I have spoken to you. Remain in me, and I will remain in you. A branch cannot produce fruit alone but must remain in the vine. In the same way, you cannot produce fruit alone but must remain in me. I am the vine, and you are the branches. If any remain in me and I remain in them, they produce much fruit. But without me they can do nothing. If any do not remain in me, they are like a branch that is thrown away and then dies. People pick up dead branches, throw them into the fire, and burn them. If you remain in me and follow my teachings, you can ask anything you want, and it will be given to you. You should produce much fruit and show that you are my followers, which brings glory to my Father.*

—John 15:1–8 NCV

c. He is an advocate

*My little children, these things I write to you, so that you may not sin. And if anyone sins, we have an Advocate with the Father, Jesus Christ the righteous. And He Himself is the propitiation for our sins, and not for ours only but also for the whole world.*

—1 John 2:1–3 NKJV

d. He is the power [authority]

*When they saw him, they worshiped him—but some of them doubted! Jesus came and told his disciples, "I have been given all authority in heaven and on earth. Therefore, go and make disciples of all the nations, baptizing them in the name of the Father and the Son and the*

> *Holy Spirit. Teach these new disciples to obey all the commands I have given you. And be sure of this: I am with you always, even to the end of the age."*
> 
> —Matthew 28:17–20 NLT

e.  He is the anointed one

> *The Spirit of the Lord [is] upon Me, because He has anointed Me [the Anointed One, the Messiah] to preach the good news (the Gospel) to the poor; He has sent Me to announce release to the captives and recovery of sight to the blind, to send forth as delivered those who are oppressed [who are downtrodden, bruised, crushed, and broken down by calamity], To proclaim the accepted and acceptable year of the Lord [the day when salvation and the free favors of God profusely abound.*
> 
> —Luke 4:18–19 Amplified

The **Holy Spirit** is the guide:

> *Then Peter opened his mouth, and said, Of a truth I perceive that God is no respecter of persons: But in every nation he that feareth him, and worketh righteousness, is accepted with him. The word which God sent unto the children of Israel, preaching peace by Jesus Christ: (he is Lord of all) That word, I say, ye know, which was published throughout all Judaea, and began from Galilee, after the baptism which John preached; How God anointed Jesus of Nazareth with the Holy Ghost and with power: who went about doing good,*

*and healing all that were oppressed of the devil; for God was with him.*
—Acts 10:34–38 KJV

## A Welcoming Community

In the four chapters of the Old Testament book of Ruth, we are privy to a cameo story of love, devotion, and redemption. It is the story of a Moabite woman who forsakes her pagan heritage in order to cling to the people of Israel and to the God of Israel. Although the author is unknown, because of her faithfulness in a time of national faithlessness, God rewards Ruth by giving her a new husband (Boaz), a son (Obed), and a privileged position in the lineage of David and Christ.

The Bible story of Ruth is a wonderful example of what "church" should be in our lives. It's important to note that in the New Testament the Greek word *ekklesia*, which is translated *"church,"* is never used in reference to a building. It always refers to a community. So when someone asks me, "Why do you go to church?" I often draw on the story of Ruth and the themes found there.

The Bible says that when Naomi and Ruth arrived in Bethlehem, *"all the city was excited because of them"* (Ruth 1:19 NKJV). These women had felt abandoned by their loved ones, spiritually discouraged, lonely, and financially bankrupt. Naomi's words, *"The LORD has caused me to suffer"* (Ruth 1:21 NLT), suggest that they were also probably a bit angry with

God. But when they arrived in Bethlehem, they were welcomed with open arms by all the people. The fact that Ruth was a Moabitess—a nation that had been in a lot of conflict with the people of Israel—was never used against her. She was made to feel just as welcome as her mother-in-law.

Church is like that. It's a community that welcomes everyone. There should be no distinction between race, gender, or socioeconomic standing, for Paul said that in Christ *"there is neither Jew nor Greek, slave nor free, male nor female"* (Galatians 3:28). God laid down this principle at the beginning of time when He said that every person is made in the image of God (Genesis 1:27).

## Finding Community

It can be unnerving to move to a new community. There are new symbols, words, norms, and behaviors to learn. It must not have been easy for Ruth, but she saw something in Naomi that she wanted as a part of her life. In order to obtain it, she was willing to give up her own way of life.

It can be hard to walk into a new church. You feel like a stranger. You don't even know where the bathroom is! But if church is anything like what it should be, you'll find people who are welcoming, who are supportive and won't condemn you for your past, who celebrate new life in Jesus Christ, who have a forgiving spirit and uphold the Word of God as the means by which a relationship with Jesus can be created, strengthened, and grown.[6]

## Church is Vindicated

In 2005, the World Outreach Conference Center (WOCC) in Chicago, IL, purchased an old YMCA building with 168 rooms to provide housing for needy people. However, when the organization applied for a single-room occupancy permit, the city denied it, allegedly because an alderman on the city council had wanted the building sold to a friend who was a real estate developer. Instead, the city rezoned the property to "manufacturing," which blocked the WOCC from using the building to further its mission. WOCC sued, and in December 2009, a panel of the Seventh Circuit Court of Appeals ruled in favor of the WOCC. Judge Richard Posner wrote that the city's action had "impeded [WOCC] in its religious mission of providing living facilities to homeless," which included victims of Hurricane Katrina.[7]

## Church for the Disabled

A new kind of church has sprung up in Toronto. It's called the "Abilities Church," and its target audience is people who are disabled physically or mentally. Ministry pastor Robert Gagnon, a victim of cerebral palsy, wasn't expected to live more than 48 hours at birth. Today, he has a master's degree in theology. The Abilities Church was founded in the fall of 2009. The group's plan is for at least fifty percent of the membership and ministry team to be disabled people. The church uses pictures to help people with severe mental disabilities to visualize the concepts presented. There are no rules for noise, walking around, or dancing.[8]

## Jordan Donates Land for Church

The Episcopal Diocese of Jerusalem recently received a gift from King Abdullah II of Jordan: two and one-half acres at the site where tradition says Jesus was baptized by John the Baptist. According to Anglican bishop Suheil Dawani of Jerusalem, the diocese will use the land to build a medium-sized Gothic church and retreat center for Anglicans from all over the world who visit the Holy Land.

Speaking at the official dedication of the site, Jordanian Prince Ghazi bin Mohammed, advisor to King Abdullah on churches in Jordan, said that the projected church and retreat center will be "an important part of Jordan's invitation to the Christian religious community to participate in collegiality and interfaith dialogue."[9]

## Bible Discovery with Errol Webster
# THE CHURCH COMMUNITY

The sanctuary built by Moses and the subsequent temple built by Solomon were considered holy and sacred because God's presence was manifest there. The temple was the center of Israelite worship. When they were unable to pray in the temple itself, they were to direct their prayers toward the temple. In the New Testament the word *temple* is applied spiritually to the church as a community of believers and not to a building. The Greek word translated "church" is *ekklesia*, which means "called out ones."

1. In speaking of the Christian church what does Paul call it? 1 Corinthians 3:16–17 *"Don't you know that you yourselves are God's temple and that God's Spirit lives in you? God's temple is sacred, and you are that temple."*

    The individual believer is also described as "a temple of the *Holy* Spirit" (1 Corinthians 6:19).

2. Upon whom is the church built? 1 Corinthians 3:11; Ephesians 2:19–21 *"For no one can lay any foundation other than the one already laid, which is Christ Jesus."*

    *"Consequently, you are no longer foreigners and aliens, but fellow citizens with God's people and members of God's household, built on the foundation of the apostles and prophets, with Christ Jesus as the chief cornerstone. In Him the whole building is joined together."*

    The church is also described as the body of Christ, with Jesus as its head (Ephesians 5:23).

3. What unity exists "in Christ"? Galatians 3:28; 1 Corinthians 12:13 *"There is neither Jew nor Greek,*

*slave nor free, male nor female, for you are all one in Christ Jesus." "For we were all baptized by one Spirit into one body—whether Jews or Greeks, slave or free."*

**The function of the church**

4. What four things were involved in the early church worship? Acts 2:42 *"They devoted themselves to the apostles' teaching and to the fellowship, to the breaking of bread and to prayer."*

5. What is the central teaching of the church? 1 Corinthians 15:1–4 *"Now, brothers, I want to remind you of the gospel I preached to you...[by which] you are saved...For what I received I passed on to you as of first importance: that Christ died for our sins according to the Scriptures, that He was buried, that He was raised on the third day according to the Scriptures."*

6. How did the early church care for the needy? Acts 2:44–45 *"The believers were together and had everything in common. Selling their possessions and goods, they gave to anyone as he had need."*

7. What commission did Jesus give to the church? Matthew 28:19–20 *"Therefore go and make disciples of all nations, baptizing them in the name of the Father and of the Son and of the Holy Spirit, and teaching them to obey everything I have commanded you. And surely I am with you always, to the very end of the age."*

**Membership in the church**

8. Who can join God's church? John 1:12 *"To all who received Him, to those who believed in His name, He gave the right to become children of God."*

Church is the family of God—a community for worship, for fellowship, for belonging.

**Source:** Signs of the Times, *November 2008.*

*The Proclamation of the Church*

# Review and Discussion

1. God purposed the local church as a gathering place for His people to hear from Him. Do you hear Him clearly? Explain.

   _____
   _____
   _____

2. "Where two or three are gathered in my name, there I am in the midst," is found in what Scripture?

   _____
   _____
   _____

3. In its singular form, *"church"* is referenced eighty (80) times in Scripture from Genesis to Revelation. Does any particular reference to *"church"* offer special meaning to you?

   _____
   _____
   _____

4. How do you recall your early experiences in church, either as a child or as an adult?

   _____
   _____
   _____

5. How meaningful is your experience in church? Explain.

   _____
   _____
   _____

***Give God the Glory!***

# Chapter Three

## The Declaration of the Church

---

*God's purpose in all this was to use the church to display his wisdom in its rich variety to all the unseen rulers and authorities in the heavenly places.*

—Ephesians 3:10 NLT

God established, and has since used, the church throughout all generations to reveal His awesome power amongst men and women. Despite aborted attempts to squash the preached word of God and the revealed truth of His word, as expressly written in *The Holy Bible*, the church has consistently and persistently declared that He is real, omnipotent (all powerful), omnipresent (perpetually present), and omniscient (all knowing). This is particularly important because the church does not necessarily represent a physical building as stated in Matthew 18:20 (KJV):

*For where two or three are gathered together in my name, there am I in the midst of them.*

Instead, *we* are the church. When we come together to *declare* His glory and richness, there He is our midst! All it takes is two to three of us, and we display His wisdom and power amongst everyone within our sphere of influence.

Baptists have a long history that dates back to the early Reformation period. John Bunyan, who wrote the well-known *Pilgrim's Promise*, became a Baptist in 1653. The Baptist missionary William Carey became a founder of Protestant cross-cultural missions when he ventured from England to India in 1783. The preaching of Charles Spurgeon, also a Baptist, attracted so many Londoners that a tabernacle seating 6,000 people was completed in 1861 to accommodate the crowds. The

Southern Baptist evangelist Billy Graham led an estimated 2.5 million people to accept Jesus as their Savior during his 60-plus years of ministry that began in 1943 and ended in 2006 when he spoke at the Festival of Hope in New Orleans, Louisiana, in the wake of Hurricane Katrina.

The largest of Baptist denominations in the United States—and, indeed, the nation's largest Protestant denomination—is the Southern Baptist Convention. However, Southern Baptists are not the only Baptist group in America. Today there are several dozen in Canada, and many in other parts of the world. According to the *World Christian Encyclopedia*, there were 52 million people in the Baptist World Alliance by the dawn of the twenty-first century.[10]

## Foundation of the Church: The Apostolic Age

In Galatians 4:4, the Apostle Paul wrote, *"But when the fullness of time came, God sent forth His Son."* Further, the Great Commission of Jesus Christ defines the church's mission in Matthew 28:19–20:

> *Jesus, undeterred, went right ahead and gave his charge: "God authorized and commanded me to commission you: Go out and train everyone you meet, far and near, in this way of life, marking them by baptism in the threefold name: Father, Son, and Holy Spirit. Then instruct them in the practice of all I have commanded you. I'll be with you as you do this,*

*day after day after day, right up to the end of the age."*

—The Message

*Therefore go and make disciples of all nations, baptizing them in the name of the Father and of the Son and of the Holy Spirit, and teaching them to obey everything I have commanded you. And surely I am with you always, to the very end of the age*

—NIV

Pentecost (fifty days after the crucifixion and ten days after the ascension of Christ) marks the birth of the church. As the Spirit filled the 120 believers who were waiting and praying, the miracle of tongues caused some observers to level the charge of drunkenness. At this point, Peter emerged as the spokesperson for the early church.

Peter dominates the first fifteen chapters of Acts. As the first among the Twelve [disciples of Jesus] to see the resurrected Christ, he emerged as the leader of the small community of believers before Pentecost (Acts 1:15). At Pentecost, he preached the Spirit-filled sermon that produced 3,000 converts. He cut through the fog of exclusive Judaism by declaring of Jesus that *"there is salvation in no one else; for there is no other name under heaven that has been given among men, by which we must be saved"* (Acts 4:12). He performed miracles, defied the Jerusalem authorities, disciplined Ananias and Sapphira, and organized helpers so the apostles could study and preach.[11]

## Our Part: The Church's Declaration

Our part, and role, to further the mission of the church is multifaceted. One-dimensional efforts to make this world a better place do not exist. There are many ways and opportunities. Let's explore.

The formation of the church continues through our collective leadership skills

—Acts 20:28

*Be careful for yourselves and for all the people the Holy Spirit has given to you to oversee. You must be like shepherds to the church of God, which he bought with the death of his own Son.*

—NCV

*Therefore take heed to yourselves and to all the flock, among which the Holy Spirit has made you overseers, to shepherd the church of God which He purchased with His own blood.*

—NKJV

We are to set our minds on spiritual things, where Jesus advocates for us continually in the presence of our Heavenly Father—Colossians 3:1–3

*If then you were raised with Christ, seek those things which are above, where Christ is, sitting at the right hand of God. Set your mind on things above, not on things on the earth. For you died, and your life is hidden with Christ in God.*

—NKJV

## GIVE GOD THE GLORY!

Ephesians 1:16–22

*I do not cease to give thanks for you, making mention of you in my prayers. [For I always pray to] the God of our Lord Jesus Christ, the Father of glory, that He may grant you a spirit of wisdom and revelation [of insight into mysteries and secrets] in the [deep and intimate] knowledge of Him, By having the eyes of your heart flooded with light, so that you can know and understand the hope to which He has called you, and how rich is His glorious inheritance in the saints (His set-apart ones), And [so that you can know and understand] what is the immeasurable and unlimited and surpassing greatness of His power in and for us who believe, as demonstrated in the working of His mighty strength, Which He exerted in Christ when He raised Him from the dead and seated Him at His [own] right hand in the heavenly [places], Far above all rule and authority and power and dominion and every name that is named [above every title that can be conferred], not only in this age and in this world, but also in the age and the world which are to come. And He has put all things under His feet and has appointed Him the universal and supreme Head of the church [a headship exercised throughout the church].*

—Amplified

We have been empowered to carry out God's plan and mission as His representatives on the earth. The Holy Spirit is, in actuality, the part of the Godhead that leads, guides, directs, comforts, and helps us in every situation, circumstance, and challenge. Trust Him and experience His power.

Acts 1:1–8

*To Theophilus. The first book I wrote was about everything Jesus began to do and teach until the day he was taken up into heaven. Before this, with the help of the Holy Spirit, Jesus told the apostles he had chosen what they should do. After his death, he showed himself to them and proved in many ways that he was alive. The apostles saw Jesus during the forty days after he was raised from the dead, and he spoke to them about the kingdom of God. Once when he was eating with them, he told them not to leave Jerusalem. He said, "Wait here to receive the promise from the Father which I told you about. John baptized people with water, but in a few days you will be baptized with the Holy Spirit." When the apostles were all together, they asked Jesus, "Lord, are you now going to give the kingdom back to Israel?" Jesus said to them, "The Father is the only One who has the authority to decide dates and times. These things are not for you to know. But when the Holy Spirit comes to you, you will receive power. You will be my witnesses—in Jerusalem, in all of Judea, in Samaria, and in every part of the world.*

—NCV

We understand and value God's Word and instruction because we can spiritually discern the

Bible. The Holy Spirit reveals it to us mentally and conceptually—John 14:17–18 and :26

> *The Friend is the Spirit of truth. The world can't accept him. That is because the world does not see him or know him. But you know him. He lives with you, and he will be in you. "I will not leave you like children who don't have parents. I will come to you.*
>
> *:26 But the Father will send the Friend in my name to help you. The Friend is the Holy Spirit. He will teach you all things. He will remind you of everything I have said to you.*
>
> —NIRV

John 16:13

> *Howbeit when he, the Spirit of truth, is come, he will guide you into all truth: for he shall not speak of himself; but whatsoever he shall hear, that shall he speak: and he will shew you things to come.*
>
> —KJV

Christ died to purchase the church, then Christ arose to give life to the church, and finally Christ ascended to be the Head of the church. Now, we fulfill our responsibility as ambassadors for Christ through repeated demonstrations of love within our respective spheres of influence (2 Corinthians 5:20), at home and abroad (Acts 1:8).

## German Sunday Law

Going to Germany for the weekend? Don't count on doing any Sunday shopping. A clause in the German constitution mandates Sunday as a day of rest and "spiritual elevation." However, a number of German states had made exceptions that permitted shopping on selected Sundays throughout the year. Berlin recently approved of Sunday shopping on ten Sundays a year, including the four prior to Christmas. The Roman Catholic Church and a coalition of Protestant churches joined with organized labor to oppose the liberalization on the grounds that retail workers needed protection from working on Sundays. Recently, Germany's highest court agreed, overturning Berlin's policy that allowed for more Sunday shopping.[12]

**GIVE GOD THE GLORY!**

# *Review and Discussion*

1. God declares that we should assemble ourselves together regularly. Do you?

2. The *church* is not necessarily a building where believers congregate. Instead, it offers a venue for corporate praise and worship. Do you agree?

3. In its plural form, *"churches"* is referenced thirty-five times from Genesis to Revelation. Can you find at least five of these references?

4. The Holy Spirit reveals to the *angel* (pastor) of the church the mood, atmosphere, and what to speak. Why does God operate this way?

5. What denomination is your church affiliated with? How does that affiliation impact your relationship with Jesus Christ?

# *Section Notes*

**Chapter One**

1 Christine Miles, "The Beginner's Guide to Church," *Signs of the Times* (Feb. 2009), 20–22.

2 Wolfgang Jenke, "Delighting in the Sabbath," *Signs of the Times* (Jan. 2008), 37.

3 *Signs of the Times* (May 2009), 5.

4 *Signs of the Times* (June 2009), 4.

5 *Adventist News Network.*

**Chapter Two**

6 Rodney Woods, "Church: Is it for you?" *Signs of the Times* (Nov. 2008), 43.

7 *Christian Newswire.*

8 *Christianweek.*

9 *Christian Century.*

**Chapter Three**

10 Arthur Patrick, "The Story of the Baptists," *Signs of the Times,* (Mar. 2009), 17.

11 James P. Eckman, Ph.D., *Perspectives from Church History,* (Wheaton, IL: Evangelical Training Association, 1996), chap. 1, 7–12.

12 *Signs of the Times* (March 2010), 4.

# ❧ Part II ❧
## What is My Role in the Local Church?

*Not forsaking the assembling of ourselves together, as the manner of some is; but exhorting one another: and so much the more, as ye see the day approaching.*
—Hebrews 10:25 KJV

*Now you [collectively] are Christ's body and [individually] you are members of it, each part severally and distinct [each with his own place and function]. So God has appointed some in the church [for His own use]: first apostles (special messengers); second prophets (inspired preachers and expounders); third teachers; then wonder-workers; then those with ability to heal the sick; helpers; administrators; [speakers in] different (unknown) tongues. Are all apostles (special messengers)? Are all prophets (inspired interpreters of the will and purposes of God)? Are all teachers? Do all have the power of performing miracles? Do all possess extraordinary powers of healing? Do all speak with tongues? Do all interpret? But earnestly desire and zealously cultivate the greatest and best gifts and graces (the higher gifts and the choicest graces). And yet I will show you a still more excellent way [one that is better by far and the highest of them all—love].*
—1 Corinthians 12:27–31 Amplified

**GIVE GOD THE GLORY!**

Membership in a local church is paramount to understanding our role within our local church. Our active participation and involvement then catapults us to a deeper appreciation for the love that God has for us. As He speaks, we listen. We listen to His voice, which manifests itself in a variety of ways, and it will ultimately mold us into our *role* that complements our spiritual gifts.

Discovering your spiritual gifts can be a daunting and time consuming endeavor, or you can choose to ask God to reveal it, or them, to you (James 1:17 and Romans 11:29). I chose the latter. My discovery process took place between 2000 and 2002, approximately seven years after my wife and I confessed Jesus Christ as our personal Lord and Savior, through conversations with God as well as various leaders in ministry whom I trusted while living in New Jersey. The conversations differed from person to person, and leader to leader, but my usual inquisitive posturing allowed God to direct my paths (Proverbs 3:6).

"Good afternoon Pastor Noonan," I said. That was my usual excited greeting to my senior pastor prior to the start of Tuesday night Bible study each week.

"Hello Kevin. How are you this fine and blessed evening," came Pastor Noonan's typical reply. He looked me in the eyes with a half grin. "I am as excited about tonight's Bible study as you are Kevin. God has a tremendous message tonight and I can't wait for you to hear it."

"Pastor, can you give me a clue? Some sort of hint? Please?" I asked.

"Yes, but please keep it to yourself. Can I trust you not to tell anyone?" he requested; hushed and almost desperate.

"Absolutely, I promise," I echoed back.

"Kevin," the Pastor began, "we are experiencing exponential growth here at Greenway United Church. It is unlike anything I've seen in my nine years as the pastor. It's a good thing to expand, grow, develop, and watch our brothers and sisters in Christ mature, but this is a critical juncture in the ministry.

"I must be obedient to God and begin the process of appointing leaders in the church. This includes all aspects of ministry leaders, not just deacons, ministers, and pastors. You happen to be one of those that God is about to elevate. You have served faithfully and your availability has been impeccable since you and your family joined in partnership with Greenway four years ago.

"This is the extent to which I can reveal my message for later tonight. It is important that all who are called to serve in a particular role in this church hear the same message at the same time," Pastor Noonan concluded. His face had a look of concern that I had never seen before.

"Wow Pastor. Your message will be quite interesting and timely. For the past five months, I've been studying the twenty spiritual gifts found in 1 Corinthians 12:4–11; Romans 12:6–8; and Ephesians

4:11–12, and learning that God freely gave us various gifts to equip us to successfully carry out our role in the body of Christ and within our respective local church," I said. He sensed my enthusiasm.

"Let's go inside Kevin and begin service," gestured Pastor Noonan. "You can start us out by leading with praise and worship," he joked.

"I don't think so sir. You know I can't carry a tune!" I laughed.

"Agreed. It was just a test to see if you knew your role," he said as we both laughed.

Later that April evening in 2001, Pastor Noonan began to teach his message that he briefly explained to me in private. The title of this thought-provoking and life-changing message was *"What is Your Role?"* The essence of this teaching was in the spirit of the vision of Greenway United Church's rapid growth from 250 members in 1997 to over 800 members at the beginning of 2001. Its vision was *"Serving the needs of people in the community and leading them to Christ."*

Pastor Noonan emphasized that he needed some help to make the vision come to life! He needed help in the form of ministry leaders that were prepared and ready to take their next step. Further, he needed others to assist him on the forward journey to leading souls to Christ. I felt that I was ready for the challenge, elevation, promotion, and increase in responsibility as long as I allowed the Lord to lead me every step along the way. At the conclusion of his message, I could not wait to hear about my appointment and next assignment. I am ready, willing, and able! Bible study ended at 9:38 p.m. and I was determined to talk to Pastor on the next day.

## What is My Role in the Local Church?

"Pastor Noonan, last night's teaching was powerful and enlightening," I said.

"Thank you, Kevin. I appreciate your kind words," said Pastor.

"You confirmed what I had been studying. That is, my spiritual gifts are teaching and exhortation (encouragement)," I revealed to Pastor Noonan for the first time.

"Kevin, I am happy to hear that and discover that you are familiar, and comfortable, with your spiritual gifts. They will serve you well in your next step in ministry as a deacon at our church. Will you accept this awesome responsibility and serve our members with the spirit of compassion, mercy, and love?" asked Pastor.

"Yes, Pastor. It will be my pleasure. Thank you, sir. I look forward to learning my new role. It is a role that I will cherish, respect, and honor," I said with passion and excitement.

*GIVE GOD THE GLORY!*

# Chapter Four

## Service to Others

*For you, brethren, were [indeed] called to freedom; only [do not let your] freedom be an incentive to your flesh and an opportunity or excuse [for selfishness], but through love you should serve one another.*
—Galatians 5:13 Amplified

*Look not every man on his own things, but every man also on the things of others.*
—Philippians 2:4 KJV

There are multiple Scriptures that reveal why Christians must live to serve others. Two are found in the New Testament: Galatians 5:13 and Philippians 2:4. Service to others removes our habitual preoccupation with self. Service to others also generates fulfillment for Christians. Service is our charge. Observe the life of Jesus during His three and one-half years of ministry. Through His humility, He openly demonstrated *love*—the motivation—and *service*—esteeming others above self—in the presence of Roman soldiers, Jews, Gentiles, Samaritans, and His disciples. In essence, Jesus was consistent in all places and before all audiences.

In its three forms, *serve, servant,* and *service,* are used interchangeably in *The Holy Bible*, 205, 489, and 142 times, respectively. God is trying to get your attention!

*The time is always right to do what is right.*
—REV. MARTIN LUTHER KING, JR.

## Bibles for Vietnam

The Scottish Bible Society is planning to send thousands of Bibles to Communist Vietnam. Elaine Duncan, the Bible Society's chief executive, explained why: *"The church [in Vietnam] is growing rapidly yet lacks the basic tool, the Bible, in sufficient quantities to strengthen existing and new Christians in their faith."* The Bible Society plans to distribute 32,000 Bibles and 15,000 New Testaments for adults alone. A separate project will send 30,000 children's Bibles to Vietnam, 10,000 Bibles, and 115,000 New Testaments. At the present time, the Scottish Bible Society is raising funds to print, ship, and distribute these Bibles.[1]

## Compassion Counts More Than Ever

Despite tough times, the USA is experiencing a compassion boom. *Parade* magazine asked 1,008 Americans what they would do if given $100,000 to donate to charity. Besides the fact that 94% of the respondents believe that it's important to be involved in a community cause, here's how they would share it:

**TABLE 2.** Charitable giving[2]

| Charity of Choice | Amout Given |
|---|---|
| Food and shelter for the needy | $15,953.21 |
| Research to cure disease | $14,311.54 |
| Disaster relief | $9308.97 |
| Animal welfare | $8783.46 |

| Youth programs | $6514.53 |
|---|---|
| Poverty relief/Job assistance | $6234.83 |
| Education | $6069.00 |
| **My religion's charity** | **$5921.93** |
| The global environment | $5340.51 |
| Public health | $4924.82 |
| Human rights | $4422.10 |
| My immediate environment | $3628.49 |
| Literacy | $2952.55 |
| **Other religious charities** | **$2262.90** |
| Promoting world democracy | $1732.32 |
| Visual and/or performing arts | $1638.83 |

## Hospital Unites Religions

Bethlehem, the birthplace of Jesus, is located in the West Bank of Israel in the Middle East. The region is one of the most contested pieces of real estate in the world. The contention is religious, between Jews, Muslims, and Christians.

However, the three faiths are coming together to construct a hospital in Bethlehem. "Christians and Muslims will serve together at the hospital and will receive additional training at some of the leading hospitals in Jerusalem," says Dr. Scott Harrison, an orthopedic surgeon whose organization, CURE International, is assisting with the construction of the US$165 million facility. The new hospital will be next to the Shepherd's Field, the spot where tradition says that shepherds first learned of Jesus' birth.[3]

## Chaplains Pray with Fire Victims

The Billy Graham Rapid Response Team is a group of 2,500 chaplains and ministry volunteers from across the United States who responded to the spiritual needs of the victims of disaster. More than 100 of these chaplains responded to the fires in Southern California in October 2007 to help victims make it through the despair of losing their homes.[4]

## The Benefits of Service

Christian conduct, in the light of the times in which we live, is personified in 1 Peter 4:10. In this context, the Apostle Paul teaches us to serve one another through God's unmerited favor (grace):

> *Each of you has received a gift to use **to serve others**. Be good servants of God's various gifts of grace.*
>
> —NCV

As stated earlier, service to others preempts our preoccupation with self. In Philippians 2:4, the Apostle Paul teaches the saints at Philippi on the subject of meekness and unity. Through this experience we can grasp his central thought: Only in Christ is real unity and joy possible.

> *Each of you should look not only to your own interests, but also **to the interests of others**.*
>
> —NIV

In Galatians 5:13–15, the Apostle teaches on the subject of liberty and love for one another as Christian men and women. We have been called unto liberty and through love we are to serve one another. In essence, this is why the Word prompts us to love thy neighbor as thyself.

> *It is absolutely clear that God has called you to a free life. Just make sure that you don't use this freedom as an excuse to do whatever you want to do and destroy your freedom. Rather, use your freedom **to serve one another in love**; that's how freedom grows. For everything we know about God's Word is summed up in a single sentence: Love others as you love yourself. That's an act of true freedom. If you bite and ravage each other, watch out—in no time at all you will be annihilating each other, and where will your precious freedom be then?*
>
> —The Message

## *Review and Discussion*

1. Jesus teaches us that *"It is more blessed to give than it is to receive."* Why did He teach this philosophy?

   _____
   _____
   _____

2. How do you define *service*?

   _____
   _____
   _____

3. Identify ways that you currently, or within the last year, serve others within your sphere of influence.

   _____
   _____
   _____

4. What service did you receive within the last five years that is/was particularly memorable? Why?

   _____
   _____
   _____

5. Fulfillment is achieved through our service to others. How do you explain this biblical principle?

   _____
   _____
   _____

***Give God the Glory!***

# Chapter Five
## Enjoy God's Blessings

*Blessed be the God and Father of our Lord Jesus Christ, who hath blessed us with all spiritual blessings in heavenly places in Christ: According as he hath chosen us in him before the foundation of the world, that we should be holy and without blame before him in love: Having predestinated us unto the adoption of children by Jesus Christ to himself, according to the good pleasure of his will, To the praise of the glory of his grace, wherein he hath made us accepted in the beloved.*

—Ephesians 1:3–6 KJV

Do you know that you are blessed? Yes, according to Ephesians 1:3–6 you are! In this context, blessed means *"worthy of praise."* When God blesses man, He confers benefits upon him; when man blesses God, he attributes praise to Him.

Where are these blessings located? In heavenly places; that is, in heaven. As the Christian's citizenship (Philippians 3:20), high priest (Hebrews 4:14), hope (Colossians 1:5), and inheritance (1 Peter 1:4) are all "in heaven," as His treasure (Matthew 6:20–21), and affection (Colossians 3:1–2) are to be "in heaven," so also the Christian's blessings are "in heaven." These spiritual benefits are granted to the believer and are retained in heaven for us, being progressively dispersed to us on earth in accordance with our need and Christian growth.

Further, Ephesians 1, verses 11 and 12 describe the inheritance that we have obtained as predestinated according to the purpose of God Almighty. As God's treasure, Christians are the apple of His eye; we are the special heirs of His love. He is then determined to care and provide for His people who are His heritage.

A blessing can be defined as the gift of God's grace. As blessed people, we are the recipients of God's favor. In turn, we are to be a blessing to others through our actions and words.

Now that you know, enjoy God's blessings!

## How Spiritual are We?

*Parade's* survey reveals a nation looking heavenward—but with its feet firmly planted on the ground of modern life. Spiritually speaking, Americans are a very practical people; moderate and tolerant in ways that would have astonished our grandparents.

Our nation was built on a foundation of strong faith, and in some respects, that hasn't changed. In fact, 69% of Americans believe in God, 77% pray outside of religious services, and 75% believe it's a parent's responsibility to give children a religious upbringing. But even though 45% of respondents called themselves religious, 50% said they rarely or never attend worship services.

**TABLE 3.** How spiritual are we?[5]

| **Religion's Purpose:** |
| --- |
| 40% say it holds the truth |
| 22% say that religion has no place in their lives |
| 19% say it helps teach morals and ethics to children |
| **Reasons we pray:** |
| 72% pray for the well-being of others |
| 60% pray for forgiveness |
| 21% pray for material things |
| **Our new beliefs:** |
| 82% would marry someone of a different faith |
| 59% say that all religions are valid |
| 24% say they are spiritual but not religious |

***GIVE GOD THE GLORY!***

## God's Plan for Your Blessing

God's plan for your life includes blessing you so that your overflow of grace and favor will spill over to others. Do you see that you are already blessed? It is not something that *will* happen; it is something that has *already* occurred!

> *God's purpose was that we Jews who were the first to trust in Christ would bring praise and glory to God.*
> —Ephesians 1:12 NLV

> *All praise to God, the Father of our Lord Jesus Christ, who has **blessed us** with every spiritual blessing in the heavenly realms because we are united with Christ. Even before he made the world, God **loved us** and **chose us** in Christ to be holy and without fault in his eyes.*
> —Ephesians 1:3–4 NLV

For those that trust in God and seek Him, blessings and favor become the norm. Receive your blessings with joy. Continually fill your heavenly clouds with praise and allow God's blessings to rain down upon you.

> *And God will generously provide all you need. Then you will always have everything you need and plenty left over to share with others.*
> —2 Corinthians 9:8 NLT

*Enjoy God's Blessings*

Be a good steward of your abundant resources and your blessings will multiply:

*"Bring all the tithes into the storehouse so there will be enough food in my Temple. If you do," says the Lord of Heaven's Armies, "I will open the windows of heaven for you, I will pour out a blessing so great you won't have enough room to take it in! Try it! Put me to the test!"*

—Malachi 3:10 NLT

## Power in Worship

If you ask Christians to define the ultimate purpose of their lives, many will say leading other people to faith in God. But believing that we exist to bring other people to a faith in God is incomplete.

From Genesis to Revelation (and before and beyond), creation has existed for one purpose: to worship God. The act of worship brings us to a state of joy in the presence of God. The writer of Hebrews says in chapter 12, verse 28:

*Therefore, since we are receiving a kingdom which cannot be shaken, let us have grace, by which we may serve God acceptably with reverence and godly fear.*

—NKJV

In Revelation, the final battle between good and evil is waged, and the players identify themselves in one way: by whom and how they worship. In a flashback to the Creation story, and angel shouts, Revelation 14:7, *"He preached in a loud voice, Fear*

*God and give him praise, because the time has come for God to judge all people. So worship God who made the heavens, and the earth, and the sea, and the springs of water"* (NCV).

The people of God are identified by their worship of the God of creation. Worship is also the identifying mark of those who have chosen to go against God. Revelation 14:11 says, *"The smoke of their torment will rise forever and ever: and they will have no relief day or night, for they have worshiped the beast and his statue and have accepted the mark of his name"* (NLT).

Genesis says that everything God made during Creation week was good. Then He established a day as a memorial of His creation: a day of worship called Sabbath. He set the earth on a repeating seven-day cycle, the seventh of which has been eternally set aside for worship. That's the Genesis story. And it's still our story. In Isaiah 66:23, God declares that in the new earth, we will be worshipping forever. *That is our purpose.*

If worship is so important, and it's something we should be focusing our energy on, then we need to have some simple ways to get started. One mnemonic is the word *power:* There is **POWER** in worship.[6]

**P**rayer—John 16:23–24

*And in that day you will ask Me nothing. Most assuredly, I say to you, whatever you ask the Father in My name He will give you. Until now you have asked nothing in My name. Ask, and you will receive, that your joy may be full.*

—NKVJ

**O**bey—Ecclesiastes 12:13 and Romans 12:1–2

*Let us hear the conclusion of the whole matter: Fear God, and keep his commandments: for this is the whole duty of man.*

—Ecclesiastes 12:13 KJV

*So here's what I want you to do, God helping you: Take your everyday, ordinary life—your sleeping, eating, going-to-work, and walking-around life—and place it before God as an offering. Embracing what God does for you is the best thing you can do for him. Don't become so well-adjusted to your culture that you fit into it without even thinking. Instead, fix your attention on God. You'll be changed from the inside out. Readily recognize what he wants from you, and quickly respond to it. Unlike the culture around you, always dragging you down to its level of immaturity, God brings the best out of you, develops well-formed maturity in you.*

—Romans 12:1–2 The Message

**W**ord—2 Corinthians 3:18, Psalm 119:104–105, and Matthew 4:10

> *So all of us who have had that veil removed can see and reflect the glory of the Lord. And the Lord—who is the Spirit—makes us more and more like him as we are changed into his glorious image.*
>
> *—2 Corinthians 3:18 NLT*

> *I gain understanding from your precepts; therefore I hate every wrong path. Your word is a lamp to my feet and a light for my path.*
>
> *—Psalm 119:104–105 NIV*

> *Then Jesus said to him, Away with you, Satan! For it is written, You shall worship the LORD your God, and Him only you shall serve.*
>
> *—Matthew 4:10 NKJV*

**E**xpress—Psalm 150

> *Praise ye the LORD. Praise God in his sanctuary: praise him in the firmament of his power. Praise him for his mighty acts: praise him according to his excellent greatness. Praise him with the sound of the trumpet: praise him with the psaltery and harp. Praise him with the timbrel and dance: praise him with stringed instruments and organs. Praise him upon the loud cymbals: praise him upon the high sounding cymbals. Let every thing that*

hath breath praise the LORD. Praise ye the LORD.

—KJV

**R**each out—Micah 6:8, Matthew 5:23–24, and Matthew 25:40

*The Lord has shown you what is good. He has told you what he requires of you. You must treat people fairly. You must love others faithfully. And you must be very careful to live the way your God wants you to.*

—Micah 6:8 NIRV

*So if when you are offering your gift at the altar you there remember that your brother has any [grievance] against you, Leave your gift at the altar and go. First make peace with your brother, and then come back and present your gift.*

—Matthew 5:23–24 Amplified

*And the King will answer and say to them, Assuredly, I say to you, inasmuch as you did it to one of the least of these My brethren, you did it to Me.*

—Matthew 25:40 NKJV

...and, finally, in 1 Corinthians 10:31–33,

*So whether you eat or drink, or whatever you do, do it all for the glory of God. Don't give offense to Jews or Gentiles or the church of God. I, too, try to please everyone in everything I do. I don't just do what is best for me; I do what is best for others so that many may be saved.*

—NLT

## Living God's Way

Being a Christian is a great lifestyle. The Bible gives many principles for healthful living for the body, mind, and emotions. For example, the Bible provides instruction on the principles of dress that help the Christian to make good choices. It also provides principles concerning the use of money, practical and spiritual benefits of giving generously, and relationships. And it gives practical instruction about spiritual aspects of living, such as prayer.

So there are many Christians who might exclaim, "*I love being a Christian.*" However, is it possible to follow the Bible's lifestyle principles closely, yet in all of that "doing good" still displease God? Can one pray for an hour each day and have God say, "*I have a complaint against you!*" (Micah 6:2). Is it possible to dress right, give right, talk right, and worship right, and still be rejected by God? According to the Bible, the answer is **Yes** as the prophet Micah points out a little further on (6:6–7).

*Enjoy God's Blessings*

God's people had failed Him. In spite of God's complaint against the people of Judah, He referred to them as "his people" (verses 2, 5). Even though He was disappointed with their behavior and their thinking, He did not disown or reject them, because He wanted them to grow in their relationship with Him and with each other. By this act, God demonstrated the same grace and mercy that He called upon His people to demonstrate to each other. He ever reminded them of His mighty act of grace when He redeemed them out of slavery at the hand of the Egyptians.[7]

**TABLE 4.** Do you feel your life has important meaning or purpose?

| Religious Affiliation | Affirmative Response |
|---|---|
| Christians | 93 percent |
| Hindus | 92 percent |
| Muslims | 91 percent |
| Buddhists | 90 percent |
| Jews | 88 percent |
| Non-religious | 83 percent |

**Source:** *Gallop Poll, based on telephone and face-to-face interviews with about 1,000 adults in 84 countries during 2007.*

## Court Says, Protect Christians

Since August 2008, Christians in the Indian state of Orissa have been under severe attack by Hindu extremists. Roman Catholic Archbishop Raphael Cheenath filed a petition with the Indian Supreme Court for protection and compensation for destroyed church property. On January 5, 2009, a three-judge panel told the state government that it will not "tolerate persecution of religious minorities." The court ordered the state government to protect Christians or "quit office." About 500 people, most of them Christians, have been killed since the violence began, and tens of thousands have been displaced.[8]

## Youthful Perspectives

The next generation of leaders and visionaries are particularly interested in success. To them, success may be defined by material wealth as seen on television and heard on radio day-by-day. However, God's view is much larger than possessions or position. So, does the next generation value spirituality and what do they think about God?

**TABLE 5.** Youth's opinions on the meaning of spirituality in the USA

| In the U.S. | |
|---|---|
| Believing there's a purpose to life | 41 percent |
| Believing in God | 33 percent |
| **In INDIA:** | |
| Being true to one's inner self | 38 percent |
| Believing in God | 33 percent |

*Based on a two-year survey by the Search Institute's Center for Spiritual Development of 7,000 youth, ages 12 to 25, in 17 countries on 6 continents.*

Bible Discovery with Errol Webster
# *GREAT EXPECTATIONS*

The Bible presents the Christian life as a spiritual battle (Ephesians 6:10–17). Renowned Christian thinker Francis Schaeffer says, "It is a life and death struggle over the minds and souls of men [and women] for all eternity, but it is equally a life and death struggle over life on this earth."

We live in a world that has largely forgotten the God of the Bible. While people are still quite religious, their "religion" is either secularism or a vague form of pantheism (god is everything-ism). How should a Bible-believing Christian live in such a world?

1. Where is a Christian's citizenship? Philippians 3:20 *"Our citizenship is in heaven. And we eagerly await a Savior from there."*

2. To what should Christians not conform? Romans 12:2 *"Do not conform any longer to the pattern of this world, but be transformed by the renewing of your mind. Then you will be able to test and approve what God's will is—his good, pleasing and perfect will."*

3. Whose kingdom should we seek? Matthew 6:33 *"Seek first his [the Father's] kingdom and his righteousness, and all these things [that we need] will be given to you as well."*

4. Whose temple is the Christian's body? 1 Corinthians 6:19-20 *"Do you know that your body is a temple of the Holy Spirit...? You are not your own; you were bought at a price. Therefore honor God with your body."*

5. What guidelines does Paul give for right thinking? Philippians 4:8 *"Whatever is true, whatever is noble, whatever is right, whatever is pure, whatever is lovely, whatever is admirable—if anything is excellent or praiseworthy—think about such things."*

6. What overriding principle should guide the Christian? 1 Corinthians 10:32 *"Whatever you do, do it all for the glory of God."*

Jesus says that we should love God with all our heart, soul, strength, and mind, and our neighbor as ourself (Luke 10:27).

7. What should motivate Christian behavior? 1 John 4:9-10 *"This is how God showed his love among us: He sent his one and only Son into the world [as an atoning sacrifice for our sins] that we might live through him."*

God wants a wholehearted response of gratitude from us. The Bible is clear that a Christian will practice discernment. Jesus said, *"No [man] can serve two masters"* (Luke 16:13).

Paul counsels, *"Test everything. Hold on to the good. Avoid every kind of evil"* (1 Thessalonians 5:21–22). We are not to accept everything that comes to us as good. There are choices to be made, and they need to be intelligent, informed choices, motivated by God's gracious forgiveness and love.

**Source:** Signs of the Times *(July 2009)*

*Enjoy God's Blessings*

## *Review and Discussion*

1. Blessings flow from God to us through our obedience to His word. Identify two recent blessings that you remember.

   _____
   _____

2. God loves us so much that He gave His only Son Jesus. Why do you believe this was God's plan to reconnect us to Him?

   _____
   _____

3. Do you measure the benefits of your blessings? Why or why not?

   _____
   _____

4. Enjoying God's blessings can be accomplished many different ways. Describe some.

   _____
   _____

5. Blessings are defined as God's favors. How are blessings manifested in your life?

   _____
   _____

*GIVE GOD THE GLORY!*

# Chapter Six
## *Your Role, Your Church*

---

*So each of us will have to answer to God.*
—Romans 14:12 NCV


*So then every one of us shall give account of himself to God.*
—Romans 14:12 KJV

*Give God the Glory!*

We were born into the earth with a divine purpose (Jeremiah 29:11–14) and designated spiritual gifts (Romans 6:8–11; 1 Corinthians 12:4–11; and Ephesians 4:11–12). Understanding what they are, and how they are manifested, is the centerpiece of most struggles that we face as Christian men and women. Lack of knowledge in this area prevents us from maximizing our divine role(s) in life.

Our primary role in the local church is to assist and support our pastor to fulfill the vision that was given by God. Through our service, this can, and should, be accomplished with joy. It takes a collective and concerted effort to help all members to recognize and acknowledge their role in the church.

> *"The government can't fix this. The church has to."*
> — TROY DUGAN, FROM OHIO, WHILE IN HAITI TO PROVIDE RELIEF TO THOUSANDS OF HAITIANS WHO ARE WITHOUT FOOD, WATER, AND MEDICAL CARE FOLLOWING THE JANUARY 12, 2010 EARTHQUAKE.

## Church Groups Hope to Help Kids and Give Encouragement

American law has firmly established that teachers may not lead prayers *in* schools. But nothing stops anyone from praying *for* schools.

Two local women established groups last year to promote the well-being of Canton City Schools through prayer. Canton City Schools Prayer Teams, started by retired teacher Annie Simon, sends three people to every school once per month to pray. Canton City Schools Christian Fellowship, started by Lathrop School librarian Georgia Robinson, is an occasional gathering of school employees for prayer.

"Annie got started and I got started, and we didn't know about each other until the middle of last year," Robinson said.

The two groups will collaborate August 6 on a prayer program to kick off the school year. The event at McKinley High School will run from 3:00 p.m. to 5:00 p.m.

The prayer teams, Simon said, are not allowed in the school buildings, but they either walk around the outside or stay in the car, following a one-hour format in which they pray and read Bible verses on topics such as violence, competition, and hypocrisy.

In a school context, the last might mean covering up bad things at home. Students "don't want you to know what went on at home," Simon said. "They'll yell at you, but it's not really you. We know as teachers that this happens, and we want to deal with it through prayer. If we bring it into the open, things will change. Maybe not right away, but they will change."

The prayer teams wear name tags when they are on school property, "so guard knows who we are and that we're not there to steal a child," Simon said. They also call ahead to let officials know that they're coming; at some schools, principals will give them lists of concerns to pray for.

The teams tend to comprise pastors and their wives, and some parents; teachers are busy working. Simon said, "We do have people in the building that pray, but they use their lunch hours."

Both Simon and Robinson hope for increased participation. Robinson's church, Dueber United Methodist, has adopted Dueber School, providing the kids with back-to-school supplies, snacks, and volunteers to help out in class. "Church leaders have to encourage their congregations to be strong in this," Robinson said. But for herself, "I'm leaving it in God's hands. That's what I hope to see."

"We would like to see all churches involved," Simon said. "We have a lot of needs."

The two groups' activities pass legal muster. Robinson said, "I am employed by Canton City Schools, but I have a heart for children, and I want to be faithful in the direction God has showed me. Church volunteers in the schools," she said, "are not quoting Scripture. They're just there to listen to that child read, or give them a hug. A lot of children come in and that's the only hug they get all day."

Simon said, "We're not trying to pull them into this church or that church…It's to help children and make a difference in the community. If praying's going to help

*Your Role, Your Church*

a child act better, do better, keep them off drugs...well, then, that's what we will do."[9]
*Reprinted courtesy of "The Repository," Canton, OH, by David Lewellen.*

## China's New Bestseller

Is it Karl Marx's *Communist Manifesto*? No. Atheist Richard Dawkins' book *The God Delusion*? No again. It's *The Holy Bible*.

In the past 20 years, the Amity Printing Company in Nanjing, China, has printed more than 50 million copies of the Bible, 43 million of them for distribution within China and the rest for export to other countries. The printing plant, a joint venture between the Amity Foundation (an organization of Chinese Christians) and the United Bible Societies, is approved by the Chinese government. The printing of the 50 millionth Bible, celebrated at the company's plant in December 2007, was attended by representatives of the Chinese government. Amity Printing is the only organization in China that prints Bibles with government approval.[10]

## Preventing Suicide

The Anglican Church of Canada's Council of the North has raised $94,000 to develop a program for reducing suicide among Aboriginal young people in the vast northern part of the country. Only fifteen percent of Canada's population lives in this region, but the suicide rate among youth between the ages of 15 and 24 is five to six times higher than the Canadian average. The Council of the North blames the residential schools of earlier years for much of the problem. In an effort to Christianize Aboriginal children, church-related schools (some but not all were Anglican) tried to dissociate Aboriginal youth from their culture. The children ended up confused, feeling like the only way out was to kill themselves. The Council will identify resources that are available to help the young people and guide local Anglicans in becoming a part of the solution.[11]

## Sunday Off is Okay

When Paul Royse applied for a job as a security officer with the Oklahoma Office of Juvenile Affairs, he asked for Sundays free so he could attend church. His supervisor agreed, on condition that he work the desirable night shift. Royse accepted the offer. When the agency hired a new supervisor, Royse resubmitted his request—and was denied. When Royse refused to work Sundays during church time, he was fired. The Alliance Defense Fund (ADF) sued the state on Royse's behalf and won. Royse received his back wages.

Kevin Theriot, a legal counsel with ADF, pointed out why they won. "The courts have held that when you have a sincerely held religious belief and it wouldn't cause an undue hardship for the government employer to accommodate that belief, then they have to."[12]

## Your Role—An Examination

Our talents, skills, and abilities vary from person to person. In parallel, our spiritual gifts are equally diverse. Upon closer examination, however, we have similar responsibilities in the body of Christ so that others will come to know and experience Him. They are:[13]

- To **Evangelize**—Matthew 28:19–20 (Amplified).

  *Go then and make disciples of all the nations, baptizing them into the name of the Father and of the Son and of the Holy Spirit, Teaching them to observe everything that I have commanded you, and behold, I am with you all the days (perpetually, uniformly, and on every occasion), to the [very] close and consummation of the age. Amen (so let it be).*

- To **Enlarge your Faith**—Matthew 19:26 (NCV).

  *Jesus looked at them and said, "For people this is impossible, but for God all things are possible."*

- To **Develop a Vision of the Unreached**—Matthew 9:37 (NIRV).

  *Then Jesus said to his disciples, "The harvest is huge. But there are only a few workers."*

- To have **Compassion for the Lost**—Luke 10:19 (NLT).

  *For the Son of Man came to seek and save those who are lost.*

- Understanding the **Value of a Person**—Matthew 16:26 (NKJV).

  *For what profit is it to a man if he gains the whole world, and loses his own soul? Or what will a man give in exchange for his soul?*

  Matthew 12:11–14 The Message:

  *He replied, "Is there a person here who, finding one of your lambs fallen into a ravine, wouldn't, even though it was a Sabbath, pull it out? Surely kindness to people is as legal as kindness to animals!" Then he said to the man, "Hold out your hand." He held it out and it was healed. The Pharisees walked out furious, sputtering about how they were going to ruin Jesus.*

  Luke 12:7 NIV:

  *Indeed, the very hairs of your head are all numbered. Don't be afraid; you are worth more than many sparrows.*

## Morning Glories

The women at Refreshing Spring Church of God in Christ in Riverdale, Maryland come early to pray on Easter Sunday morning, as they have done every Sunday for decades. In the Book of Matthew, Jesus says do not pray just so others may see you. Hours before the congregation fills the pews, more than a half a dozen "prayer warriors" gather in the open spaces of the sanctuary and draw shawls around their shoulders so that even in the presence of one another, they may be private with God.

They walk and chant, they kneel and pray, they lie on the floor face down with their arms outstretched to say, "Have your way, O God, I love your way, Jesus. In spite of your way, You still come to see about us, Lord. Not one of your words has fallen to the floor," and their voices break with the ardor of their faith. They pray for the choir, the ushers, President Obama and his family.

To intercede with God on behalf of others is one of the highest orders of Christian life, Prayer Warrior Deidra Weathers explains before services begin. And although she does not say it, it is also one of the most unseen. To wake up earlier than everyone else, to arrive at the church two hours before service begins, and maintain a fiercely prayerful intensity for others who may not even know that is what you are doing is a calling for only the deeply devout.

> "Some people are called to intercede...You're standing in the gap for somebody else."
> —DEIDRA WEATHERS

There are about a dozen at Refreshing Spring, mostly women but a couple of men. They try to remain upright, faithful, reverent, so that they may be "in right standing with God" and that their words might reach heaven. "We're praying for the people who don't know God, that God will open their eyes," says Weathers.[14]

## Life or Death?

Maribel Perez, a 36-year-old mother of two, needs a lung transplant to extend her life and free her from an oxygen tank. She breathes in short puffs, panting almost, through a hole cut into her trachea and covered demurely with a patch of gauze. Clear tubes connected to a noisy machine in the living room of her small Alexandria, Virginia apartment pump pure oxygen into her nostrils. Crossing the room can leave the 36-year-old woman breathless. Crying sometimes feels like drowning.

Twice in the past two years, she has been told to prepare to die. Twice, she has been rejected for a lung transplant because her case was deemed too difficult. Twice, she has nearly been sent home to Peru because doctors told her there was nothing more they could do here, and if there were, her insurance wouldn't pay. She refused to believe them.

Then, doctors, social workers, friends, family, priests, politicians, and strangers coalesced as a veritable army of guardian angels around her. They pushed for treatment and insurance. They found loopholes, hospital beds, and ventilators. They prayed. They set up a "Save Maribel" Web site and Facebook page. They called news conferences in which Perez tearfully pleaded for her life. They raised $60,000 to save her.

## Perez had become a Jehovah's Witness.

So it was nothing less than shattering when, miraculously, in early February 2010, one of the world's largest lung-transplant programs, at the University of Pittsburgh Medical Center, agreed to take her, and Perez said no. Her reason had nothing to do with breath. It was because of blood.

Perez had become a Jehovah's Witness. The religion teaches that blood is sacred, the seat of one's soul, and that in the Bible, God specifically prohibits the consumption of blood, whether by mouth or through veins in a transfusion. Many Jehovah's Witnesses carry cards explaining that in an emergency they are not to receive blood and that no medical practititioner will be held liable if they die as a result.

On January 7, 2010, after one of many visits from fellow Jehovah's Witnesses, Perez told her husband, Lorenzo, that she had signed a medical directive refusing a blood transfusion. Hearing that, he said, was like being slammed in the chest. "I had been fighting so hard for so long to keep her alive, I felt betrayed," he said in Spanish. "I was so angry. It was like I didn't know her anymore." His wife had chosen to die.

In a panic, Lorenzo called out to his wife's army of guardians. They descended upon her like avenging angels. How could she sign something like this? The Witnesses could be wrong, they pleaded; other faiths interpret the Bible differently. When that failed to move her, they called her a hypocrite. Told her that she had wasted so many people's time and faith. Then they softened. How could she leave her two children after struggling so mightily to stay with them? How could a loving God want her to choose death?

* * *

Four years ago, Perez began getting dizzy and falling. She could never seem to catch her breath. A friend took her to a free lung clinic in the District run by the National Institutes of Health for the homeless and uninsured. There, Mark Gladwin diagnosed severe pulmonary fibrosis. The doctor began to follow her closely. She was so young to be terminally ill. The only way to extend her life was a lung transplant, which can cost at least a half million dollars. With no money, immigration papers, or insurance, Perez's prospects were poor. Caught between borders, political policy, and medical ethics, her life hangs in existential balance.

*The only way to extend her life was a lung transplant, which can cost at least a half a million dollars.*

In 2007, she was repeatedly hospitalized and sent to a hospice, where doctors recommended that she return to Peru to die in her mother's care. But friends and advocates found the Kaiser Permanente Bridge program, which offers three years of discounted insurance to the uninsured. She healed enough to go home.

In the fall of 2008, she contracted pneumonia. Again, she was hospitalized. Again, doctors told her to prepare to die. Instead, she spent a year at the Specialty Hospital of Washington, with social worker Paula Hammond calling Kaiser every two weeks for approval to extend her stay. Hammond arranged for surgeons from Inova Fairfax Hospital, the area's only lung transplant center, to evaluate Perez. They said the operation would be too risky.

Last spring [2009], Laura Wilson, 81, a friend who met Perez through a neighbor and became like a mother to her, learned that Gladwin had moved to Pittsburgh to become chief of the pulmonary division there. She appealed to him: Maribel has insurance now! You can help her now! Gladwin agreed to see Perez if Kaiser would pay for the transplant and intensive follow-up care.

Perez could not contain her joy. "I want to be a part of my children's lives," she said then. "For a mother, even one more day is precious." But Kaiser at first refused to pay for the transplant, Perez's doctors said, telling them that Pittsburgh was not in Kaiser's network. Kaiser officials would not comment on Perez's case.

Her advocates wrote letters and sent appeals and, finally, Kaiser agreed to cover the transplant as an out-of-network expense, meaning Perez needed about $80,000 for the co-payment. Her advocates set up a fund through the Catholic Archdiocese of Arlington and had news conferences pleading for donations here and in Peru. Their efforts netted $30,000. Then Wilson found the Ray Tye Medical Aid Foundation in Massachusetts, which agreed to match those funds.

About 1,400 lung transplants per year are done in the United States, compared with 15,000 kidneys and

2,200 hearts. The procedure is fairly new and survival rates are low, averaging five to seven years, said Joseph Pilewski, medical director of Pittsburgh's lung transplant program. It's a therapy of last resort. "If your other option is a 90 percent chance of dying within the year," Pilewski said, "then a lung transplant is a good option."

Perez has no other options, her doctors say. Hospitals in Peru, where Kaiser

*Caught between borders, political policy and medical ethics, her life hangs in existential balance.*

recommended she return last summer, could not handle her case, they say, nor could her damaged lungs survive a trip there.

"As a physician, if we were to be distracted by someone's insurance status, their immigration status, or other sociopolitical variables . . . then we lose sight of our primary mission: to take care of people," Gladwin said. "Maribel is a young woman. She has young children. She's the kind of person a transplant was designed for. From a social-justice standpoint, you could ask: Why is it fair to give a lung transplant to a 65-year-old with emphysema who's smoked for 40 years and not to a young mother?"

In mid-December, Perez and her husband traveled to Pittsburgh for five days of testing. In a December twenty-third letter, the medical team deemed her an "acceptable candidate for transplant." She would join about 30 people on their waiting list. Her army of guardian angels rejoiced. Then, early last month, they noticed she was no longer returning their calls.

* * *

After she signed the directive refusing transfusions, Perez was in torment, she said. She knew she was signing away her last chance at life. She curled into herself on the single bed in the room she shares with her 12-year-old daughter. She blew out short streams of breath to calm herself. She couldn't sleep. God had resurrected her, lifting her from deathbeds and despair. Was it really His will that she now give up and die?

*The word of God was the only thing that sustained her.*

Perez was raised Catholic, but a neighbor who was a Jehovah's Witness impressed her with his knowledge of the Bible. Two years ago, she began attending services and Bible study classes. Lorenzo went a few times, but it wasn't for him. Still, he was happy that his fragile wife had found a place of solace. What no one understood, she explained later, was that in her darkest hours, when she lay dying in the hospice, and throughout that long, lonely year at Specialty Hospital, the word of God was the only thing that sustained her. Twice, she'd thought of ripping out the life-sustaining tubes that tethered her to the wall. Her belief in God stayed her hand. She wanted desperately to do what He wanted.

That weekend, her mother called from Peru and begged her to change her mind and have the operation. Her doctors called. Her sister, a nurse, chimed in from Italy. Her sister-in-law reminded her of another relative, a Jehovah's Witness who refused a transfusion and died, leaving two toddlers behind. Fellow Witnesses continued to visit and urged her to stay strong, assuring her that just as soldiers die on the battlefield to defend their country, sometimes Jehovah's Witnesses die to protect the integrity of God's law. Lorenzo barred the Witnesses from the house, told the children they could no longer be part of the congregation and threatened that if Perez continued to refuse the transfusion, their marriage of nineteen years would be over.

> *Her heart told her that God wanted her to choose life.*

Her children, schooled by the Jehovah's Witnesses, told her they'd be sad if she died but were proud of her for following her faith. Perez feared less for her eternal life than that God would punish her by taking her life if she went ahead with the transplant. "I was worried God wouldn't let me live after the operation," she said. Three days later, Perez told Lorenzo she'd changed her mind. "I began to think how much I loved my children, these marvelous gifts from God," she explained, gulping for air as tears rolled down her face. "God loves. He does not demand that we follow rules. The rules are ours." Her heart told her that God wanted her to choose life.

Now, Lorenzo said, it is as if they are approaching the door to the future with the key in their hand, ready to turn the lock. Perez, who has difficulty walking into the next room, must once more travel to Pittsburgh to sign a new directive, permitting doctors to use blood during her operation. But first, Kaiser doctors now say she must regain the 14 pounds her already-thin frame has lost since she got out of the hospital. The transplant doctors want to know how she will pay for medical care once her insurance expires. She doesn't know but hopes that in Peru, it will be cheaper.

She is still not used to the bustle of activity in the small apartment after so long in a lonely hospital room. Her son, Jason, a fourth-grader, wanders in to tell about his day before running to the living room to play a computer game. Lorenzo shuffles through the endless paperwork that grows out of a serious illness. And her daughter, Diana, sings her a new pop song, holding the handle of her mother's portable oxygen tank like a rock star's microphone. The two giggle. They pinkie-swear on a secret that they promise to talk more about later, once the lights are out, when they will drift off to sleep, together.

Perez no longer talks to Jehovah's Witnesses, nor they to her. It is hard, she said. They are like her family. But the religion "disfellowships," or excommunicates, members who disobey its teachings. Contacted by a reporter and asked about Perez, a member of her congregation said, "She is not a Jehovah's Witness," and hung up. [15]

## Why Must I Come to Church?

A short answer to a potentially complex question is: **To hear the gospel.** That is precisely why we come to church. Revelation 1:1–20 (NIV) describes in detail *what was, what is, and what is to come*. It is written to the local church:

1. **Prologue**
   *The revelation of Jesus Christ, which God gave him to show his servants what must soon take place. He made it known by sending his angel to his servant John,*
   *Who testifies to everything he saw—that is, the word of God and the testimony of Jesus Christ.*
   *Blessed is the one who reads the words of this prophecy, and blessed are those who hear it and take to heart what is written in it, because the time is near.*

2. **Greetings and doxology**
   *John, To the seven churches in the province of Asia: Grace and peace to you from him who is, and who was, and who is to come, and from the seven spirits before his throne,*
   *And from Jesus Christ, who is the faithful witness, the firstborn from the dead, and the ruler of the kings of the earth. To him who loves us and has freed us from our sins by his blood,*
   *And has made us to be a kingdom and priests to serve his God and Father—to him be glory and power for ever and ever! Amen.*
   *Look, he is coming with the clouds, and every eye will see him, even those who pierced him; and all the peoples of the earth will mourn because of him. So shall it be! Amen.*

*"I am the Alpha and the Omega," says the Lord God, who is, and who was, and who is to come, the Almighty.*

## 3. One like a Son of Man

*I, John, your brother and companion in the suffering and kingdom and patient endurance that are ours in Jesus, was on the island of Patmos because of the word of God and the testimony of Jesus.*

*On the Lord's Day I was in the Spirit, and I heard behind me a loud voice like a trumpet,*

*Which said: "Write on a scroll what you see and send it to the seven churches: to Ephesus, Smyrna, Pergamum, Thyatira, Sardis, Philadelphia and Laodicea."*

*I turned around to see the voice that was speaking to me. And when I turned I saw seven golden lampstands,*

*And among the lampstands was someone "like a son of man," dressed in a robe reaching down to his feet and with a golden sash around his chest.*

*His head and hair were white like wool, as white as snow, and his eyes were like blazing fire.*

*His feet were like bronze glowing in a furnace, and his voice was like the sound of rushing waters.*

*In his right hand he held seven stars, and out of his mouth came a sharp double-edged sword. His face was like the sun shining in all its brilliance.*

*When I saw him, I fell at his feet as though dead. Then he placed his right hand on me and said: "Do not be afraid. I am the First and the Last. I am the Living One; I was dead, and behold I am alive for ever and ever! And I hold the keys of death and Hades.*

*"Write, therefore, what you have seen, what is now and what will take place later.*

*"The mystery of the seven stars that you saw in my right hand and of the seven golden lampstands is this: The seven stars are the angels of the seven churches, and the seven lampstands are the seven churches."*

This passage of Scripture reveals three essential reasons that we must actively attend church. Besides hearing the gospel (good news), we learn to know God (His attributes, characteristics, mannerism, and consistent ways), know ourselves (through recurring self-examination), and how to relate to others (compassion, patience, and service).

1. To know God means that we:
    a. Trust Him,
    b. Obey Him, and
    c. Depend upon Him.
2. To know ourselves, we learn how:
    a. To accentuate our situations/strengths,
    b. To want to strengthen our weaknesses, and
    c. To solve problems and make decisions based upon His Word.
3. To know how to relate to others, we understand the intricacies of:
    a. Respecting authority,
    b. Operating within our spiritual gifts, and
    c. Understanding our role(s) in our local church.

## *Review and Discussion*

1. Do you value your current role in your local church?
   _____
   _____
   _____

2. How does your role in your local church bring joy to others?
   _____
   _____
   _____

3. Do you feel that your role in your local church is meaningful to God's overall plan for mankind? Why?
   _____
   _____
   _____

4. What is/are your spiritual gift(s)? How do you know for sure?
   _____
   _____
   _____

5. Are you striving toward helping your local church achieve its mission and vision? How?
   _____
   _____
   _____

## *Section Notes*

### Chapter Four

1 *Christian Today*.

2 Michael J. Berland, "Compassion Counts More than Ever," *Parade* magazine, (Mar. 7, 2010), 4.

3 *Christianpost.com*.

4 *PR Newswire*.

### Chapter Five

5 Christine Wicker, "How Spiritual are We?" *Parade*, (Oct. 4, 2009), 4.

6 David Edgren, "Power in Worship—Is worship going to church? Is it singing, praying, or reading the Bible," *Signs of the Times*, (Oct. 2008), 27.

7 Rodney Woods, "Living God's Way." *Signs of the Times*, (Jul. 2009), 45–48.

8 "Religion Today Summaries," *Signs of the Times*, (May 2009), 4.

### Chapter Six

9 Evangelist Annie L. Simon, "Called to Pray: Sharing How a Community School Prayer Outreach Ministry is Established," *The Repository*, 41.

10 www.amityfoundation.org.

11 Frank Stirk, www.christianweek.org.stories.php?id=694, (accessed 2010)

12 www.OneNewsNow.com/Legal.Default.aspx?id+166116, (accessed Aug. 2010).

13 "The Church at Study," (Wheaton, IL: Evangelical Training Association, 1992).

14 Lonnae O'Neal Parker, *Washington Post*, (April 5, 2010).

15 Brigid Schulte, "A Matter of life, Death, and Faith: Religious Objection Complicates Young Mother's Decision on a Transplant," *Washington Post*, (Feb. 17, 2010).

# ❦ Part III ❦
## How Do I Glorify God by Fulfilling My Role in the Local Church?

*And all things are of God, who hath reconciled us to himself by Jesus Christ, and hath given to us the ministry of reconciliation.*
—2 Corinthians 5:18 KJV

*But all things are from God, who through Jesus Christ reconciled us to Himself [received us into favor, brought us into harmony with Himself] and gave to us the ministry of reconciliation [that by word and deed we might aim by bring others unto harmony with Him].*
—2 Corinthians 5:18 Amplified

I credit my maternal grandmother, *Granny*, for leading me to Christ. Of course, I am eternally grateful to my mom and dad for their diligence and training (Proverbs 22:6), but my personal relationship with our Heavenly Father, through Jesus Christ, is a direct result of Granny's nurturing and speaking into my life that dates back to 1968. It continued into my initial years in college in the early 1980s. As I recall, through her words and deeds, Granny was preparing me for ministry work. I didn't know or understand then, but as I reflect upon my life, her intervention was pivotal and influential.

Acknowledging a call to ministry is a first step. Understanding our role, as a result of the call, is a key component in God's overall plan for our lives. It may take several years to learn and develop. All of the details of the multiple conversations between Granny and I are vague, but I can imagine how many of those meaningful times transpired, especially when I was very young. God was, indeed, the centerpiece.

"...Thank you Jesus for blessing this house, my husband, my children, and my grandchildren. Amen." Granny concluded one of her hundreds of prayers by her bedside.

"Granny?" I whispered cautiously. "Are you done?"

*Part III—How Do I Glorify God?*

"Yes, Kevin. I'm finished talking to the Lord for tonight. What is it?" Granny asked as she arose from her knees.

"Why do you love the Lord?" I asked with a spirit of curiosity and naiveté.

"Well, that's an easy one Kevin. I love the Lord because God *is* Love. He loves us so much and provides everything that we need so that our lives are fulfilled. He also gave us spiritual gifts that we use in the church and in our homes to bring Him glory," explained Granny in simple terms.

"Awesome!" I shouted.

"I raised your mom to always put God first and to remember to attend church as often as possible. It's good for the soul. That is where you hear from God through your pastor. I see you as a pastor one day when you grow up. Your mom has done a good job raising you in the church and I appreciate the programs that are available for you, and your brother, at Ebenezer Baptist Church. Keep up the good work Kevin," Granny pronounced.

"Thanks, Granny. How do you know that I will become a pastor, Granny?"

"God told me Kevin. As you know, I pray several times a day. God has revealed to me that your role in the church will be as a pastor. God has already blessed you with the gifts of leadership, teaching, and encouragement. As He reveals these to me, I, in turn, reveal them unto you. They will each develop as you grow and learn more about God. God wants you to know," said Granny.

"Wow, I don't know what this all means right now, but I believe it. Thanks for letting me know. When will I know for sure that I am supposed to pursue this?" I questioned with a renewed interest.

"The Lord will reveal it to you, Kevin, at the right time in your life. Maybe when you are 25-years-old or perhaps when you turn 40-years-old. The time will be just right, according to God's divine plan. After you graduate from college and begin working, you will get to a point where that particular line of work is no longer fulfilling and God will prompt you to make a change—a change that will bring fulfillment in your role in your local church," Granny explained.

"It all sounds so exciting Granny. I can't wait. I will continue to go to church with my mom and pay attention in Sunday school and other youth programs. It's interesting to watch you pray. You must be good at it because I see you on your knees all the time talking to God. Sometimes, I can hear you too. Thanks for your prayers," I said looking up at Granny's smile.

"Ultimately Kevin, your fulfillment is evidence that you are operating in your spiritual gifts. Continue down that path and God will bless your efforts, motives, and good works. I will always be praying for you," explained Granny.

# Chapter Seven
## Good Works

*Let your light so shine before men, that they may see your good works and glorify your Father in heaven.*

—Matthew 5:16 NKJV

# GIVE GOD THE GLORY!

The Scripture is clear, in its revelation, that our *good works* ushers forth glory to God (Matthew 5:16). *"Ye are the light of the world"* in verse 14 describes the essential mission of the Christian to the world. Our light is to clearly shine forth into the darkness of human depravity. Darkness is the absence of light. Darkness alone cannot dispel the light, but the smallest light can dispel the greatest darkness. Throughout this world, God is using men, women, girls, and boys in significant ways that manifest *good works*.

## European Union Addresses Persecution

An estimated 100 million Christians worldwide suffer persecution for their faith, including, in some cases, death. The European Union (EU) has taken steps to define the actions that the embassies of member EU countries can take to protect the rights of Christians and religious minorities in countries where they are persecuted. The EU will use the World Watch List of Persecution published by Open Doors, a non-denominational organization that monitors the treatment of Christians in countries violating religious freedom. Dr. Carl Moeller, president and CEO of Open Doors USA, said, "Christians around the world are becoming more and more marginalized every year.

They are caught in the crossfire in places like Iraq, Iran, and North Korea. So this is a positive sign by the EU to promote religious freedom globally." Open Doors identifies North Korea as the number one persecutor of Christians, followed by Iran, Saudi Arabia, and Somalia.[1]

## Death for Egyptian Christian?

In Egypt, all citizens must register their religion with the government. Following his decision to become a Christian, Muslim-born Maher Ahmad El-Mo'otahssenm Bellah El-Gohary applied for a change of religious registry. When opposing attorneys recommended that he be condemned to death, El-Gohary tried to obtain papers authorizing attorney Nabil Ghobreyal to act as his proxy representation in court. However, staff members at the registry office swore at Ghobreyal and beat him to the point that he had to resign from representing El-Gohary. As a result, El-Gohary, who had gone into hiding, will have to represent himself openly in court. "I believe God will protect me," he said. "It's a hard decision, but I have to go."[2]

## Muslims Apologize

At 6:00 a.m. on October 10 [2007], a group of 300 Muslims vandalized the New Apostolic Christian Church in the Pakistani village of Gowind, near the border with India. They broke windows, plastered dung on the walls, and cut the wires to the church's loudspeakers. Following the attack, Muslim clerics called for a jihad against the Christian "infidels."

Two days later, however, three Muslim community leaders signed a statement apologizing for the vandalism. The statement was signed in the presence of Christian leaders, the police, and about 100 Muslims. The document stated, "We apologize to the Christians for desecrating the church and hurting their religious sentiments."[3]

## Canadian Apology

In 1920, the Canadian government passed a law requiring the Aboriginal children attend church-operated boarding schools operated by Presbyterians, Anglicans, Roman Catholics, and the United Church of Canada. The Canadian government financially supported the schools.

Beginning in the 1980s, a number of former students accused the schools of abusing them physically and sexually, and this led to a class action lawsuit. The result was a Can$1.9 billion compensation package distributed among 65,000 survivors of the schools. On June 11, 2008, Canadian Prime Minister Stephen Harper and other government leaders apologized for the government's role in forcing these children from their homes into the schools and for the abuse they suffered.

"I was very encouraged by their determination to make sure that this apology is seen as a beginning, and that it will be accompanied by actions that will significantly improve the quality of life for First Nations people in this land," said Archbishop Fred Hiltz, head of the Anglican Church of Canada.[4]

## Building Bridges of Hope

Moved by a plight a world away, one man takes action. Arriving at the Blue Nile in Ethiopia after hiking fifteen miles from the nearest dirt road into a gorge almost as deep as the Grand Canyon, American Ken Frantz surveyed piles of rebar, stacks of wooden decking, tons of concrete, and spans of steel cable that men and mules had lugged down on footpaths to the banks of the African river. Frantz, 60, planned to turn the piles of building materials into a new suspension footbridge to replace a 360-year-old stone bridge he had already repaired—twice. Over the centuries, flooding had washed out the bridge so often that it had earned the name Sebara Dildiy, Amharic for "broken bridge."

In this remote corner of Ethiopia, Sebara Dildiy is critical to the lives of hundreds of thousands of Amhara highlanders: almost all of them live without running water or electricity and they depend on footpaths for their commerce and well-being. "If this bridge is broken, their lives are broken," said Yirgalem Ambachew, president of the Bahir Dar Rotary Club in northern Ethiopia. The next-nearest river crossing is nearly a week's walk away.

Frantz, a former builder from Yorktown, Virginia, USA, is the founder of Bridges to Prosperity (www.bridgestoprosperity.org), a nonprofit that constructs and repairs bridges in Asia, Africa, and South America. He formed the organization after seeing a photo of Sebara Dildiy in National Geographic in 2001. The image showed Ethiopian villagers crossing the swollen Blue Nile by looping themselves and their cattle to a frayed rope held by 10 men on each side of the broken span.

"The picture didn't do justice to the need," he said, choking up as he described people so desperate to cross the river that they would put their lives at risk to do it. He decided on the spot to dedicate himself to fix the broken bridge—and more.

*Villagers and volunteers rebuilt the span together.*

After traveling to Ethiopia for the first Sebara Dildiy repair, Frantz learned that a simple footbridge could boost economic activity and improve life for isolated populations around the world. He identified a need for a half million of these bridges—then set out to start building them.

He first took Bridges to Prosperity to Nepal to learn about bridge-building techniques from the Swiss group Helvetas, which had designed a simple cable-suspended bridge that could be built with local materials and labor, as long as someone could supply the cable. While there, he participated in a joint venture to build a bridge over the Kamro Khola River, which swells to become virtually impassable during monsoon seasons.

From Nepal, Frantz went to work in Indonesia, where, in 1992, fourteen children had died crossing a poorly constructed bridge over the Way Sekampung River on their way to school. In Ethiopia, he set up a training program for young engineers. Soon, Bridges to Prosperity expanded its reach to South America, with a bridge over Peru's Huambramayo River, which rages so violently in the rainy season that people on one side of it were isolated from all public services for four months a year.

Along the way, Frantz enlisted others to join his quest. One recruit was Avery Bang, a 25-year-old American civil engineer he met when she was volunteering in Peru. "I think Ken hired me because I didn't have the experience to know that things couldn't be done," she said.

Today, the organization has constructed more than forty bridges in seven countries, including El Salvador and Honduras. With partners, they have built seven others in Nepal, Sudan, Kenya, Bolivia, Indonesia, Mali, and Rwanda, and over the next few years, they plan to focus their efforts in Zambia, Ghana, Liberia, Guatemala, and Nicaragua. Frantz hopes to start programs in twenty countries by 2020 and to lead the construction of 200 new bridges a year.

Thanks to the efforts of Bridges to Prosperity, villagers in far-flung locales around the world can travel across otherwise impassable rivers to attend schools, find jobs, reach markets to sell crops and livestock, and visit clinics to get their children medical care.

GIVE GOD THE GLORY!

> *A simple footbridge can help change the lives of so many people.*

Trade rose almost as soon as Sebara Dildiy was repaired in 2002. Zoe Pacciani, international program director for Bridges to Prosperity, witnessed how local farmers got better prices for their crops when they sold them across the river. The farmers used the extra money to replace leaky thatch roofs with tin. "What seems like a simple thing—a footbridge—has changed the lives of so many people," Pacciani said.

Unfortunately, the repaired Sebara Dildiy washed away again during a flood in 2006. Undaunted, Frantz arranged to fix the bridge while planning to build a new one. Bridges to Prosperity only works in places where it can count on local support and labor—both of which were in evidence at the Sebara Dildiy site. Ethiopian villagers and volunteers mixed concrete and bent rebar alongside the Bridges to Prosperity team, which included two of Frantz's four brothers, Forrest and Marty, who hammered in wooden planks as the cables were set.

Also at the site was a 20-year-old woman named Banchamlak, whom Frantz treats like a daughter. She is a living example of the bridge's remarkable impact. When she was six, Banchamlak was burned in a household accident that left her with one arm fused to her torso. Thanks to Frantz and that first bridge repair, she was able to cross the Blue Nile to get medical care that allowed her to regain the use of her arm. After undergoing several operations, she made a remarkable recovery and graduated from high school. Today she attends college with the financial assistance of Bridges to Prosperity and the Bahir Dar Rotary Club. "I want to be a doctor," she said. "If there had been no bridge, I don't know what would have happened to me."

In November, Frantz and his team completed the new bridge, the fiftieth project for Bridges to Prosperity, at the spot where its work first began. "This is symbolic of fixing a larger problem worldwide," Frantz said. "More than a billion people live in extreme poverty, but it's a problem we can solve if we all join together."

*Bridge repair is symbolic of fixing a larger problem.*

At the inauguration ceremony for the bridge, Frantz teared up as he proudly watched laden mules make the crossing. From now on, Sebara Dildiy—no longer the broken bridge—will need another name.[5]

## Review and Discussion

1. We have a mandate from God to make Him clear and visible in the earth. How are you contributing to this mandate?

   _____
   _____

2. God is glorified through our *good works*. What did Jesus teach us about this in "The Sermon on the Mount"?

   _____
   _____

3. Why are others counting on our *good works*? Give some examples.

   _____
   _____

4. An expression of our love for God is demonstrated through *good works*. How?

   _____
   _____

5. Love compels us to give. How is your gift to others measured in terms of brotherly love?

   _____
   _____

# Chapter Eight

## Togetherness

*I'm praying not only for them But also for those who will believe in me Because of them and their witness about me. The goal is for all of them to become one heart and mind—Just as you, Father, are in me and I in you, So they might be one heart and mind with us. Then the world might believe that you, in fact, sent me. The same glory you gave me, I gave them, So they'll be as unified and together as we are—I in them and you in me. Then they'll be mature in this oneness, And give the godless world evidence That you've sent me and loved them In the same way you've loved me.*

—John 17:20–23 The Message

**GIVE GOD THE GLORY!**

We must learn to understand that even though the United States Constitution declares that all men are created equal, this does not mean that all men are identical. We are brothers and sisters, children of a holy Heavenly Father. We must learn to accept our differences, without making wars out of minor disagreements.

The biblical term of "forbearance" is probably best understood as tolerance. Tolerance has been defined as a "willingness to recognize and respect the beliefs or practices of others." It is a key to developing unity. Yet we have a habit of stretching and adapting word meanings to suit our personal opinions.

> *I refuse to accept the view that mankind is so tragically bound to the starless midnight of racism and war that the bright daybreak of peace and brotherhood can never become a reality.*
> *— REV. MARTIN LUTHER KING, JR.*

If we are to live with forbearance for others, it means we can no longer fight the ugliness we find in the world with our own "Christianized ugliness." We have no right to confront their twisted values with our own twisted "Christianized" values, the kind of values that supposedly permit hypocrisy and judgmental attitudes to dwell side by side with righteousness and holiness.

True unity is not achieved by leaving our differences hidden, but by dealing with them in the open air of Christ's mercy. Just as a ship has many cabins, so God's kingdom has room for many opinions. But just as a ship has just one main deck, it is on this common deck where we come out of our cabins to stand **together**.[6]

## It's Your Attitude

Our attitude is an outward expression of our internal thoughts. Jesus reminds us of this during His first public sermon—The Sermon on the Mount. This New Testament teaching is powerful and thought provoking. Throughout chapters five, six and seven of Matthew, Jesus teaches His disciples, along with multitudes of curious onlookers and observers, about the proper attitude concerning love, almsgiving, prayer, fasting, wealth, judging, treatment of others (The Golden Rule), and introduces the first of multiple parables (The Parable of the Two Builders).

However, in the midst of His teaching about these diverse topics, He begins with the 'Be-Attitudes.' In laymen's terms, I equate this to *"the **attitude** you ought to be."* I realize that this is not proper English, but it gets to my point. It expresses our *attitude* toward God and ultimately fosters togetherness amongst God's people. In Matthew 5:4–12, the character and attitude described by our Lord are unattainable by self-effort.

GIVE GOD THE GLORY!

Instead, they are developed in the Christian by the work of the indwelling Holy Spirit:

*"**Blessed** are they that mourn: for they shall be comforted.*

***Blessed** are the meek: for they shall inherit the earth.*

***Blessed** are they which do hunger and thirst after righteousness: for they shall be filled.*

***Blessed** are the merciful: for they shall obtain mercy.*

***Blessed** are the pure in heart: for they shall see God.*

***Blessed** are the peacemakers: for they shall be called the children of God.*

***Blessed** are they which are persecuted for righteousness' sake: for theirs is the kingdom of heaven.*

***Blessed** are ye, when men shall revile you, and persecute you, and shall say all manner of evil against you falsely, for my sake.*

***Rejoice, and be exceeding glad**: for great is your reward in heaven: for so persecuted they the prophets which were before you."*

—KJV

Having announced the kingdom of heaven as "near," Jesus declares the principles of that kingdom. Those worth noting include:
1. In this sermon, Jesus states the perfect standard of righteousness demanded by the law (Matthew 5:48), thus demonstrating that all men are sinners, habitually falling short of the divine standard, and that, therefore, salvation by works of law is an impossibility, and
2. Our Lord reaffirms and declares that the attitude of men toward the Mosaic law of the Old Testament will determine their place in the kingdom (Matthew 5:19).

Jesus taught that the world seen from God's viewpoint is tilted in favor of the oppressed. This teaching emerges in The Sermon on the Mount and other statements of Jesus:
— Matthew 19:30; Mark 10:31; Luke 13:30 "...the first shall be the last," and
— Luke 14:11 & 18:14 "...he who humbles himself will be exalted."

But why would God single out the oppressed for special attention? In retrospect, the weaker we feel, the harder we lean on God. The poor, the hungry, the mourners, and those who suffer are blessed (Matthew 5:3–6) because their lack of self-sufficiency is obvious to them every day. They must turn somewhere for strength. People who are rich, successful, and beautiful may go through life relying on their natural gifts. But people who are needy, dependent, and dissatisfied with life are more likely to welcome God's free gift of love. Thus, suffering helps us to:
- Realize our urgent need for redemption,

- Experience our dependence on God and our interdependence with *one another*,
- Distinguish between necessities and luxuries, and
- Respond to the call of the gospel because we may have become so desperate that we cry out to God.[7]

Togetherness can be defined as two or more who desire the same thing in the same way with the same end result. It works by love through three levels of fellowship:

**Perfecting**: With those in authority over us (Ephesians 4:11–13). They teach us how to mature, develop, and grow as Christians, and are divinely appointed as leaders within the local church.

*He is the One who gave some the gift to be apostles. He gave some the gift to be prophets. He gave some the gift of preaching the good news. And he gave some the gift to be pastors and teachers. He did it so that they might prepare God's people to serve. If they do, the body of Christ will be built up. That will continue until we all become one in the faith and in the knowledge of God's Son. Then we will be grown up in the faith. We will receive everything that Christ has for us.*

—NIRV

**Edifying**: With those who are peers (Romans 14:19). This is the building up of ones faith' principle in which we choose to live peaceably with others.

> *Let us therefore follow after the things which make for peace, and things wherewith one may edify another.*
>
> —KJV

**Ministry:** With those under our authority (1 Corinthians 3:5). As ministers, one who serves, our mandate is to permeate our environments with well-intentioned motives. These include a desire to do good, to serve, and to strengthen those within our sphere of influence.

> *After all, what is Apollos? And what is Paul? We are only people who serve. We helped you to believe. The Lord has given each of us our own work to do.*
>
> —NIRV

Our togetherness is our greatest strength!

### *Baptized together*

In I Corinthians 12, Paul compared the church to the human body with its various members: Eyes, nose, mouth, hands, and feet. Each member has certain spiritual gifts, often based on the person's natural talents, by which he or she is able to serve others. That's why Paul sometimes spoke of the church as "the body of Christ" (1 Corinthians 12:27 and Colossians 1:24).

What does this have to do with baptism? In 1 Corinthians 12:13, Paul said that "we were all baptized by one Spirit into one body." The body we are baptized into is "the body of Christ," the church. So baptism is a ceremony by which we are united with other Christian believers in church fellowship.[8]

## Review and Discussion

1. Togetherness is expressed through unity. In your view, is your church unified?
   _____
   _____

2. What suggestions can you offer to unify the multiple church denominations across the globe?
   _____
   _____

3. There is power in togetherness, yet many churches still operate in isolation. Why do you think this persists?
   _____
   _____

4. Why does Satan work so hard to prevent togetherness amongst the saints? What is his fear?
   _____
   _____

5. What are your views on the concept of togetherness? How is it manifested?
   _____
   _____

# Chapter Nine

## Stay in Your Lane

*I therefore, the prisoner of the Lord, beseech you that ye walk worthy of the vocation wherewith ye are called, with all lowliness and meekness, with longsuffering, forbearing one another in love.*

—Ephesians 4:1–2 KJV

*And we pray this in order that you may live a life worthy of the Lord and may please him in every way: bearing fruit in every good work, growing in the knowledge of God.*

—Colossians 1:10 NIV

*Give God the Glory!*

Ephesians 4:1–3 offers an encouraging appeal by a powerful and thought-provoking teacher—Paul the Apostle—to stay in our lane relative to our individual and collective work in the ministry.

> *I therefore, the prisoner of the Lord, beseech you that ye walk worthy of the vocation wherewith ye are called, with all lowliness and meekness, with longsuffering, forbearing one another in love; Endeavouring to keep the unity of the Spirit in the bond of peace.*
>
> —KJV

In this New Testament book, he is emphasizing the need for unity in the midst of the important city of Ephesus, located on the West Coast of Asia Minor, where this church was founded. As the most favorable seaport in the Roman province, the city was the most important trade center west of Tarsus and was a cultural center with a population of 300,000 people. Divided into two parts, this book addresses the position (what) of the Christian and the practice (how) of the Christian, to include the privileges and responsibilities, respectively.

To walk worthy of our vocation means that we are to live in a manner befitting the divine call or invitation (vocation), which summoned us to salvation. Further, these verses begin to spell out what constitutes the *"walk worthy"* of verse 1. Noble conduct includes

*Stay in Your Lane*

humility, patience toward others, and bending over backward to maintain unity, or harmony, among God's people.

## Carrying the Cross

Arthur Blessitt literally follows Christ's admonition to *"take up the cross"* (Mark 10:21). He has walked more than 38,000 miles in 315 countries, island groups, and territories, carrying a twelve-foot cross for Jesus! His trek has carried him to all seven continents, including Antarctica. He has been through fifty-two countries that were at war, and he has been arrested or jailed twenty-four times, though not for committing any crimes.

It began some forty years ago at five in the morning. Blessitt says that Jesus spoke to him and said, *"Arthur, take the cross off the wall of your building, carry the cross on foot. Identify my message on the highways, [and] road-sides where people are."* Today, Blessitt is listed in the Guinness Book of World Records for taking "the world's longest walk."[9]

## Christian Fined

A Christian in Algeria was detained for five days, given a one-year suspended sentence, and fined US$460—for carrying a Bible. He was also accused of publishing and distributing illegal religious materials. The man, who requested anonymity for his own safety, told Christian friends that the authorities who detained him pressured him to return to Islam. His conviction is the most recent in a wave of detentions and court cases against Protestants and Catholics in Algeria. Since January 2008, police and provincial officials have closed up to half of Algeria's Protestant congregations.[10]

## Personal Qualities

Some personal qualities that encourage us to better understand and serve in our respective roles are:[11]

**Personal and corporate prayer** (1 Thessalonians 5:17 and Matthew 6:9–13)

*Pray without ceasing.*

—1 Thessalonians 5:17 KJV

**The Lord's Prayer—A Pattern for Prayer...**

*After this manner therefore pray ye: Our Father which art in heaven, Hallowed be thy name. Thy kingdom come, Thy will be done in earth, as it is in heaven. Give us this day our daily bread. And forgive us our debts, as we forgive our debtors. And lead us not into temptation, but deliver us from evil: For thine is the kingdom, and the power, and the glory, for ever. Amen.*

—Matthew 6:9–13

**Positive attitude** (Matthew 5:4–12 and Philippians 2:5; See *'Be-Attitudes'* in chapter 8 of this book)

*You must have the same attitude that Christ Jesus had.*
                                —Philippians 2:5 NLT

**Regular church attendance** (Hebrews 10:25)
*Not forsaking the assembling of ourselves together, as is the manner of some, but exhorting one another, and so much the more as you see the Day approaching.*
                                —NKJV

**Proper Stewardship** (Malachi 3:10–11)
*Bring all the tithes into the storehouse, that there may be food in My house, and try Me now in this, says the LORD of hosts, If I will not open for you the windows of heaven and pour out for you such blessing that there will not be room enough to receive it. And I will rebuke the devourer for your sakes, so that he will not destroy the fruit of your ground, nor shall the vine fail to bear fruit for you in the field, says the LORD of hosts.*
                                —NKJV

## How do I Function in the Church?

We function in the local church through the ministry and the operation of the Holy Spirit. The Holy Spirit is our helper, comforter, counselor, guide, and discerner. It is a necessary and essential element to effectively function in the local church. We are developed in the church through the ministry of the Holy Spirit.

*I tell you the truth, anyone who has faith in me will do what I have been doing. He will do even greater things than these, because I am going to the Father. And I will do whatever you ask in my name, so that the Son may bring glory to the Father. You may ask me for anything in my name, and I will do it.*

### Jesus Promises the Holy Spirit

*If you love me, you will obey what I command.*

*And I will ask the Father, and he will give you another* **Counselor** *to be with you forever—*

*The* **Spirit of truth**. *The world cannot accept him, because it neither sees him nor knows him. But you know him, for he lives with you and will be in you.*

*I will not leave you as orphans; I will come to you.*

*Before long, the world will not see me anymore, but you will see me. Because I live, you also will live.*

*On that day you will realize that I am in my Father, and you are in me, and I am in you.*

*Whoever has my commands and obeys them, he is the one who loves me. He who loves me will be loved by my Father, and I too will love him and show myself to him.*

*Then Judas (not Judas Iscariot) said, But, Lord, why do you intend to show yourself to us and not to the world?*

*Jesus replied, If anyone loves me, he will obey my teaching. My Father will love him, and we will come to him and make our home with him.*

*He who does not love me will not obey my teaching. These words you hear are not my own; they belong to the Father who sent me.*

*All this I have spoken while still with you.*

*But the **Counselor, the Holy Spirit**, whom the Father will send in my name, will teach you all things and will remind you of everything I have said to you.*

—John 14:15–26 NIV

*Nevertheless I tell you the truth; It is expedient for you that I go away: for if I go not away, the **Comforter** will not come unto you; but if I depart, I will send him unto you.*

—John 16:7 KJV

### Paul in Ephesus

*While Apollos was in Corinth, Paul was visiting some places on the way to Ephesus. There he found some followers and asked them,*

*Did you receive the **Holy Spirit** when you believed? They said, We have never even heard of a **Holy Spirit**.*

*So he asked, What kind of baptism did you have? They said, It was the baptism that John taught.*

*Paul said, John's baptism was a baptism of changed hearts and lives. He told people to believe in the one who would come after him, and that one is Jesus.*

*When they heard this, they were baptized in the name of the Lord Jesus.*

*Then Paul laid his hands on them, and the **Holy Spirit** came upon them. They began speaking different languages and prophesying.*

*There were about twelve people in this group.*
—Acts 19:1–7 NCV

### The Gentiles Hear the Good News

*Then Peter replied, I see very clearly that God shows no favoritism.*

*In every nation he accepts those who fear him and do what is right.*

*This is the message of Good News for the people of Israel—that there is peace with God through Jesus Christ, who is Lord of all.*

*You know what happened throughout Judea, beginning in Galilee, after John began preaching his message of baptism.*

*And you know that **God anointed Jesus of Nazareth with the Holy Spirit** and with power. Then Jesus went around doing good and healing all who were oppressed by the devil, for God was with him.*
—Acts 10:34–38 NLT

*While Peter was still speaking these words, the **Holy Spirit** fell on all who were listening to the message.*

*And the believers from among the circumcised [the Jews] who came with Peter were surprised and amazed, because the **free***

***gift of the Holy Spirit*** *had been bestowed and poured out largely even on the Gentiles.*

*For they heard them talking in [unknown] tongues (languages) and extolling and magnifying God. Then Peter asked,*

*Can anyone forbid or refuse water for baptizing these people, seeing that they have received the **Holy Spirit** just as we have?*

*And he ordered that they be baptized in the name of Jesus Christ (the Messiah). Then they begged him to stay on there for some days.*

—Acts 10:44–48 Amplified

The above demonstrate clearly that our internal development, by the indwelling power of the Holy Spirit, organizes us, sanctifies us, anoints us, and directs us. Hence, we are *made* functional through the operation of the Holy Spirit.

## Review and Discussion

1. The whole is only as good as its parts. Do you believe this and why?

2. The chain is only as strong as its weakest link. Describe what this means to you.

3. God has given us spiritual gifts to strengthen the body of Christ and the world universally. Why don't we all have the exact same spiritual gifts?

4. Understanding our unique place in the overall plan of God is special. What steps have you taken to know and understand yours?

5. Patience keeps us planted in our designated place until God promotes us toward our next step in ministry. Will you stay in your lane until God releases you?

# *Final Thoughts*

This book is atypical in its approach in magnifying the criticality of the church, and its inherent power. Through numerous global examples that reveal a servant's heart, and the unselfish deeds of men and women of God, I am certain that we can make this world a better place.

Miraculous events are happening all around us on every continent on the globe. Our connection with the church universal, in essence, makes us brothers and sisters in Christ. Brothers and sisters care for one another, nurture one another, pray for one another, show concern for one another, laugh together, cry together, and encourage one another. In other words, unconditional and brotherly love should be our passion, zeal, and motivation at all times and in all situations.

My intent is to change the focus of the *church* as we have known or been taught. It is not merely a building with walls and a roof. Instead, we (God's children) are the church. It is comprised of people as we have learned in Matthew 18:20. In the spirit of serving this world as ambassadors for Christ (2 Corinthians 5:17–20), our time has come to unleash the power within us as was done in the early church (Acts 2:42–47) through:

1. Instruction: *"continued stedfastly in the apostles' doctrine,"*
2. Fellowship: *"and fellowship,"*
3. Observance of the ordinances: *"breaking of bread,"*
4. Corporate prayer: *"prayers,"*
5. Effective outreach: *"fear came upon every soul,"*
6. Common cause: *"had all things common,"* and
7. Mutual assistance: *"parted them to all men, as every man had need."*

Through these acts, we can realize and live out the three primary focus points in this book—What is the Church?; What is my Role in the Local Church?; and How Do I Glorify God by Fulfilling My Role in the Local Church? The answer to each of these questions resides on the inside of us and operates by the orchestration of the Holy Spirit (Acts 1:8).

# Establishment of the Local Church–A Pictorial View

*GIVE GOD THE GLORY!*

## CHURCH HISTORY

*Establishment of the Local Church*

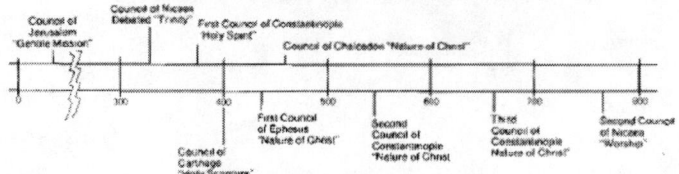

# GIVE GOD THE GLORY!

*Establishment of the Local Church*

**GIVE GOD THE GLORY!**

## *A Prayer for the Local Church*
©2010 by Kevin Wayne Johnson

*Heavenly Father, I come to You in the name of Jesus,*
*With a grateful heart for the opportunity to pray.*
*It is my sincere desire that You help us all*
*To understand 'The Power in the Local Church' today.*

*I pray for churches universal,*
*Both near to us and far away.*
*That Your Holy Spirit would reveal its presence*
*To all that desire to acknowledge Your way.*

*Hear my prayer, O Lord*
*As I know You always do.*
*That we be able to capture the essence of the church:*
*To unite ourselves in love and in accordance with Your truth.*

*Your Word established the local church,*
*Against which the gates of hell cannot prevail.*
*So as we stand upon this simple truth,*
*We also commit ourselves to excel.*

*'Ekklesia' defines the church*
*As one who is "called out."*
*We will live according to righteousness*
*'Cause that's what it's all about.*

*I pray also Father*
*That Your power is felt within.*
*And that Your ministers of reconciliation, which we are,*
*Strive to teach others to live without sin.*

*Through our good works, we choose to give You glory,
That which You desire and richly deserve.
During worship service, we cherish the preached Word
As we gladly depart to serve.*

*We love the church with all of our heart
Because of all that it means to us.
Love, joy, comfort, rest, peace, anointing, and feeling Your presence
Are embedded into our very consciousness.*

*We love you today Father
For adopting us into the body of Christ.
We know that You loved us so
That we could never repay You for the paid price.*

*The church is our refuge,
There's no safer place to be.
It's a public place intended for private intimacy,
Just between You and me.*

*So this prayer is intended to reach the world
From the state of Alaska to the country of New Zealand.
Where millions of local churches reside
To spread the gospel throughout the land.*

*I lift up this prayer
In the name of Jesus.
For there is no other name by which men can be saved
And in that name we can enjoy eternal rest!*

*God bless the church. A-men!*

# Section Notes

**Chapter Seven**

1 www.open-doorsusa.org.

2 Crosswalk.com.

3 "Building Bridges of Hope," www.open-doorsusa.org.

4 Christian Century.

5 Daniel Glick, "Building Bridges of Hope," *Parade* magazine, (Mar. 7, 2010).

**Chapter Eight**

6 Tommy Tenney, "God's Dream Team: A Call to Unity," *The Prescription for Unity: Keys to Developing Unity Servanthood—The Womb of Unity,* chap. 4, 60–61.

7 *Our Daily Bread,* (Jun. 17, 2010).

8 Marvin Moore, "Why Baptism Matters," *Signs of the Times,* (Oct. 2009), 14.

**Chapter Nine**

9 www.blessitt.com.

10 Compass Direct News.

11 Deacons as Leaders.

# Give God the Glory!

## The Power in the Local Church

### Kevin Wayne Johnson

A Reader's Guide

# A Conversation with Kevin Wayne Johnson

## Facilitated by Linda Pate

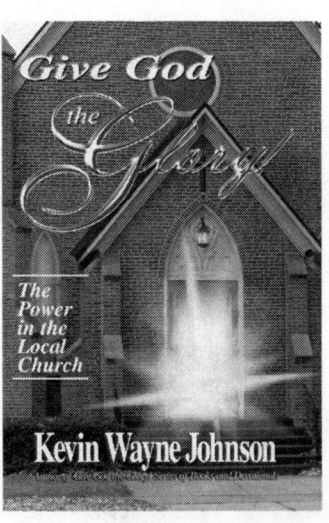

Recorded on May 27, 2010

# The Interview

MS. PATE: Well, Kevin Johnson, I'm just so thankful to have you on today to, um, allow me to do a interview.

MR. JOHNSON: Yes, thank you as well.

MS. PATE: And I'm excited for being here for this interview.

MR. JOHNSON: Thank you for being available.

MS. PATE: I mean I'm excited about what you're doing. Oh, you're very welcome, and thank you for granting me this opportunity to interview you tonight and talk about what you're doing. And I'm really excited.

MR. JOHNSON: Outstanding, outstanding.

MS. PATE: Before we get started, yeah, before we get started, Kevin, um, tell our readers a little bit about yourself.

MR. JOHNSON: Well, I'm a native of Richmond, Virginia. My dad served twenty years in the United States Marine Corps and mom was always there for us, kind of taking care of my brother and I; he's three- and-a-half years younger than I am.

And I've been working now in the federal government for twenty-five years at a number of civilian agencies and defense agencies. I've been blessed to have worked at the mid-level and senior levels of the federal government, really for the past fifteen years, both in New York City and primarily and predominantly in the Washington, D.C. area. Been married seventeen years and, um, my wife and I together, we have three precious sons, ages twelve, thirteen, and fourteen. They're very, very actively involved in a lot of different sporting activities. Doing well in school.

And also seventeen years ago, my wife and I, together, confessed Jesus Christ as our personal Lord and Savior and we've been walking according to God's word ever since that time. I've responded to the call that's on my life, and so that's why I'm a writer. And I'm also a preacher of the gospel and most recently I was appointed Pastor of Ministry at my local church in Columbia, Maryland. We have about 2,500 plus members and growing. And I'm just excited.

About eight years ago God gave me a vision to author a book—just one book. The book is titled *Give God the Glory!*, and that's based on a lot of research and I also researched my name. It's a relatively common name so I use my full name when I write, Kevin Wayne Johnson, to distinguish me from other Kevin Johnsons who have written books in the past.

The subtitle of the first book is *Know God and Do the Will of God Concerning Your Life*. And it's really a book that helps my readers to understand the significance of personal relationships, both, um, with other people and with our Heavenly Father, God Almighty. Once that was finished and it was picked up for national distribution as a self-published book, the Lord then gave me a very clear vision to write a series of books, hence the *Give God the Glory!* book series.

So currently, we'll be releasing Labor Day weekend, 2010, book number seven in the *Give*

***God the Glory!*** series and that title would be *The Power in the Local Church.*
So that's, that's just a little bit about me—
MS. PATE: Wow.
MR. JOHNSON: —and what I've been doing. I'm very actively involved as a Christian man in my community, in my family, in my church. Um, our ministry has expanded internationally with relationships in the United Kingdom. Our books are sold around the world. It's been just a phenomenal blessing. And in 2010, we're looking at the blessed opportunity to have our books translated into four languages and, uh, we're really, really excited about that.
MS. PATE: Wow. You've done so much, it seems, and tell our readers again, how many books are in the series?
MR. JOHNSON: Well, initially there, the vision was to have nine books in the series and we're on number seven now. Now that was the original vision a number of years ago. That has since grown because we do devotionals, um, we do study guides.

Soon we'll have a work book and so it has actually expanded beyond just nine books but that was the original vision, to have the nine books focusing on five key areas. Relationships, again, personal relationships with men and women and with our Heavenly Father, and then giving God the glory in the work place in terms of what that means. And then giving God glory in our families, so helping us to understand the role of the man as a husband and a father. The role of the woman as a wife and mother. And then the two roles of the children, to honor and obey. All scripturally based and then, now we're moving into what it means to give God the glory in the local church.

So we'll be writing the initial book that will be released Labor Day weekend, 2010, and then probably within the next, I'm just guessing right now, but within the next eight to twelve months we'll follow up with a devotional that will also focus on the power in the local church.

And then we'll follow up with—

MS. PATE: Wow.

MR. JOHNSON: —a workbook that further defines what it means to give Him glory in the work place.

MS. PATE: Uh-huh.

MR. JOHNSON: The book was actually published back in 2003, but probably 2011 or 2012 we're going to do a work book. And then the last two books in the series will focus on give God the glory even while we're at rest and relaxation. And I'm excited about those.

MS. PATE: Wow. Yeah.

MR. JOHNSON: And that will be in the future, probably 2013/2014. So, you know, we've gone beyond the original vision of just nine books and it's actually expanded out.

And I'm also submitting my stories to other publications that compile different books, anthologies, et cetera. So I'm also a contributing author in three other books as well. Bringing the total books up to probably fifteen or sixteen.

MS. PATE: Wow. So now you say the seventh book is the *Power in the Local Church*.

MR. JOHNSON: Correct.

MS. PATE: Tell us what that book, you know, is about. What is the power in the local church?

MR. JOHNSON: I want, I want my readers to really understand the significance of church in and of itself and not to think of church as just a building or a place where we go.

Church is wherever you and I go. God's Word teaches us that where two or three are gathered together in His name, there He is in the midst. So whether it's a tent, whether it's at the ball park, whether it's at the skating rink, the local restaurant; wherever we go, you and I, there is the church. It's beyond just a building with a cross on the front.

And so, what I'm looking to do, throughout nine chapters in this particular book, approximately two hundred pages, is to really give people some real good insight and some really good examples that I've extracted that really touch the entire globe. I use examples from Peru, from New Zealand, Australia, all throughout Europe, Canada, South America, and of course, the United States where people are coming together and creating communities and within those communities they're literally worshiping the Lord in the traditional sense of what we think of as the church. So I'm looking to teach people about, you know, what is the church. And the church was actually established in the Book of Matthew, chapter sixteen, and verse number eighteen.

MS. PATE: Hum.

MR. JOHNSON: And then I want to get into what is our role in the church. In other words, why do we go to church? It has to be beyond tradition, it has to be beyond because momma and daddy said so, it has to be beyond, you know, like a social network. I want us to understand the significance of going to church. We go to church to hear from God. And I want people to understand that.

And then last, but not least, I want people to understand, and all of my readers around the globe, and we have lots of examples in the book that show you very clearly about how to do this, is how do we actually glorify God by fulfilling our role in the church.

MS. PATE: Huh.

MR. JOHNSON: So everyone of us was born with a purpose and everyone of us has at least one spiritual gift which are freely given by God and when we choose to use that purpose and spiritual gift in our role, we make life so much better for everybody around us.

So I talk about the fact that good works and togetherness, and by staying in our lane, in other words, recognizing what our role is in the local church, that's how we get to really, truly understand what it means to give God the glory in the church. So everything is spiritually based. It's Bible-based, I use a lot of examples from all points of the globe because I'm really, truly trying to reach a global audience and helping people understand the significance and the power that's in the local church. That power that really resides within us and where we go, we take the church with us. It's beyond just the four walls of a building that has a cross on the top. And that's the core message that I'm trying to get to my readers.

MS. PATE: That's exciting and wonderful!

MR. JOHNSON: Oh, yeah, I'm excited about it.

MS. PATE: Yeah, I am too. I can't wait to get a copy so that I can read because I think it's so very

*Reader's Guide*

important that we really understand what going to church really means and how we have power.

MR. JOHNSON: Exactly.

MS. PATE: So, tell our readers, you know, when you say global, what does that mean?

MR. JOHNSON: That means there are six plus billion people on the planet and I believe that God Almighty has expanded our territory so that we can have the, the reach, um, to get the message that Jesus is Lord to my brothers and sisters in Argentina, in Seattle, Washington, in Toronto, Canada, in New Zealand, Australia, all parts of Europe, Russia, the United Kingdom, the Pacific Rim, Africa.

I truly believe that and there are readers at all points of the globe that need to understand the significance of what it means, Jesus is Lord. And so this is just an avenue that the Lord has given me, through *Writing for the Lord* Ministries, and through **Give God the Glory!** book series to reach these people.

And so when I say global reach, when I look at the relationships that I've already established in the eight short years that I've been writing, and the number of people that I've gotten to know and who in turn know me, and through the thirteen strategic partnerships that I've formulated through distribution, um, I am truly at a point where I can reach people all over the world and know how to do it. So that's why, that's why we're definitely aiming to reach all points of the globe.

And that's why I use all of these different examples in the book. There are examples about what it means, the power in the local church, I'm using examples that I've found, that I've researched that, that literally cater—

MS. PATE: Uh-huh.

MR. JOHNSON: —to different people all over the globe. So that's exactly what I mean by that.

MS. PATE: Okay. And do you feel, Kevin, that globally, you know, because its based on your culture?

MR. JOHNSON: Right.

MS. PATE: And how you worship and how you feel the power. You know, globally, well, will it bring some clarity to our culture here in the United States or will that book be able to tap in no matter where you live?

MR. JOHNSON: Yeah. Yeah.

MS. PATE: You'll understand your power and your purpose.

MR. JOHNSON: Exactly. I specifically wrote it so that it doesn't just reach the American reader, but all of the readers in the Eastern hemisphere as well as the Western hemisphere of the globe would be able to relate because I'm using very, very key and simple scriptural examples that would cater to everyone. So my readers in Australia would be able to relate; and my readers in New Zealand would be able to relate. And my French and Spanish brothers and sisters would be able to relate. And all of my brothers and sisters in South America would be able to relate, as well as my brothers and sisters here in the United States.

And that's, that's the way that the Lord has led me to read this book because they're the ones that He told me to go out and reach and that's exactly what I'm doing.

I've already done it in part. But He's saying to continue to do that because these people need to get a hold of what you're writing and I'm using you as the messenger to reach them. So, by faith, that's exactly what I'm doing and like I said, Labor Day weekend, 2010, it will be released and we've been getting the word out since November of last year. So there are literally millions of people that know it's coming and they're delighted.

MS. PATE: I am too...

MR. JOHNSON: Yeah. Yep, prayerfully they'll catch the vision and the Word teaches us to walk by faith and not by sight and that's exactly what we're doing.

MS. PATE: Wow. Well, I am so excited about what you're doing and what you've been doing. And some of your books in this series, hasn't it been translated into other languages as well?

MR. JOHNSON: Yeah, what, what we, a couple of things happened. We had some real serious negotiations with one of the major French publishers that was very, very close to going forward. They decided not to, at this particular juncture, but we're looking at Burmese, Falam, and there's another language in the country of Myanmar (Burma). They're already on board, we're just working out some final details to make that happen. We've already got the confirmation. That is a done deal.

And then we're in negotiations with the Russian publisher out of Moscow and I'm confident that that will happen as well. And then as we continue to go forward, there is a company that we have that represents our foreign rights and translations services, et cetera, and they're continuing to, you know, constantly negotiate with these different agents around the world.

The vision is to have the books translated into twenty-two languages over a period of time and we're confident and we're walking by faith that will happen as well so that we can truly reach readers that need to be helped to read a book in a language other than just English.

MS. PATE: Wow.

MR. JOHNSON: Yep.

MS. PATE: You're doing such a great work and I applaud you and you have such great support from your family as well, being obedient to the voice of the Lord.

MR. JOHNSON: Absolutely.

MS. PATE: And you know, it's so important that we are obedient, um, you know, and I just know that you have a story to tell. And your books have done so well, even in the times where the economy and, you know, things of that nature so I just know that, you know, um, you're doing a great work and I truly applaud you for doing what you do.

Now I want...will you be touring? How will the readers, how can they get in contact with you if they wanted to order the book?

MR. JOHNSON: Yeah, the main way, Linda, to, eh, to reach me is, of course, either through my blog or through the Web site. Our Web site is, um, patterned after our ministry. So the ministry is *Writing for the Lord* Ministries and the Web site www.writingforthelord.com or www.writingforthelord.org. We own both of those. My blog, and I blog on a very regular basis, is

*Reader's Guide*

http://GiveGodtheGlory.wordpress.com and we're out there quite a bit writing about different things that are going on.

So those are two very easy ways to catch me. Now on the Web site, there's an events calendar so I'm always posting either where I am or where the books are being represented, because I have a number of companies that represent my books at different venues, you know, whether it's the International Christian Retail Show or Book Expo America or any of the major regional shows. Even some of the local shows on the East Coast, et cetera.

A lot of the engagements that I have at churches and conferences and conventions, all of the information is right there. We're very proactive in keeping that events calendar up to date. So any time a person wants to, to come out and just kind of catch up on what we're doing, they can go right to the events calendar.

I'm doing a number of events. Like I said, we have the Hampton Minister's Conference coming up next week, for example. Um, I got the confirmation through Urban Ministries today that I'll be signing there with them. You're talking about over ten thousand ministers at Hampton University in Hampton, Virginia. And there's a number of other events coming up during the summer time and then even into the fall as we release the book.

So, and it's available basically everywhere that books are sold. Once you have distribution in place, you're good to go. Amazon.com, here in the United States, Amazon.com in Canada.

Amazon.com in the UK. And like I said, we have, uh, relationships with thirteen what I call strategic distributors all over the world to help us get the message out.

So we're excited and if anybody has any questions or wants to shoot an e-mail or anything like that, just reach me through the Web site and we'll be as responsive as we can.

MS. PATE: Well, I, I want to thank you again, Kevin, for coming on. This is Kevin Wayne Johnson, the author of the *Give God the Glory!* series and he's got his new book coming out, *Power in the Local Church*. It will come out, again, the end of this month, after Memorial Day.

MR. JOHNSON: No, no, no. Labor Day. Labor Day weekend, 2010.

MS. PATE: Oh, Labor Day. Oh, so I was rushing it.

MR. JOHNSON: Yeah, Labor Day weekend, 2010.

MS. PATE: I wanted it to come out Memorial Day. Labor Day weekend is when I want it to come out.

MR. JOHNSON: Yeah, well, I'll tell you what, the draft, the initial draft, will be ready this weekend, Memorial Day weekend, but that's just the draft. The final version will be released to the general public and to the Christian marketplace Labor Day weekend, 2010.

MS. PATE: Labor Day. And so now can they go on your Web site and read an excerpt of your book or no?

MR. JOHNSON: Well, not yet. But I will, during the summer of 2010, I am going to be posting on the Web site probably Chapter One. The book leading up to Chapter One, I will more than likely post it there.

*Reader's Guide*

MS. PATE: Okay.

MR. JOHNSON: If not the entire chapter, at least part of it so people can take a look at that and that will help to whet their appetite. But absolutely, I want to give people some access to that. And then also, when you go to Amazon.com, I'll have the 'Search Inside the Book' feature as well so some of the readers can go in and take a look at some of that information as well.

MS. PATE: Okay. Well, you've given us great information and I know that they will be excited about getting a new series, *The Power in the Local Church*.

So, Kevin, I want to thank you for coming on tonight and sharing that information with our readers, and I look forward to you and continue to be blessed in the Lord, and I know we'll be talking again soon.

MR. JOHNSON: All right. Well thank you so much, Linda, for the opportunity, I really appreciate it.

MS. PATE: Okay, and I will talk to you soon.

MR. JOHNSON: Okay, thanks again.

MS. PATE: Thank you.

MR. JOHNSON: All right, bye-bye.

MS. PATE: Bye-bye.

---

**Linda Pate** *is the owner of Precious Memories Reading and Collectibles Bookstore, Richmond, Virginia, and the host of her literary talk show on www.Talkshoe.com. An active member of Mount Gilead Baptist Church in Williamsburg, Virginia, Mrs. Pate is an advocate for authors of all genres and serves as a distinguished faculty member at selected writer's conferences across the United States. Mrs. Pate may be contacted as follows: Online4books@gmail.com and www.preciousmemoriesreading.com.*

*GIVE GOD THE GLORY!*

*Reader's Guide*

# Reading Group Questions and Topics for Discussion

1. Based upon what you've read in this book, how has your perspective on the local church changed, if at all?

2. Added emphasis on different versions of the Bible were incorporated to reach a global audience. Did you find the multiple versions helpful?

3. Several real life examples were used to highlight the blessed gift of serving. What are your thoughts on selected examples that were used?

4. Together, we accomplish much more than when we operate independently. Do you agree? Why?

5. What is your favorite portion of church service? Lead a discussion on this topic.

6. In Part II—*What is my role in the local church?*—how would you describe *your* role in *your* local church?

7. Do you believe that it is every member's responsibility to support the vision of your pastor or does that responsibility belong only with the leadership team within your local church?

8. According to Matthew 5:16, our good work(s) glorifies God. What does this mean to you? Cite some specific examples.

9. What will you do *today* to make your church better? How will you achieve them?

10. During the praise and worship portion of church service, do you consistently experience the presence of the Lord?

11. Have you discovered your purpose? Do you know your spiritual gift(s)?

12. Describe the *power* in the local church that you feel during your worship services. Do you ever feel that same *power* in other environments?

# Selected Bibliography and Recommended Reading

*Baltimore Sun* Newspaper.

Bottke, Allison. *God Answers Prayers—Military Edition: True Stories from People Who Serve and Those Who Love Them.* Eugene, OR: Harvest House Publishers, 2005.

Discovery Series Bible Study. *What Does the Bible Say About Patience?* Grand Rapids, MI: Discovery House Publishers.

Dockery, Karen, Godwin, Johnnie, Godwin, Phyllis. *The Student Bible Dictionary.* Uhrichsville, OH: Barbour Publishing, Inc., 2000.

Eckman, James P. Ph.D. *Perspectives from Church History.* Wheaton, IL: Evangelical Training Association, 1996.

Evangelical Training Association. *The Church at Study: Sunday School Ministry for the 1990s.* Wheaton, IL, 1992.

Farrington, Karen. *Historical Atlas of the Holy Lands.* New York, NY: Checkmark Books, 2003.

*Kairos* magazine. Clarence, NY: Kairos Publishing, a division of Eagles' Wings.

*Lifelines* magazine. Grand Rapids, MI: Bethany Christian Services.

*Men's Devotional Bible*, NIV, with Daily Devotions from Godly Men. Grand Rapids, MI: Zondervan Publishing House, 1993.

*Merriam Webster's Dictionary of English Usage.* Springfield, MA: Merriam-Webster Publishers, 1994.

Miner, Margaret, and Hugh Rawson, eds., *A Dictionary of Quotations from The Bible*. New York: Penguin Group [A Signet Book], 1990.

*Nelson's Complete Book of Bible Maps & Charts: Old and New Testaments.* Nashville, TN: Thomas Nelson Publishers, 1993.

*Parade* magazine. New York, NY: Parade Publications.

Prime, Derek and Begg, Alistair. *On Being a Pastor: Understanding Our Calling and Work.* Chicago, IL: Moody Publishers, 2004.

RBC Ministries, *Our Daily Bread—For Personal and Family Devotions.*

Rees, Erik, with Foreword by Rick Warren. *S.H.A.P.E.: Finding & Fulfilling Your Unique Purpose for Life*, Small Group Study Guide. Grand Rapids, MI: Zondervan, 2002.

Schultz, Samuel J., Th.D. *Old Testament Survey, Part I—Genesis to Esther*. Wheaton, IL: Evangelical Training Association, 1991.

Sheffield, Robert (compiler and contributor). *Deacons as Leaders*. Nashville, TN: Convention Press, 1991.

## Selected Bibliography

*Signs of the Times* monthly magazine. Nampa, ID: Pacific Press.

Simon, Annie L. *Called to Pray: Sharing How a Community School Prayer Outreach Ministry is Established.* Longwood, FL: Xulon Press, 2003.

Smith, Gary V., Ph.D. *Old Testament Survey, Part II - Job to Malachi.* Wheaton, IL: Evangelical Training Association, 1991.

*Smith's Bible Dictionary.* Uhrichsville, OH: Barbour Books.

Strong, James. *Strong's Exhaustive Concordance of the Bible.* Peabody, MA: Hendrickson Publishers.

*The Beaufort Gazette* newspaper.

*The Holy Bible,* The King James Study Bible, King James Version. Nashville, TN: Thomas Nelson Publishers, 1988.

*The Holy Bible*, The New Open Bible Study Edition, King James Version Study Bible. Nashville, TN: Thomas Nelson Publishers, 1990.

*The Holy Bible,* The Scofield Study Bible, New International Version. New York: Oxford University Press, 2004.

*The International Standard Bible Encyclopedia.* Hendrickson Publishers, 1996.

*The Washington Post* newspaper.

Tenney, Tommy. *God's Dream Team: A Call to Unity.* Ventura, CA: Regal Books, 1999.

*USA Today* newspaper.

*U.S. News & World Report* magazine. New York, NY: U.S. News and World Report, Incorporated.

Vaughn, Randy William. *The World Christian Desk Reference and Almanac: Facts, Statistics, Surveys, Data and History.* Piscataway, NJ: Inspirit Press, 2001.

Vines, W.E., Unger, Merrill F., White, William, Jr. *Complete Expository Dictionary of Old and New Testament Words.* Nashville, TN: Thomas Nelson Publishers, 1984, 1996.

# Index

Algeria, persecution of Christians in, 131–32
A&M Body Shop, 17
attitude, 123–27, 132–33

baptism, 13, 127
Baptists, 42–43
believers fellowship, 24–25
Bibles, 61, 87, 131–32
blessings, 67–68, 70–71
Bridges to Prosperity, 116–119

charitable giving, 61–62t
children, church groups helping, 85–87
China, Bible in, 87
Christianity, growth of, 6
   milestone dates in the, 7
Christians, apologies to, 114
church
   changing the focus of the, 139–40
   declaration, 42, 45–48
   definitions, 10–11, 13
   foundation, 43–44
   function of, 38
   a gang hideout becomes a, 17
   how to function in, 133–37
   is vindicated, 35
   major historical events in the, 20
   mission, 43–44
   original word for, xix–xx, 10
   people's role in, 84

role of local, 53–57
what happens at, 11–12
why God wants us to go to, 27–33
*See also specific topics*
church attendance, 133
    reasons for, 99–102
church growth, 19
church terminology, 12–13
communion, 13
community, 37–38
    finding, 34
    a welcoming, 33–34
compassion, 89
    counts more than ever, 61

denomination, 13
disabled, church for the, 35–36
discipline, 25
doxology, xxvi, 13, 100

Egyptian Christians, persecution of, 113
*ekklesia* (church), xix–xx, 10
Ethiopia, 115–119
European Union (EU), addressing persecution, 112–113
evangelization, 89

fellowship of the believers, 24–25
fire victims, chaplains praying with, 63
forbearance, 122. *See also* tolerance

German Sunday law, 49
glory, xxvi
God
    is our source, 27–29

living the way of, 76–77
obedience to His command, 26–27
why He wants us to go to church, 27–33

Holy Spirit
   is the guide, 32–33
   Jesus' promising the, 134–35
hospital uniting religions, 62

India, Christians in, 77-78
Islam. *See* Muslims

Jehovah's Witnesses, 92–99
Jesus Christ, 101–102
   is an advocate, 31
   is divine, 30–31
   is head of the church, 29–32
   is the anointed one, 32
   is the power (authority), 31–32
   promises the Holy Spirit, 134–35
Jordan, donating land for church, 36

life, meaning/purpose of, 77t
Lord's Prayer, 132

membership in church, 38
Muslims, 113–114

obedience, 73
   to God's command, 26–27
offering, 12

pastoral oversight, 26
Paul in Ephesus, 135–36

Pentecost, 44
personal qualities, 132–33
power, xix, 31–32
praise, 11
prayer, 12, 73
   reasons for, 69t

religion, purpose of, 69t
religious persecution and religious freedom, 77–78,
      112–115, 131–32
Ruth, book of, 33–34

Sabbath, 14–16
   ideas for a, 16
sermon, 12
service, benefits of, 63–64
singing, 11
spirituality, 69
   youth's opinions on the meaning of, 78t
stewardship, proper, 71, 133
suicide (prevention), 18, 87–88
Sunday, time off from work on, 88

tolerance
   defined, 122
   *See also* religious persecution and religious freedom

Vietnam, Bibles for, 61

welcome, 11
winding up, 12
World Outreach Conference Center (WOCC), 35
worship, 25
   power in, 71–76

*Order additional copies of this book:*

# Give God the Glory!
# The Power in the Local Church
Book #7, © 2010
ISBN: 978-0-9705902-5-1
Price: $19.95
Pages: 208
Hardcover Dimensions: 5.5" x 8.5"

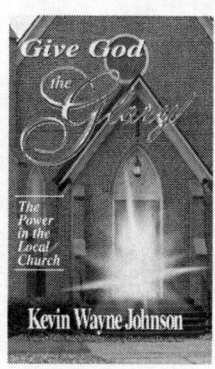

Name: _____
Address: _____
City: _____
State/Zip Code: _____
E-mail: _____

Mail order form with check or money order to: *Writing for the Lord* Ministries, 6400 Shannon Court, Clarksville, MD 21029. Please add $3.00 for shipping and handling. We also accept payment through PayPal—Kevin@writingforthelord.com.

## *Give God the Glory!* STUDY GUIDE
## Know God and Do the Will of God Concerning *Your* Life

Book #6, © 2008
ISBN: 978-0-9705902-2-0
Price: $15.00
Pages: 160
Paperback Dimensions: 8.5" x 11"

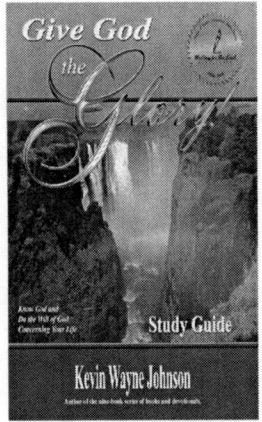

Name: _____
Address: _____
City: _____
State/Zip Code: _____
E-mail: _____

Mail order form with check or money order to: *Writing for the Lord* Ministries, 6400 Shannon Court, Clarksville, MD 21029. Please add $3.00 for shipping and handling. We also accept payment through PayPal—Kevin@writingforthelord.com.

# *Give God the Glory!*
## Know God and Do the Will of God Concerning *Your* Life

Book #1, © 2001; Fifth Printing
ISBN: 978-0-9705902-0-6
Price: $10.99
Pages: 162
Paperback Dimensions: 5.5" x 8.5"

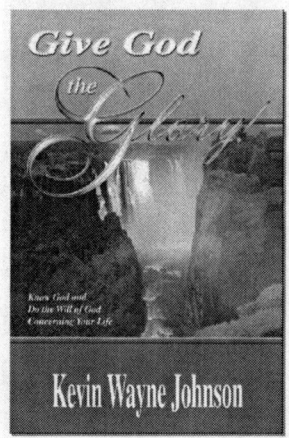

Name: _____
Address: _____
City: _____
State/Zip Code: _____
E-mail: _____

Mail order form with check or money order to: *Writing for the Lord* Ministries, 6400 Shannon Court, Clarksville, MD 21029. Please add $3.00 for shipping and handling. We also accept payment through PayPal—Kevin@writingforthelord.com.

## *Give God the Glory!*
### Called to be Light in the Workplace
Book #2, © 2003; Second Printing
ISBN: 978-0-9705902-1-3
Price: $14.95
Pages: 187
Paperback Dimensions: 6" x 9"

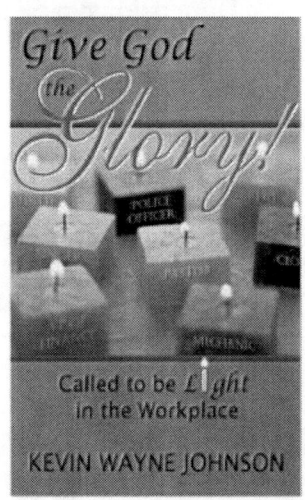

Name: _____
Address: _____
City: _____
State/Zip Code: _____
E-mail: _____

Mail order form with check or money order to: *Writing for the Lord* Ministries, 6400 Shannon Court, Clarksville, MD 21029. Please add $3.00 for shipping and handling. We also accept payment through PayPal—Kevin@writingforthelord.com.

# *Give God the Glory!*
## Let Your Light So Shine, a devotional/gift book
Book #3, © 2004; Third Printing
ISBN: 978-0-9752572-9-6
Price: $7.95
Pages: 54
Paperback Dimensions: 5.5" x 6.5"

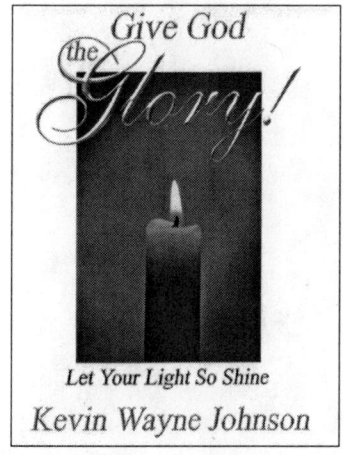

Name: _____
Address: _____
City: _____
State/Zip Code: _____
E-mail: _____

Mail order form with check or money order to: *Writing for the Lord* Ministries, 6400 Shannon Court, Clarksville, MD 21029. Please add $3.00 for shipping and handling. We also accept payment through PayPal—Kevin@writingforthelord.com.

## *Give God the Glory!*
### The Godly Family Life
Book #4, © 2005; Second Printing
ISBN: 978-0-9705902-3-7
Price: $13.00
Pages: 200
Paperback Dimensions: 6" x 9"

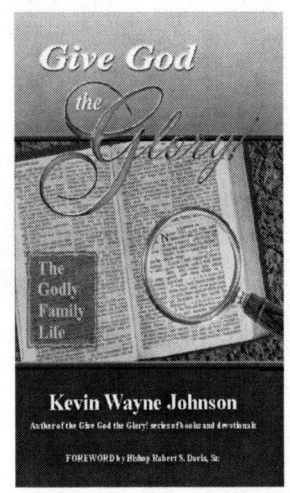

Name: _____
Address: _____
City: _____
State/Zip Code: _____
E-mail: _____

Mail order form with check or money order to: *Writing for the Lord* Ministries, 6400 Shannon Court, Clarksville, MD 21029. Please add $3.00 for shipping and handling. We also accept payment through PayPal—Kevin@writingforthelord.com.

*Give God the Glory!*
**Your Role in Your Family, a devotional/gift book**
Book #5, © 2006; Second Printing
ISBN: 978-0-9705902-4-4
Price: $7.95
Pages: 56
Paperback Dimensions: 5.5" x 6.5"

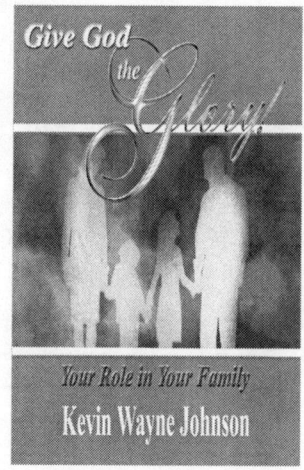

Name: _____
Address: _____
City: _____
State/Zip Code: _____
E-mail: _____

Mail order form with check or money order to: *Writing for the Lord* Ministries, 6400 Shannon Court, Clarksville, MD 21029. Please add $3.00 for shipping and handling. We also accept payment through PayPal—Kevin@writingforthelord.com.

*GIVE GOD THE GLORY!*

# Other books featuring Kevin Wayne Johnson's writings:

Blended Families:
An Anthology
© 2006

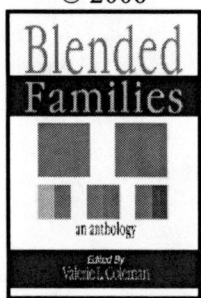

ISBN: 978-0-9786066-0-2
Price $14.95
Paperback

The Secret: His Word
Impacting Our Lives
© 2007

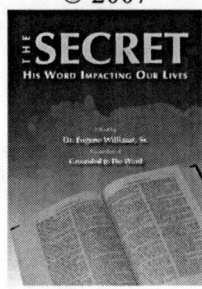

ISBN: 978-0-6151797-6-6
Price: $12.95
Paperback

Name: _____
Address: _____
City: _____
State/Zip Code: _____
E-mail: _____

Mail order form with check or money order to: *Writing for the Lord* Ministries, 6400 Shannon Court, Clarksville, MD 21029. Please add $3.00 for shipping and handling. We also accept payment through PayPal—Kevin@writingforthelord.com.

*Now unto him that is able to keep you from falling, and to present you faultless before the presence of his glory with exceeding joy. To the only wise God our Saviour, be glory and majesty, dominion and power, both now and ever. Amen.*

—Jude 1:24–25 KJV

*God is strong and can help you not to fall. He can bring you before his glory without any wrong in you and can give you great joy. He is the only God, the One who saves us. To him be glory, greatness, power, and authority through Jesus Christ our Lord for all time past, now, and forever. Amen.*

—Jude 1:24–25 NCV

LaVergne, TN USA
25 September 2010
198386LV00001B/2/P